Learn to
INVEST and TRADE
on WALL STREET

R. M. Kuklin

MERCANTINE PRESS
Lincoln, Nebraska

Library of Congress Card Catalog Number: 79–64472

International Standard Book Number: 0–933962–00–2 (cloth)

International Standard Book Number: 0–933962–01–0 (paper)

Published and distributed by:

Mercantine Press

4351 Washington Street

Lincoln, Nebraska 68506

Foreword

This is a very basic book. The language is simple for a reason. During twenty years of teaching grammar I learned that to teach anything new, simplicity is necessary for comprehension. I learned that you could use no "fifty-dollar" words; I learned that you had to give examples and explain carefully; and I learned that you had to present each section in great detail and review as you went along, because few students were able to grasp new material completely the first time it was introduced.

When I decided I wanted to learn about investing and trading on the stock market, I turned to books to learn. I found them interesting and from each one I gleaned a little something, but they were not basic enough. It were as though the authors were talking about gerunds and participles when I still hadn't learned subject and verb. I needed a book that had the diagram _Children ⌐ play_.

I continued to buy books and to research other books in our public library. Finally I decided to take notes on my reading and began making use of some of the technical tools a few of the authors advocated. As my notes expanded and my understanding grew, I began to learn the basics of the stock market.

When I read one author's statement that he wished "there were a vast body of informed writing on what the stock market is really all about, but alas there is not," I agreed with him and decided to write my own book to help others who are interested in this field of investment but don't know how to begin. This book represents years of research, and I hope you will find it helpful.

Acknowledgments

I would like to acknowledge and thank the following people for their permission to use the charts and reproductions illustrating this book:

Mr. Allen O. Felix
The New York Stock Exchange
11 Wall Street
New York, N.Y. 10005

Mr. Donald S. Jones
Securities Research Company
208 Newbury Street
Boston, Mass. 02116

Mr. Richard Pucci
Standard & Poor's Corporation
345 Hudson Street
New York, N.Y. 10014

Mr. Alan R. Shaw
Smith Barney, Harris Upham & Co., Inc.
1345 Avenue of the Americas
New York, N.Y. 10019

Mr. Jerome Sterling
M. C. Horsey & Company, Inc.
Salisbury, Maryland 21801

I also wish to thank Helen Cowles and the members of my family for checking the manuscript and making helpful suggestions. But mostly I wish to thank Harry, my husband and best friend, for his encouragement and support.

Contents

1 For Beginners, Both Men and Women
Shows the Difficutly Beginners Have Encountered in
Wanting to Learn About Investing in Stocks   1

2 Why You Should Be in the Stock Market
Investing in Stocks Is a Business Just Like Every Other
Business, Yet Has Many Advantages Over the Others   6

3 What Are Stocks?
How Companies Are Formed and Shares Issued, and How
Shares Are Traded in the Market   12

4 Where to Get Information about Stocks
How to Read the Financial Page of a Newspaper, the
Stock Guide, Stock Reports, and Listing Requirements
for Companies on the New York Stock Exchange   16

5 Understanding the Dow Theory
The Historical Background of the Theory, What It Is,
and How Consistently It Has Been Working   26

6 Timing, the Primary Tool
Timing Techniques: Cycles, Years, Months   34

7 Keeping Track of the Stock Market
How to Compute a Moving Average, the Dow-Jones
Industrial Average Ten-Week and Forty-Week Moving
Averages for 1974–1977, and How They Can Be
Interpreted   40

8 The Advance-Decline Line
How to Compute One, and the Dow-Jones Advance-
Decline Line for 1974–1977   54

9   Keeping Track of Individual Stocks
How to Keep Track Through Price Changes, an Example
of One, and How to Interpret It   63

10   Individual Stocks—Moving Averages
How to Keep Track of an Individual Stock Through
Moving Averages, and an Example of One   72

11   Keeping Track of Stocks through Charts
How to Chart, and Examples of Line Chart, Bar Chart,
and Point and Figure Chart   86

12   Making Your Investment List
How to Decide on Companies to Follow: 52 Investment
Groups on the New York Exchange and Companies in
Each   103

**13   How to Evaluate a Company through Fundamental
Analysis**
Interpreting a Balance Sheet and What Each Item in
One Means   123

14   Analyzing the Profit and Loss Statement
How to Read a Profit and Loss Sheet. What the P/E
Ratio Means, What Are Yield, Cash Flow, Good
Management   133

15   Volume: an Additional Technical Tool
Theories about Using Volume to Make Investment
Decisions   139

16   You and Your Stockbroker
How to Choose One, What to Expect, and Commissions   147

17   How to Begin Your Investment Program
Suggestions for Several Different Ways to Begin   151

18   Your Buying Strategy
Buying in a Bear Market, in a Bull Market, Timing Guide,
Low-Priced Stocks, High-Priced Stocks, Institutional
Stocks, Averaging, Diversification, Options, Etc.   156

19   Your Selling Strategy
When to Sell, Stop-Loss Orders, Amount of Profit or
Loss to Take, Tax Selling, Etc.   174

20 The Short Sale
What It Is, How to Use It   183

21 The Human Element
How Your Emotions Affect Your Investment, and Some
Suggestions for Control   195

Glossary   201

Index   211

CHAPTER 1

For Beginners, Both Men and Women

The world of stock market investment is an exciting one, a risky one, a challenging one, and one that can bring great financial rewards. In this country it became organized in 1792 when a group of 24 men met under a buttonwood tree on Wall Street in New York City and agreed to meet daily to buy and sell securities. Brokers have continued buying and selling stocks and bonds at almost the same site ever since.

In the past this world of finance has always held a fascination for men. They were anxious to build up estates to provide for their families, and many looked upon Wall Street investments as an ideal way for accomplishing this. Many felt security lay in investing in the growing companies of America, in the dividends and interest received, and in their increased value as the years went on.

Others found the financial game of short-term investing an alluring one and were willing to take greater risks in order to build up fortunes. Unfortunately, statistics show that few succeeded, primarily because they did not know how to go about making profitable investments. They did not prepare themselves by learning the basic skills necessary for making the correct moves. They assumed that being intelligent is enough, and did not realize that emotions play as large a part as does intelligence in successful investment.

Young men today are equally as fascinated with the market as were their fathers. If you are one who is anxious to become a successful investor, your first problem is, where do you start? You might take an investment course—as I did—and see some films and hear some lectures on what stocks are and how they are bought and sold and end up still not knowing where to start. Or you might visit

1

the New York Stock Exchange on Wall Street—as I did twice—see a cartoon, and learn even less. Or you then turn to the library.

The principal difficulty for the beginner is to find a book in which the author has gathered all the basics together and has written about them in simple, nontechnical language. Gerald Loeb, in his book *The Battle for Investment Survival*, airily writes that he won't go into any great basic detail because he assumes his readers have studied other books on this. I have spent years reading and studying these other books and, unfortunately, have found few that start at the beginning. As much for myself as for others, I started taking notes as I read on items I felt could be used in a successful investing program. I have gathered these together in this book, and hope it will show you, step by step, how to master the art of investing in the stock market.

Men are not alone in wanting to learn more about how to become successful investors. So too are women who seek independence in this area. Some are career-minded and support themselves. Many women are the principal providers for their families and are interested in improving their financial position through investments. One place they can do this on their own is in the stock market.

Although for many years more women than men have owned stock, comparatively few women do their own investing and trading in the market. Gerald Loeb, the author mentioned previously, who was one of the most respected investment authorities in the 30's and 40's on Wall Street, remarked that he had few women clients, and the passing years have done little to change this. In 1977 a young college professor on the television program "Wall Street Week" expressed puzzlement that he had only two women in his classes on finance.

One reason so few women have been involved in the stock market has been the protective attitude of husbands who buy stock in their wives' names and then assume that if anything happens to them, their wives would be taken care of. They feel all the widows have to do is collect the dividends, and if they need advice, there are plenty of men in the financial field to help them.

But what of the women who might want to learn more? A difficulty those women who might have become interested in handling their own investments have encountered has been the chauvinistic attitude of men that higher finance is beyond their understanding.

An example of this intolerance is the complaint of a young teacher friend that her father had laughed at her when she said she wanted to learn about investing on Wall Street. She had heard her father and brothers discussing their investments, and now that she was working, she had money to invest too. In fact, she was earning even more money than the brothers were. His advice to her was, "Just ask the boys what they buy and buy the same," as though learning to invest on her own would be beyond her.

Unfortunately, many women themselves are convinced that Wall Street investing takes skills beyond their capabilities. Because they think they are not good at math, many women think they would not be good at investing in stocks. Neither belief could be farther from the truth. A number of writers on the stock market emphasize strongly that nothing more than elementary school arithmetic is necessary for successful investing. All a person needs to know is how to add, subtract, divide, and to understand simple fractions and percentages. And to make things even easier, quicker, and more accurate, an inexpensive calculator can do all the arithmetic computations for the investor.

One reason beginners have been frightened of the stock market is the attitude of many writers and professionals in the market who look upon investing and trading on Wall Street as a fierce game. They love the excitement of competition for profits; they consider it a war against the nameless "they" who are out to take their money away. To them it's the violence of professional football or the razzle-dazzle of the Harlem Globetrotters. But it need not be considered in that light. A better game to compare it with is bridge, and both men and women are excellent bridge players. Playing with both cards and stocks requires skill and art and intuition. In both bridge and investing, the players must take time to develop a "feel" for the game. As one writer on the market put it, only an experienced player knows when not to finesse.

Some beginners, both men and women, may be worried because the term "speculation" is frequently used when speaking of trading with stocks, and many people equate this term with gambling. Yet speculation in stocks is a legitimate form of trading for profit and has never been condemned by any church or state. In fact, many religious organizations have large sums invested in the market, just as do some government agencies with surplus funds. After all, to speculate simply means, according to Webster's dictionary, "to engage in a risky business venture on the chance of making huge profits." There are many people who are speculators in the real estate business, who buy property hoping to sell at a profit, yet nobody refers to them as gamblers. Nor is there the same attitude toward antique dealers, or coin dealers, or art dealers, even though they too buy and take a chance on making a profit. They are all risk takers because their prices rise and fall, just as stocks do.

To be successful in the stock market takes as much knowledge and skill and art as it does to be successful in the antique, the coin, and the art business. To be considered a gambler in one and not in the others is most unfair—worse, unreasonable.

Many beginners find that Wall Street jargon is very confusing. It takes weeks to learn that "bull" means the market is going up, and that "bear" means that the market is going down. How these terms ever came to be used no one knows. Also the sensationalism of the language used in writing about the market is disturbing. Writers use such terms as "pigs" and "panic" and "risk" and "fear" and "greed" as though these emotions exist only in the stock market. People who overvalue their houses when they try to sell them are not called "pigs"; they are considered smart operators if they get their price. Anyone in any legitimate business wants to make as much profit as possible and fears too great a loss in times of difficulty, yet no such terms are attached to them. It would be an improvement to use a lot less emotional terms in the Wall Street business too.

Potential investors, particularly women, are intimidated in reading about financial news. They might encounter some sensational headlines, like (when the market has taken a 10 per cent reversal) "Stock Market Loses $5 Billion in 80 Point Drop." (I am just guessing at the figures.) Of course, the previous year it had gained over a hundred points, so the headline could have been "Stock Market Gains $6 Billion in 100 Point Spurt." Tossing such big figures about can make many people fearful. When all the stores in the country reduce their linens 20 per cent or so in January, no paper headlines "Merchandisers Lose a Billion Dollars in January White Sales." They instead advertise heavily to stimulate sales, and their customers just look at it as a good time for everyone to get bargains. The stock market is no different. People wait for January white sales to buy linens; if they aren't ready to buy that month, they know they can get the same bargains in July. New investors need to learn they have the same opportunities for bargains in the stock market; these times when stock prices are cheaper come just as periodically.

In writing this book I have tried to keep in mind the person who may know nothing about stocks and the market. I have illustrated every step of the learning process with material I have found valuable, and I have tried to use figures and explanations that are easy to understand. Many of the chapters will require study, but if you will put forth the effort to learn, you will find your new skills absorbing and financially rewarding.

CHAPTER 2

Why You Should Be in the Stock Market

Despite the excitement and suspense it generates, investing in the stock market can be a conservative activity and should not be equated with gambling on the horses or with playing war games. It is true investors are taking chances, but they are also taking chances when they cross the street. But just as they protect themselves by crossing the street with the green light, so can beginning investors protect themselves by learning all they can about the fundamentals and techniques of stock market investing and trading.

It is interesting that business people are not considered chance takers, yet they are. A manufacturer invests a fortune in a plant, has to put up with raw material problems, production problems, employee problems, sales problems; yet he is willing to risk his money so he can make a profit. Most years he probably will, but some years he won't, at least not as much.

Men and women who open up retail stores also take chances. They take a chance that they can make money in spite of high rents, dishonest employees, shoplifters, rising costs of their products, season sales, competition, taxes, government restrictions, and a host of other things.

And who is a greater chance-taker than a dry-land farmer! He spends many thousands of dollars on equipment and seeds, plants his corn and wheat, and knows full well there will be years the rains won't come and he'll lose his shirt.

It is in this business sense that investing in the stock market is a risk. It is in the sense of deliberately going into the business of investing in the stock market, knowing that some years you will make a good profit, other years a little, and some years none.

A person entering into the investment field should have the same attitude as a person opening a clothing store or a boutique. These retailers expect to make their normal profit on the greater percentage of their merchandise. But they know that as the season wanes, they need to start reducing their prices. So they will make a smaller profit on part of the balance of the merchandise, barely get their money back on some, and take a loss on a little. This is the retailing game.

This is what stock market investors should expect too. They should expect to make a good profit on 60 per cent to 70 per cent of their trades, barely get their money back on some, and cut their losses before they get too deep on the rest. This is the stock market trading game.

Just as successful clothing merchants spend many years learning their business, so too must the successful investors spend years learning the necessary skills. They must learn to be good buyers, to learn what stocks will probably go up so they can sell at a profit. They have to learn how to buy at the right time and how to sell at the right time. They have to learn the fundamentals about choosing companies to follow and the techniques for keeping track of the pulse of the market. They don't learn this overnight.

Investing in the stock market should be looked upon as just another type of business. It is one of the easiest small businesses to get into or out of. One advantage is that age is no factor, and the skills can be practiced just as successfully by a young person beginning a career or by a retiree interested in adding zest to leisurely living. It can bring extra money for luxuries and be great fun. It can banish boredom and bring a sense of adventure to one's life. One writer described the active traders on Wall Street as the most alive men he knew!

Going into the stock market business can be an excellent avocation for the woman who wishes to be a homemaker and yet would like to learn a skill which could be profitable for herself and for her family. And why not include the family? It could be a shared interest with the husband; it could be a shared interest with the children. Many math classes in junior high school have a unit on investing in the stock market as a basis for learning math skills. Many high school economics classes have a similar unit. And college students taking business courses have stock market units which encourage them to become life-long investors in stocks. It could make for lively conversation around the dinner table!

Successful investing demands more skill, insight, and discipline than most investors are willing to put into it. Many successful businessmen and professionals assume that because they are doing well in their own fields, they will have no difficulty making money in the market. Unfortunately, there is no carryover. Success as a doctor does not insure success as a stock investor. Those who consistently win in the market are aware that intelligence is not enough. They need to study and learn the moods of the market; they need to confront their own emotions and learn to control them; they need to study their own mistakes so as not to repeat them. They need to devote time to learn the psychology of the market so they can confidently make their own decisions, based on study and skill and insight.

How much can intelligent investors make in the stock market if they are fairly active and are willing to learn a moderate amount of the necessary skills? Most writers feel 20 per cent per year is not an unreasonable goal. Some, less modest, aim at doubling their money in several years, and others envision that 20 per cent profit for each trade with five trades a year equals 100 per cent, or twice as much money as you start out with.

There are over 25 million investors in the stock market today, and they trade about 40 per cent of the shares bought and sold each day. The other 60 per cent is traded by institutions such as pension funds, mutual funds, insurance companies, and banks. In 1976 the New York Stock Exchange averaged over 21 million shares a day. This average means about 8 million shares each day for the small investors. They are not all losing money!

There is no denying that there is a risk in buying stock, but for most people this risk is much greater than it needs to be. To avoid this loss they must be willing to devote three to five hours each week to the subject of investment. Buying and selling stocks require careful and thorough study. In his book, mentioned previously, Gerald Loeb feels that devoting time to investment can, in many cases, increase a person's wealth more than the way in which he earns his living. He feels that taking time from one's business to learn to trade in the stock market can often be more profitable than the business itself.

It should be remembered that there is risk in any form of investment. You might lose some of your money if the value of your investments in real estate, or antiques, or art should go down. Or you might put your money in the bank and risk losing part of the value of your dollars through inflation. Even the banks and insurance companies are investing more and more in common stocks because records show that the average stock has made a higher rate of gain and provided a greater protection against inflation than most other forms of investment.

Some of the reasons that investing in Wall Street has advantages is that the prices of stocks are continually listed in the daily paper, and stocks can easily be bought or sold at quoted prices, plus a commission. An alternative form of investment—real estate, for example—cannot be bought or sold as readily, also involves a commission, and does not give the same protection against fraud. The real estate business does not have a Securities and Exchange Commission, mandated by Congress, breathing down its neck.

The rise of the investment funds, with their billions of dollars, might lead a prospective investor to think he could never do as well on his own. Actually, the small investors have a better chance of making money than the large institutions. For one thing, they have the advantage of being able to buy and sell much more easily. Their relatively small number of shares does not disturb the basic trend of prices. In spite of higher commissions, they can make a profit on a smaller increase in prices than can an institution.

According to statistics, a large mutual fund needs a 31 per cent increase in price to sell a stock and reinvest without losing money, because they buy or sell many thousands of shares at a time. Their big block of shares increases the price they have to pay when they buy and depresses the price when they sell. This is because such large numbers cannot be bought or sold at one time but must be transacted piecemeal. When other investors become aware of such volume, their rushing in to buy or sell too affects the price for the funds. This same 31 per cent can yield the small investor a handsome profit. Nor do the funds perform so well that their returns average more than the market as a whole. Some funds do better than the market, some do about the same, and some do much worse—which is what individual investors do on their own too.

One important point which needs stressing is that the money small investors use to invest in Wall Street must be money that they do not need for everyday living expenses. They should have a savings account for emergencies and adequate insurance for their needs. Then, and only then, should they think of investing in the stock market.

How much money do you need to begin your program? You can start with less than $500. Does this sound like a lot of money? Let's consider some hobbies that you or your friends might have. Photography? Did you buy a good camera, and lenses and other equipment? Have you added to this the film and the costs of developing this film? Of course, you do get a great deal of pleasure and satisfaction in creating pictures to keep and to display and to discuss with friends. But unless you become a professional photographer, you get no monetary rewards for your work. The same money invested intelligently in the stock market can increase your original investment many times over. And you can get equal pleasure in discussing with others your great interest, to say nothing of the personal satisfaction you get from achieving success. Have you taken up skiing and taken a few trips a year to ski resorts? For the same price you can have an absorbing hobby which not only involves you the year round, but which can also make money for you.

New investors might wonder about the safety of their investments in the stock market. They know that most banks and savings and loan companies have their accounts insured by the federal government, but they are not sure about how safe their accounts are with the brokerage firms. In the late 1960's, because of antiquated methods of keeping records, many prestigious brokerage firms were shown to be unable to handle the volume of paper work brought about by a greatly increased volume of business. This failure to keep up with modern methods forced many mergers and consolidations and a few outright collapses before the incompetents were weeded out of Wall Street. This closing of many firms brought about the 1970 Securities Investor Protection Corporation Act, which provides federal protection for each account. Recently amended, the act provides a total protection of $100,000 for each account, with up to

$40,000 in cash or all in securities, for investors who still have accounts in brokerage firms when they go out of business.

Also, in the late 1960's business was booming so greatly that an arrogance descended upon the brokerage business and many firms refused to handle small accounts. However, the market declines in 1970 and 1974 chastened many of these firms, and there are few now which have any minimum requirements for the amount of money or the number of shares in any order. The New York Stock Exchange, in answer to criticism about small accounts, has established an Investors Service Bureau to supply small investors with the names of firms in their areas that handle accounts of all sizes. The bureau's address is 11 Wall Street, New York, New York 10005.

CHAPTER 3

What Are Stocks?

If you wanted to go into business for yourself, would you have enough money to take care of all your needs? If you do, lucky you. If you don't have the money, you have three choices: You could scrounge around and borrow from relatives and friends, perhaps with reluctance lest they become too involved with your venture. Or you could borrow money from some bank or lending institution and worry about meeting your deadline of payments. Or you could follow the basis of capitalism and the entire free enterprise system, become a company and raise capital through the sale of common stock.

What is common stock? Let's try to explain by following Mr. and Mrs. Smith through their new business venture. It works something like this: These two young people invent a new hair cutter to use in their barber-beauty shop business, and they are convinced that they can sell these to every barber and beauty operator who sees it. They patent the new invention and decide they want to manufacture it themselves. Unfortunately, they haven't the $50,000 it would take to rent a building, buy the necessary machinery, buy the materials needed, pay for labor, advertise it, and sell it.

So the couple decides to form a company and sell shares to friends, relatives, and anyone willing to take a chance that the venture will prove profitable. Since everyone can't afford to put in the same amount of money, they issue 5,000 shares at $10 each. Some people buy more than others, but they are able to raise the money they need.

Every person who owns a share of stock is a part owner of the company. As they can't all get together to discuss major decisions, they elect a board of directors to oversee the operations of the company. They can attend an annual meeting open to all stockholders, and they are all sent an annual report from the board on how well the company is doing. Stockholders who cannot attend the annual meeting are asked to sign a proxy, a statement which authorizes one of the directors to vote for them. Each share entitles them to one vote.

One reason for a person to invest in the company is the hope of sharing in its profits. If it has earned $5,000 its second year in business, the board of directors might decide to keep half of the profits to put back into the business and divide the balance among the shareholders. Each person would get $.50 for each share owned, a 5 per cent return on the investment.

Another reason for investing in the company is the hope of someday selling the shares for more than the $10 that was paid for each one. How much will the price be at the time he wants to sell his stock? Only whatever someone else is willing to pay for it. The value of the company (the assets it owns) is not the deciding factor in determining the price of its stock. If another investor thinks the company will continue to grow in sales, that it will continue to pay part of its profits each year to owners of the stock, that its stock will go up in price, the buyer might be willing to pay more for the stock than the seller had paid for it. So the original investor has profited in two ways—capital gain as well as dividends.

Where can the investor find a buyer? In the markets where stocks are bought and sold. The stock exchanges themselves do not buy or sell the stock. They simply act as a place to get the buyers and the sellers together. In this way they resemble the real estate companies with whom you list your house when you want to sell it. You set your price to them and their agents try to sell it for your price or to the highest bidder. For this the seller gives the agent a commission. In the stock exchanges there are also prices that the sellers ask and prices that the buyers bid. The seller might want to get $12 a share for his stock, but the buyer is willing to pay about $11.50. If each consents to buy and sell "at market," the two brokers try to get the best price that they can at the moment of sale for their client; so the two might agree on $11.75. Both the buyers and the sellers pay commission.

Let's pretend the above transaction occurred on the floor of the

New York Stock Exchange in order to show what else might occur there. Suppose the broker for the person who wanted to sell the stock could find no one who wanted to buy it. Or suppose the broker who wanted to buy the stock could find none for his client. In either case the broker turns the order over to another broker, a specialist in that stock who confines his activities to only a particular few of the stocks listed. This specialist puts the order in his book and assumes the responsibility for executing it for a share of the commission. He has the right to buy the stock for himself or sell from his own holdings. He is obligated to buy or sell to maintain "a fair and orderly" market when one of his stocks is moving up or down too rapidly. If necessary he must borrow stocks he needs to fulfil his function.

When the term "stock market" is used, it is necessary to understand that there is more than one market. For the private investors there are three markets which predominate: the New York Stock Exchange, the American Stock Exchange, and the over-the-counter market, which is a collection of stock dealers from every part of the country. Shares of 1,550 major U.S. corporations are traded (which means bought and sold in Wall Street jargon) on the New York Stock Exchange daily. The American Stock Exchange lists about 1,000 companies, but they usually are newer and more speculative, and most of their shares sell for less than on the larger New York exchange. Most of the rest of the companies listed, comprising many thousands of both large and small companies, are traded in the over-the-counter market. In addition, there are about 15 regional exchanges which function very much like the New York Stock Exchange.

With thousands and thousands of companies listed in all the exchanges, you must make an important decision. The first thing you need to realize is that, since you are a beginner, you need as much safety as you can possibly get. You will find this margin of safety in the New York Stock Exchange list of 1,550 companies, because their requirements for being listed are so exacting. These are the requirements as stated in their *1977 Fact Book*:

> Listing Requirements: To be listed on the New York Stock Exchange, a company is expected to meet certain qualifications and to be willing to keep the investing public informed on the progress of its affairs. The company must be a going concern, or be the successor to a going

concern. In determining eligibility for listing, particular attention is given to such qualifications as: 1) the degree of national interest in the company; 2) its relative position and stability in the industry; and 3) whether it is engaged in an expanding industry, with prospects of at least maintaining its relative position.

Initial Listing—While each case is decided on its own merits, the Exchange generally requires the following as a minimum:

1. Demonstrated earning power under competitive conditions of $2.5 million before Federal income taxes for the most recent year and $2 million pretax for each of the preceding two years.
2. Net tangible assets of $16 million, but greater emphasis is placed on the aggregate market value of the common stock.
3. Market value of publicly held shares, subject to adjustment depending on market conditions, within the following limits:
   Maximum $16,000,000
   Minimum $ 8,000,000
   Present   (5/1/77) $16,000,000
4. A total of 1,000,000 common shares publicly held.
5. 2,000 holders of 100 shares or more.

Listing Agreement: The listing agreement between the company and the Exchange is designed to provide timely disclosure to the public of earnings statements, dividend notices, and other information which might reasonably be expected materially to affect the market for securities. The Exchange requires actively operating companies to agree to solicit proxies for all meetings of stockholders.

With the above high standards you can see why you, as a beginning investor, should stick to those companies listed on the New York Stock Exchange. And for an added margin of safety, you need to confine your transactions to common stocks. Leave to the more sophisticated investors the more complicated vehicles of investment.

CHAPTER 4

Where to Get Information about Stocks

The beginner learning any new skill has to practice using the tools the skill calls for. If you took home economics in school and were assigned to a cooking class, you had to first learn to read and interpret the recipe in the cookbook for the simple dish you were about to prepare. You had to learn what all the abbreviations for the measurements stood for, how to mix the ingredients together, and then how to cook the food.

As in a cookbook, the information about the stock market has its own "recipes" containing abbreviations you need to learn. The following reproduction is taken from the New York Stock Exchange's booklet *You and the Investment World*. It is written in simple language and will teach you to read the financial pages of any paper.

Reading from left to right, the first important point of information it gives is in the high-low columns, which tell you the highest price and the lowest price the stock sold for during the year. Notice that Am T&T fluctuated almost 12 points, meaning $12, that year.

After the high-low comes the name of the company, followed by the dividend it last paid, which would be important to an investor who bought the stock for income. The P/E ratio column is defined in note by No. 6. This will be discussed in greater detail in a later chapter.

The sales column tells you how active the stock is by how many shares changed hands the previous day, which gives an indication of the interest held by investors. The high-low-close columns give you that day's fluctuation in price, and also enable you to see that the stock price is near the year's high by comparing the close column with the year's high-low columns. The net change shows the price is still rising.

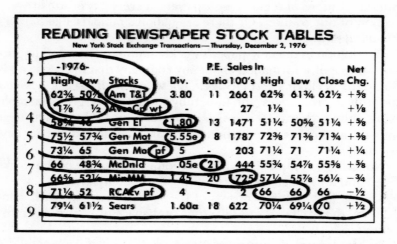

READING NEWSPAPER STOCK TABLES
New York Stock Exchange Transactions — Thursday, December 2, 1976

	-1976-				P.E.	Sales In				Net
	High	Low	Stocks	Div.	Ratio	100's	High	Low	Close	Chg.
3	62¾	50⅞	Am T&T	3.80	11	2661	62⅜	61¾	62½	+⅝
	1⅞	½	AveoCp wt	-	-	27	1⅛	1	1	+⅛
4	58¾	46	Gen El	1.80	13	1471	51¼	50⅝	51¼	+⅝
5	75½	57¾	Gen Mot	5.55e	8	1787	72⅜	71⅜	71¾	+⅜
6	73¼	65	Gen Mot pf	5	-	203	71¼	71	71¼	+¼
7	66	48¾	McDnld	.05e	21	444	55¾	54⅞	55⅝	+⅝
	66⅝	52½	MinMM	1.45	20	725	57¼	55⅞	56¼	-¾
8	71¼	52	RCA cv pf	4	-	2	66	66	66	-½
9	79¼	61½	Sears	1.60a	18	622	70¼	69¼	70	+½

1. Abbreviated name of the corporation issuing the stock. The stocks listed are common stocks unless an entry after the name indicates otherwise.

2. Wt stands for warrant. As with stocks, the price range indicates the highest and lowest prices per share paid for this warrant on the Exchange during the year – In this case, $1.87½ and $0.50.

3. Rate of annual dividend — for this stock, $1.80. This amount is an estimation based on the last quarterly or semi-annual payment.

4. Letters following the dividend number indicate additional information. Here, for example, the "e" designates the stated amount as declared or paid so far this year. Other symbols are explained in tables appearing in newspapers.

5. "pf" following the name indicates a preferred stock.

6. The price of a share of stock divided by earnings per share for a 12-month period.

7. This column shows the number of shares reported traded for the day, expressed in hundreds–for this stock. 72,500. This number does not include stocks bought in odd-lot quantities, that is, in quantities less than 100 shares for most stocks. The letter "z" preceding an entry indicates the actual number of shares traded.

8. The highest price paid for this security during the day's trading session was $66.00 – the lowest, $66.00. Cv. pf. stands for convertibile preferred.

9. The closing price or last sale of the day in this stock was at $70.00 per share. And this, Thursday's closing price, is $0.50 more than the closing price of the previous day–as indicated by the " + ½."

Your own daily paper may give you complete coverage of the stocks on the New York Stock Exchange. You need not make use of the daily figures unless you wish to keep track of a particular stock in which you are interested. The Sunday paper, which gives the weekly summary, is important. Following many stocks daily involves more time than you need to spend; besides, stocks may fluctuate greatly from day to day but usually seem to even out at the end of the week. Keeping track then on a regular weekly basis is essential for success in the market.

Your own Sunday newspaper probably gives this weekly summary of the New York Stock Exchange listings. If it doesn't, there are the

Sunday editions of regional newspapers in every city of size in every section of our country. Or there are national tabloids, like *Barron's Financial Weekly*.

In addition to the newspaper's weekly summary, a second important source of information about any company that interests you is Standard & Poor's *Stock Guide*. These stock digests are issued monthly to brokerages, and hopefully you should be given a sample copy without charge by a broker eager for your business. The next four pages show a reproduction of the *Stock Guide* and instructions for use.

Notice how complete the information is about each of the stocks listed and how much you can learn about the company:

1. The first column consists of the symbols used for each company by the exchanges to save time and space in recording transactions.

2. The second column gives the names of the companies and the markets where they are traded. You will be interested only in those traded on the New York Stock Exchange (NYS), discussed in the last chapter.

3. The earnings and dividends ranking is a score given by Standard & Poor based on a formula covering the past eight years. A+ is the highest ranking.

4. Par value is explained later. It is not important in evaluating a company.

5. The next two columns tell how many financial institutions hold the stock and the number of shares they have. This might influence your thinking about a company. You might feel that heavy institutional investing is a safety factor and indicates the company has been investigated by experts and they feel its stock is a good investment.

6. The principal business column gives important information about the company. You might be unaware of all the areas in which business is done.

7. Price range. This gives the highest price and the lowest price at which the shares were sold for the calendar years indicated, the past year, and the present year. These are important to show the trading range of the stock. This will be discussed in greater detail later.

8. The next column indicates the sales in the past month, given in hundreds. This information is important because you want to follow only those stocks that are reasonably active, so you can buy and sell

with greater ease. Active means at least 25,000 shares were traded the previous month.

9. The percentage of dividends, the years they have been issued, and the latest payments are of interest to investors who wish to get the greatest possible annual yields for income. They are also an indication of the solidarity of the company.

10. This covers the rest of the columns. The P/E ratio is the ratio of price of a share to the earnings of the company. The financial position gives the assets and liabilities of the company as shown in its balance sheet. Capitalization shows the long-term debt of the company and the number and kind of shares it has issued. The earnings-per-share column covers the last five years for comparison. All these are discussed in later chapters.

A third source of information is Standard & Poor's *Stock Reports*, which can be found in the reference department of many public libraries. In addition, many main and branch libraries may have other sources, such as Moody's *Stock Survey*, Value Line's *Ratings and Reports*, Moody's *Handbook*, the daily publication *The Wall Street Journal*, and *Barron's Financial Weekly*. These are just some of the sources available.

There are also hundreds of company annual reports available. You may send for them through the publications; or your own library probably has some of these and would welcome your using its facilities. And don't overlook the fact that many banks carry financial manuals, as do all brokerage offices.

The stock reports give a wealth of information not available from the one line in the *Stock Digest*. From the following reproduction of the report of Addressograph Multigraph, you can see how much material it contains. On the front is a short summary of the company, giving its principal areas of business and an evaluation of its future prospects. The page also includes a five-year chart, giving you a quick comparison of the stock prices with the market as a whole. Notice how much better this stock has done than the average of the market; its price continues to go up while the market line is declining.

The back of the sheet gives more complete financial statistics from the balance sheet and the profit and loss statements over a ten-year period. It also contains a more complete description of the company's products and pertinent details a prospective investor should know.

STANDARD & POOR'S CORPORATION

#	Ticker Symbol	Name of Issue (Call Price of Pfd. Stocks)	Market	Com Rank & Pfd Rating	Par Val	Inst Hold Cos	Inst Hold Shs (000)	Principal Business	1960-76 High	1960-76 Low	1977 High	1977 Low	1978 High	1978 Low	Apr Sales in 100s	April 1978 High	Low	Last Sale Or Bid	% Div Yield	P-E Ratio
1	LG	Laclede Gas	NYS,MW,Ph	B	4	15	174	Distr nat gas in St. Louis	32½	3½	24½	8	20¼	19¾	185	20	19¾	19½	8.7	6
2	LCLD	Laclede Steel	OTC	B	20	3	50	Semi & finished steel prods	35½	3¾	18¼	8	12¾	11¼	238	12½	11	12B		6
3	LAF	Lafayette Radio Elec.	ASE	B		5	422	Sells hi-fi components, etc.	9¼	1¾	9¼	1¼	6¾	4¾	757	6¾	6⅛	6⅝		8
4	LKK	Lake Shore Mines	ASE,TS	B+		..	..	Invest in mining & bldg cos		2¾		1½	3	2¾	554	3	2½	2¾		d
5	LAKE	Lake Superior Dis Pw	OTC		10	..	6	Elec util-Wisc & Mich areas	15¾	8	13¾	11¾	12¾	11¾	74	12	11¾	11⅛B	8.8	8
6	LMR	La Maur, Inc.	ASE	B	3⅓¢	1	25	Hair care;personal grooming	40	2¾	5¾	3½		3¾	453	4		4	5.0	11
7	LMS	Lamson & Sessions	NYS	B+	5	5	271	Mfr industrial fasteners	27¼	5¾	23¾	17½	26¼	17	2718	26½	17	26¼ B	4.9	9
8	LAMS	Lamston (M.H.)	OTC,Bo	B+	5	..	..	Variety strs, NYC & environs	20½	5¼	11½	9¼	13½	11¼		13½		13½ B	9.6	5
9	LANC	Lancaster Colony	OTC	B+		1	408	Housewares: ind'l products	28¾	3¾	21	9¾	22½	18¼	1059	22½	16½	22¼ B	3.2	10
10	LNCE	Lance, Inc.	OTC	A	83⅓¢	122	130	Snack foods: vending	30	3¾	18¼	13	18½	15½	1476	18¼	16½	18¼ B	4.8	11
11	LHRT	Lanchart Indus.	OTC	NR	10¢	..	2	Mobile & modular home mfr	20¾	⅞	5¾	3¾	5½	4½	291	5½	4¾	5B	4.8	6
12	LRES	Land Resources	OTC	NR	10¢	1	108	Real estate interests	13½	½	1½		3¾	1½	819	3¾	3	3¾ B		8
13	BKF	Landmark Bkg Fla.	OTC			7	968	Multiple bank bldg, Fla	24¾	5	6¼	5¾	6½	5½	1383	6¾	6¼	6½ B	6.2	8
14	LML	Landmark Land	ASE,MW	NR	50¢	1	16	Land develop:bldg,mtls distr	30½	5	5½	2	4¾	4½	494	4¾	4¼	4¾		19
15	LNY	Lane Bryant	NYS	A	No	20	788	Apparel chain,mail order	34	5¾	14¾	12	14¾	11¾	527	14½	12½	14¾	6.1	7
16	LANE	Lane Co.	OTC	B+	5	14	706	Furniture mfr.	59	4¾	19¾	15¾	19¾	16	295	19¾	19	19¾ B	4.5	6
17	LAND	Lane Wood.	OTC	NR		..	..	Mobile hm financing:hous'g	12	1¾	⅞	1/16		1¾	803	3½	3½	3½ B		16
18	LNO	Lanco, Inc	ASE	NR		..	..	Supermkts & deptment strs		⅜	5¾	3½	5¾	4¾	113	5¾	4¾	5¾	3.2	12
19	LBP	Lanier Business Prod.	NYS,PS	NR	1	15	104	Mfr dictating eq;dstr 3M pr	25		22¾	13	25¼	18¼	943	25¼	23	23¾ B	1.7	13
20	LPI	La Pointe Indus	ASE	B		..	..	Elec/electronic components		⅜	5¾	4	6¾	4¾	199	6¾	4¾	5⅛B	5.9	8
21	LQM	La Quinta Mtr Inns	ASE	B+	10¢	6	161	Motor inn operator	8¾	1¾	16¼	11¾	23¾	13	1264	23¾	19¾	21¼ B		24
22	LARS	Larsen Co.	ASE	B+		3	27	Canned & frozen vegetables	19	4½	14½	11¾	23¾	12¼	803	19¾	13½	21½ B	6.4	12
23	LBF	LaTouraine-Bickfds Fd	ASE	B+	10¢	..	..	Pancake houses: ring mfr	4¾	1¼	2	1¾	2¾	1¼	323	1¾	1¼	1⅝B	0.7	6
24	LAUF	Laufer Co	OTC	NR	10¢	..	..	Magazine publish:talent	12¾	¾	6	3½	9¾	5¾	770	9¾	8¾	9¾ B	6.1	10
25	LF	Laurestide Fin'l	MS,TS,VS	B+	10¢	..	..	Financial services: insur	29¾	2¾	8	6¾	8¾	7	58	8¾	7¾	8¾ B		
26	LAWH	Lawhon (J.F.)Furniture	OTC	NR	5¢	..	55	Warehouse-showroom retailer	26¾	1¾	26¾	9¾		3¾	423	6	3¼	6B		24
27	LWRY	Lawry's Foods	OTC	B+	2	15	153	Specialty food products	25	1¾	17¾	11	13	10¾	227	13	12	13B	2.4	12
28	LAWS	Lawson Products	OTC	B+	No	39	398	Dstr fasteners, maint parts	21¾	2¼	17¾	9¾	11¾	8¾	1094	18¼	10¼	18¼ B	1.6	16
29	LAW	Lawter Chemicals	NYS	A+		4	82	Printing ink vehicles, resin	14¾	2¾	9¾	5¾	12¾	10½	3572	12¾	10¾	11¾ B	3.1	15
30	LAZA	Lazare Kaplan Int'l	OTC			..	..	Cutter/merchant diamonds							146					
31	LAZB	La-Z-Boy Chair	OTC	B+	10¢	8	194	Mfr of reclining chairs	46¾	4¾	20	11¾	14¾	11¾	463	14¾	13¾	13¾ B	5.2	7
32	LPET	Lear Petroleum	OTC	B+		2	21	Gas gathering: oil/gas	7¾	1¾	19¾	6¾	17¾	13¾	2808	17¾	13¾	17⅛B	0.6	10
33	LSI	Lear Siegler	NYS,Bo,MW,Ph,PS	B+		27	923	Vehicle comp:electr/commun	29¾	1¾	17¾	13¾	19¾	13¾	11533	19¾	15¾	19¾ B	4.0	6
34	Pr	$2.25 cm Cv Pfd (45)vrtg	NYS,PS	BB	No	11	92	ind'l,agric,housing prod	72¾	17¾	43¾	35½	48	35½	616	48	38½	47¾	4.7	7
35	LRI	Lee-Ronal	ASE	B+		9	265	Chemicals, electroplat proc	20½	4¾	4¾	4¼	15¼	7	422	14¼	13	14¼	4.1	8
36	LTC	Leaseway Transport	NYS,Bo	A−		50	544	All areas mtr veh transp	51¾	3¾	35½	27	33½	27½	2008	33½	32	33	4.8	8
37	LEE	Lee Enterprises	NYS	A	2½	35	272	Newspaper publish:radio,TV	25	3¾	28½	20½	29½	22¾	603	29¾	27¾	29¾	2.6	8
38	LEN	Lee National	ASE,Ph	C	2½	2	65	Fin'l sv to real estate indy	30	2¾	4¾	2¾	4¾	2¾	120	3¾	3	3½		d
39	LPH	Lee Pharmaceuticals	ASE,EPS	NR	No	1	13	Prevent/restoral dentistry	24	2¾	4½	2½	4½	4	529	4¾	4	4½		37
40	LDN	Leeds & Northrup	NYS,Bo,Ph	B+	25¢	14	398	Electronic instr. contr sys	26¾	4½	25	13	25¼	19	2266	25¾	21	25¼	2.9	10
41	LSO	Lesona Corp	NYS,Bo	B		10	138	Mfr textile & plastics mchy	59¾	5¾	23½	17	20½	16¾	933	19¾	17¾	17¾	5.8	6
42	LEGG	Leggett & Platt	NYS	A−	5	9	316	Mfr springs,etc for furn,bed	28¾	2	16¾	9¾	19¾	14¾	1149	19¾	16¾	19¾ B	2.7	7
43	LEH	Lehigh Press	ASE	B	No	1	113	Commercial printer: packag'g	17¾	2¾	8¾	5¾	9¾	8	468	9¾	9¾	9¾		3
44		Lehigh Valley Ind	NYS,Bo,MW,Ph	C	50¢	5	24	Textiles: elec prod, shoes	13¾	2¾	4¾	2¾	4¾	2¾	1965	3¾	1¾	1½		6
45	Pr	$1.50 cm Cv A Pfd (27½) vtg	NYS		No			Metal castings: sales prom	134	4¾	30¾	13	28¾	22	12	28¾	26	24B		

Uniform Footnote Explanations—See Page 1. Other: [a]$3.35,'77. [b]$1.42,'77. [c]North'n States Pwr proposes merger,$14. [d]$0.05'76.
[e]Mo Dec,pr fiscal Apr '74. [f]$0.11,'72. [g]Harlequin Enterprises has acq.about 53% of co. [h]$0.21,'76. [i]Plan go private, $3.28. [j]$1.66,'77.
[k]$0.26,'76. [l]$2.12-$0.10,'77. [m]$2.43,'77. [n]Accum on Pfd. [o]$0.40,'77. [p]$0.26,'76. [q]$1.59-$0.43,'77. [r]$1.59-$0.43,'77. [s]$0.22,'77. [t]$1.66,'77.

HOW TO USE THE STOCK GUIDE

It is necessary to read carefully the following instructions and those on Pages 1 and 6 to correctly interpret abbreviations and data in the Guide.

P-E Ratio	P-E Ratio (Price-Earnings Ratio)—See explanation on Page 1.
% Div. Yield	Yields are derived by dividing total indicated dividend rate by price of stock. Such rate is based on latest dividend paid including (†), or excluding stock. In the case of Canadian issues, prices are quoted in Canadian dollars (e) extras as indicated by footnote. Additional symbols used: (s) including stock; and (‡) including extras and stock.
Last Month OTC—Bid Prices High Low Last	Last sales on principal exchanges are closing quotations for the preceding month. In the case of Canadian issues, prices are quoted in Canadian dollars providing the first exchange listed is a Canadian exchange. In the case of over-the-counter stocks, the latest available bid price is shown under the "Last" column.
Month Sales in 100s	Trading volume is for the month indicated on the Composite Tape, in hundreds of shares.
PRICE RANGE — Historical High Low / Last Year High Low / Current Year High Low	High and Low price ranges are for the calendar years indicated. Price ranges are not exclusive for the exchange on which the stock is currently traded, but are based on the best available data covering the period of the column head. Price ranges of over-the-counter stocks are based on the best available high and low bid prices during the period, and should be viewed as reasonable approximations.
PRINCIPAL BUSINESS	This is the principal business of the company. Where a company is engaged in several lines of business every effort has been made to list that line from which it obtains the greatest proportion of its revenue. In addition, an indication of the company's rank in the industry is given where possible.
★ Inst. Hold Cos Shs. (1000)	The number of financial institutions—banks, investment and insurance companies—that hold this stock and the number of shares (000 omitted) held. See explanation on Page 1.
Par Val.	Present par value of the stock named. In determining transfer taxes, No Par issues are figured the same as $100 par.
Earns & Div Ranking	Standard & Poor's Ranking System is explained on Page 4.
STOCKS NAME OF ISSUE (Call Price of Pfd. Stocks) Market	The markets for each issue are indicated by standard abbreviations, as shown on Page 6. Stocks traded "Over-the-Counter" are indicated by the abbreviation OTC; it will be noted that some issues may have an active OTC market as well as exchange markets. 10—10 shares; 25—25 shares; 50—50 shares; all others 100 shares. Unit of Trading for stocks on the New York Stock Exchange and American Stock Exchange is indicated as follows: Abbreviations of various provisions, etc. are shown on Page 6. The Call Price of preferred stocks is shown in parentheses after the name of the issue; the date indicates year in which call price declines. Where the abbreviations has been necessary. Where the name of the company is not followed by the designation of any particular issue of its stock, it is the common or capital stock that is referred to. Names shown in this column are not necessarily the exact corporate title of the company. Also, because of space limitations, the occasional use of abbreviations has been necessary.
Ticker Symbol	Ticker symbols on listed issues are those of the exchange first listed in "Market" column. OTC stocks carry NASDAQ Trading System symbols. Supplementary symbols as would appear on the ticker tape after symbol, such as "Pr" for preferred stocks, etc., are indented.
INDEX	The index numbers are a visual guide to the columnar data.

COMMON AND PREFERRED STOCKS

INDEX	Cash Divs. Ea. Yr. Since	DIVIDENDS						FINANCIAL POSITION				CAPITALIZATION 000					—$ Per Shr—EARNINGS—$ Per Shr—						Last 12 Mos.	INTERIM EARNINGS OR REMARKS			INDEX
		Latest Payment Date	Ex. Div.	$ So Far 1978	Total Ind. Rate	$ Paid 1977		Cash& Equiv. Mil-$	Curr. Assets	Curr. Liabs.	Balance Sheet Date	Long Term Debt Mil-$	Shs.—Pfd.	Com.	1973	1974	1975	Years 1976	1977		Period	$—Per Share—$ 1977	1978	
1	1946	QQ0.42½ 4-3-78 3-9	0.85	1.70	1.66		8.05	82.2	67.3	12-31-77	110.	399	4363 Sp	2.46	1.75	2.78	2.22	△2.59	3.38	12 Mo Mar	△3.22	3.38	1
2	1972	0.25 2-25-77 2-7	Nil	0.25		2.77	61.9	26.0	12-31-77	39.5		1650 Dc	2.29	10.35	2.25	1.12⁰△0.53	0.06	3 Mo Mar	d0.14	0.45	2
3	1975	0.06¼ 5-20-77 4-14	Nil	0.13		3.85	45.3	18.0	12-31-77			2199 Dc	□1.63	0.91	0.18	52d1.65	d2.24	6 Mo Dec△	0.31	d0.28	3
4		g0.10 11-15-55 10-7	Nil			6.00	6.13	0.04	12-31-77	22.6		5104 Dc	□0.38	□d0.17	d0.54	0.18	0.09				4
5	1937	0.26 6-1-78 5-9	0.52	1.04	1.03	0.55	7.82	5.24	12-31-77		30	1269 Dc	1.23	1.14	1.29	1.02	1.49	12 Mo Mar	1.11	1.48	5
6	1965	QQ0.05 3-29-78 3-9	0.05	0.20	0.20	0.46	11.4	3.44	12-31-77	0.13		1363 Dc	0.65	0.11	0.42	0.56	0.56	3 Mo Mar	0.21	0.02	6
7	1942	QQ0.32½ 6-9-78 5-15	0.65	1.30	1.20	4.55	65.6	22.4	12-31-77	38.9		1785 Dc	1.67	5.44	1.11	2.61	2.80	3 Mo Mar	0.71	0.75	7
8	1945	QQ0.32½ 3-1-78 2-8	0.32½	1.30	1.10	0.92	5.6	2.44	1-31-78			315 Ja	1.29	1.57	△1.15	1.93	2.64				8
9	1964	QQ0.16 3-31-78 3-6	0.32	0.72	0.453	7.73	83.6	39.6	12-31-78	30.4		5028 Dc	1.17	0.99	1.64	1.51	1.86	6 Mo Dec△	0.84	1.25	9
10	1945	QQ0.22 4-18-78 3-6	0.473	0.88	0.806	24.0	43.1	9.42	12-31-77	30.3		8343 Dc	0.89	1.10	1.44	1.53	1.64	12 Wk Mar	0.34	0.37	10
11	1977	Q0.06 4-4-78 3-13	0.12	0.24	0.20	n/a	5.11	2.70	12-31-77	1.47		844 Sp	0.69	0.02	0.59	△0.57	0.88	6 Mo Mar	0.32	0.29	11
12		None Paid		Nil		Equity per shr $7.49			12-31-77	*94.5		3064 Sp	0.92	0.55	d0.60	0.01	0.21	3 Mo Mar	0.03	0.11	12
13	1970	Q0.10 3-31-78 3-13	0.20	0.40	0.36	Book Value $7.95			12-31-77	1.53	200	7181 Dc	0.99	1.00	d0.20	d0.49	△0.82	3 Mo Mar	△0.20	□0.22	13
14		2.50 10-21-58 10-10	Nil			Equity per shr $3.72			12-31-77	7.33		3081 Dc	*0.54	d0.26	d0.20	*0.12	△0.22				14
15	1941	Q0.22½ 6-1-78 5-8	0.42½	0.90	0.80	15.7	122.	43.5	1-28-78	13.8		4724 Ja	1.75	1.61	1.87	□•1.78	2.12	3 Mo Mar			15
16	1922	Q0.18 4-10-78 3-20	0.33	0.87	†0.70	25.5	64.4	8.82	12-31-77	32.3	51	2671 Dc	2.85	2.77	2.44	2.75	2.87	3 Mo. Mar	0.31	0.85	16
17		5%Stk 9-13-74 8-12	Nil			Equity per shr $1.82			3-11-78	9.31		1385 Dc	d0.56	³d1.43	d5.36	0.95	△0.18	24 Wk. Mar	0.32	0.40	17
18	1975	S0.08 3-15-78 2-23	0.08	0.16	0.12	n/a	11.7	7.98	9-2-77	7.73		1024 Sp	0.46	0.52	0.91	1.38	1.36	9 Mo.Feb	1.08	1.40	18
19	1977	S0.15 6-1-78 5-8	0.15	0.40	0.20	0.44	56.4	27.0		0.13		4235 My	0.74	0.93	1.14	0.95	1.60	6 Mo.Feb		0.28	19
20	1967	S0.15 1-31-78 12-27	0.15	0.30	0.25	0.19	7.93	3.44	6-30-77			693 Je	0.79	0.71	d0.45	0.59	0.58	6 Mo Dec△	△0.22	△0.28	20
21	1936	None Since Public		Nil		2.76	5.50	5.68	2-28-78	62.7		1807 My	□0.68	0.64	0.61	0.94	1.36	9 Mo Feb	0.86	1.34	21
22		Q0.22 3-28-78 3-13	0.22	0.88	0.86	0.61	2.95	18.4	8-31-77	6.19		755 My	1.64	1.96	2.89	1.65	1.80	9 Mo Feb	1.21	1.85	22
23		None on new company		Nil		2.76	8.62	3.26	12-31-77	4.44		2715 Dc	△0.20	△0.18	△△0.10	△0.26	△0.21	3 Mo Mar	•0.03	•0.03	23
24	1976	0.066 8-10-77 7-19	0.066	0.07	0.066	1.65	4.52	2.29	12-31-77		638	1159 Mr	0.03	d0.05	0.13	0.47	1.00	9 Mo Dec△	0.52	1.05	24
25	1970	g0.12½ 3-31-78 3-6	g0.12½	0.50	g0.50	Equity per shr $11.38			12-31-77	*227.		4130 Dc	1.29	0.60	1.04	1.19	□1.39	3 Mo Dec△			25
26		None Paid		Nil		0.48	9.23	8.37	10-31-77	1.12		*2919 Ja	Nil	†0.10	d0.13	•0.18	0.25	9 Mo Oct△	•0.19	0.26	26
27	1958	†0.10 2-15-78 1-19	†0.10	0.31	†0.29	0.84	14.0	6.10	9-30-77	2.97		1519 Dc	0.87	0.01	1.41	1.48	P1.69		•0.19		27
28	1973	0.07 4-21-78 3-27	0.07	0.28	0.40	5.95	22.3	6.07	12-31-77			3312 Dc	0.72	0.98	1.19	1.28	1.55				28
29	1959	0.10 3-1-78 2-8	0.10	0.40	0.40	16.3	33.7	4.25	12-31-77		p11709 Dc		0.42	0.46	0.47	0.63	0.69				29
30	1977	0.06 5-26-78 5-3	0.06	0.24	0.06	1.27	17.4	3.08	2-28-78			1127 My	1.47	1.73	1.73	0.64	1.24	9 Mo Feb	0.83	1.82	30
31	1963	0.18 3-10-78 2-10	0.18	0.72	0.68	10.8	61.2	11.7	1-31-78	5.47		4644 Ap	1.71	1.57	0.35	1.88	2.40	9 Mo.Jan	1.63	1.31	31
32	1977	S0.05 5-24-78 5-4	S0.05	0.10	0.086	0.52	7.76	6.18	12-31-77	17.7	1737	1278 Sp	0.90	0.47	□0.34	0.75	59△1.70	12 Mo.Dec△	0.46	△1.80	32
33	1954	QQ0.56¼ 6-1-77 4-25	0.56¼	2.25	2.25	17.6	389.	160.		170.	12333	Je	6.96	11.25	10.84	14.26	20.99	3 Mo Mar	1.65	2.24	33
34	1966	QQ0.15 3-28-78 3-8	0.15	0.60	0.44	Conv into 2% shrs com			11-30-77	0.14	1713	1483 Fb	1.41	1.29	1.06	1.55		9 Mo Nov△		1.49	34
35	1963					4.64	15.6	3.20													35
36	1965	Q0.40 4-10-78 3-15	0.80	1.60	s1.264	39.7	114.	166.	12-31-77	184.		7863 Dc	2.51	2.31	2.80	3.47	4.12	6 Mo Mar	1.13	1.73	36
37	1960	Q0.275 7-1-78 5-24	0.55	0.76	0.60	11.2	26.7	18.9	12-31-77	*47.8		4790 Sp	0.94	1.10	1.44	1.88	2.35	6 Mo Feb	0.99	1.73	37
38		0.15% 10-19-67 10-2		Nil		Equity per shr $10.27			11-30-77	50.9	75	3342 My	△0.58	△0.74	d1.25	d1.18	d1.42	3 Mo Mar	0.95	d1.04	38
39		None Since Public		Nil		1.92	5.36	10.27	12-31-77			1923 Sp	0.07	0.03	0.07	0.03	0.08	12 Mo Dec△	0.04	0.12	39
40	1939	Q0.18 4-25-78 3-27	0.36	0.72	0.50	4.14	112.	49.0	11-27-77	18.8	385	3292 My	0.42	1.03	0.80	1.30	△1.70	9 Mo Feb	1.12	1.90	40
41	1959	Q0.25 6-7-78 5-16	0.25	1.00	0.93¾	10.0	79.8	34.0	12-31-77	27.6		1785 Dc	2.77	3.70	△2.25	^63 3.19	□*3.05	3 Mo Mar	0.84	0.61	41
42	1939	0.13 5-31-71 5-8	0.13	0.52	0.44	0.95	42.2	15.8	12-31-77	19.5		2625 Dc	1.47	1.28	1.26	2.01	2.44	3 Mo Mar	0.56	0.75	42
43		0.14 10-30-71 10-8	Nil			0.48	45.6	18.9	12-31-77	10.5	223	780 Dc	0.86	0.60	0.74	1.26	p*0.08	3 Mo Mar	0.42	0.71	43
44		None Paid	66Nil			1.15	35.5	18.4	10-1-77	30.4	160	6923 Dc	d0.15	d0.14	d0.19	d0.15	p*60 0.43	3 Mo Mar	0.07	d0.08	44
45		0.75 7-3-72 6-16				Conv into 8 shrs common							5.90	5.47	d4.37	5.97		Accum $8.25 to 1-3-78			45

◆ Stock Splits & Dlrs By Line Reference Index ¹⁴-for-1,'74. ¹⁰10%,'74;15%,'75. ⁹Adj to 3%,'73;3-for-2,'78. ²²2-for-1,'77. ²³10%,'77;'78. ²³¹10%,'77;3-for-2,'78. ¹⁸Adj to 4%,'73. ³⁹3-for-2,'77. ⁴³3-for-2,'73. ²⁴³3-for-2,'73. ²⁴³5-for-4,'73,'74,'75,'76. ²³10%,'75. ¹⁷5-for-4,'77. To split 6-for-3,ex May 4. ²³10%,'74. ³⁹Adj to 4%,'77.

HOW TO USE THE STOCK GUIDE

It is necessary to read carefully the following instructions and those on Pages 1 and 6 to correctly interpret abbreviations and data in the Guide.

INDEX	The index numbers are a visual guide to the columnar data.
INTERIM EARNINGS OR REMARKS — Period — $ Per Share Comparison	Interim earnings are shown, when available, for the longest accounting interval since the last fiscal year-end. Also published in this column from time to time are references to exchanges of shares, mergers, name changes, etc. See also Financial Position column for such notations.
ANNUAL EARNINGS — Last 12 Mos.	Last 12 Mos. indicates 12 months earnings through period shown in interim earnings column, when available, or annual, if not.
ANNUAL EARNINGS — $ Per Share Latest Five Years	S & P Earnings Estimates are the final product of careful analysis by industry specialists of available relevant information. They are unofficial, however, and responsibility for their accuracy cannot be assumed. Earnings for fiscal years ending March 31 or earlier are shown under the column of the preceding calendar year.
ANNUAL EARNINGS — Yrs. End	EARNINGS are in general on a "Primary" basis as reported by company, excluding extraordinary items. More detailed information on method of reporting and usage of standard footnotes can be found on Page 1.
CAPITALIZATION — Long Term Debt Mil-$ / Shs. 000 Pfd. Com.	Long Term Debt is in millions of dollars, as 25.0—$25,000,000; 2.58—$2,580,000; 0.20—$200,000. It includes funded debt, long term bank loans, mortgages, etc. Preferred and common stocks are in shares to the nearest thousands (000 omitted), as 150—150,000; 30—30,000; 2—1,500. Outstanding shares exclude treasury stock. Figure shown under preferred shares column on company name line represents the combined number of preferred shares outstanding.
FINANCIAL POSITION — Mil-$ Cash & Equiv. Assets, Curr. Assets, Curr. Liabs., Balance Sheet Date	Where current balance sheet items are not of analytical significance, special calculations pertinent to the industry in which the company operates are presented, as "Book Value per Share" for Banks and Finance Companies, "Net Asset Value per Share" for Investment Trusts, and "Equity per Share" (stockholders) for Insurance Companies. Cash & Equivalent, Current Assets, and Current Liabilities are given in millions of dollars (000,000) omitted, as 17.0—$17,000,000; 1.75—$1,750,000; 0.18—$175,000, etc.
DIVIDENDS — Total Ind. Rate / Last Year	Total dividend payments, including extras if any, made in the preceding calendar year. For preferred dividend accumulations to latest payment due date, see "Financial Position" or Remarks column. S & P projection of dividend payments for next 12 months, used to compute % Div. Yield.
DIVIDENDS — This Year	Payments made or declared payable thus far in the current calendar year, including both regular and extras, if any.
DIVIDENDS — Ex. Div.	The date shown is that on which the stock sells "ex-dividend"; that is, the date on which it sells without the right to receive the latest declared dividend.
DIVIDENDS — Latest Payment Date	Date of disbursement of the latest payment. If an extra or stock dividend also is being paid, it is so indicated by footnote.
DIVIDENDS — Latest Payment Per $	Latest dividend payment. If at a regular established rate, it is so noted by M—Monthly, Q—Quarterly, S—Semi-Annually, or A—Annually.
Some Divs. Ea. Yr. Since	One or more cash dividends have been paid each year to date, without interruption, beginning with year listed.
INDEX	Details of stock dividends and stock splits, effected during the past five years, are reported by symbol ♦ and footnotes which carry numerals corresponding to those in "Index" column. Adjustments have been made for all stock dividends.

♦ Stock Splits & Divs By Page Reference Index.

Addressograph-Multigraph

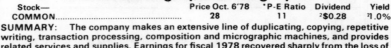

Stock—	Price Oct. 6'78	*P-E Ratio	Dividend	Yield
COMMON	28	11	[2]$0.28	[1]1.0%

SUMMARY: The company makes an extensive line of duplicating, copying, repetitive writing, transaction processing, composition and micrographic machines, and provides related services and supplies. Earnings for fiscal 1978 recovered sharply from the loss of fiscal 1977, reflecting the absence of write-offs as well as substantially wider operating margins. Aided by moderately higher revenues and wider margins, share earnings for fiscal 1979 could advance over 25%. Quarterly cash dividends were resumed in April, 1978 following omission since June, 1974.

SALES & OPER. REVENUES (Million $)

Quarter:	1977-8	1976-7	1975-6	1974-5
Oct.	149.0	135.7	133.8	140.0
Jan.	164.1	144.1	134.9	143.2
Apr.	167.7	156.5	146.6	146.0
July	185.8	159.9	157.6	155.1

Based on a preliminary report, revenues for the fiscal year ended July 31, 1978 rose 11.8% from those of the year before, reflecting higher unit shipments of all products. Margins widened on cost efficiencies stemming from the higher unit volume. Following the absence of fiscal 1977's $15.3 million charge for discontinued operations and $8.0 million payment from Xerox, pretax income totaled $36,657,000, versus a pretax loss of $10,371,000. After taxes of $15,400,000 (42.0%), against $3,633,000, net income amounted to $21,257,000, in contrast to a net loss of $14,004,000. Share earnings equaled $2.54, versus a net loss of $1.70. Results for fiscal 1977 were before a charge of $5,294,000 ($0.64 a share) from the cumulative effect of an accounting change.

[3]COMMON SHARE EARNINGS ($)

Quarter:	1977-8	1976-7	1975-6	1974-5
Oct.	0.24	d0.03	0.06	0.10
Jan.	0.52	d0.09	0.13	0.12
Apr.	[4]0.81	0.18	0.27	0.12
July	0.97	d1.74	0.36	0.44

PROSPECTS

Near Term—Revenues for the fiscal year ending July 31, 1979 are expected to rise about 10% from the $666.6 million of fiscal 1978, with higher unit volume accounting for the major part of the gain. Service revenues and sale of duplicating supplies should be up moderately.

Margins should widen, aided by increased production and cost efficiencies stemming from the higher unit volume. Thus, earnings for fiscal 1979 could rise to about $3.25 a share from the prior year's $2.54. Dividends, resumed in April, 1978, were raised to $0.07 quarterly, from $0.05, with the October 10, 1978 payment.

Long Term—The company has an established position in the business machines market but the offset duplicator business faces increasing competition from high-speed plain-paper copiers.

RECENT DEVELOPMENTS

In August, 1978 the company reached an agreement to acquire ECRM, Inc. for some $5.4 million in cash. ECRM manufactures electronic text editing, optical character recognition, and high resolution laser scanner/facsimile systems for text processing and newspaper production. Previously, in June, AIN acquired Infortext, Inc., a producer of intelligent terminal systems which monitor, control and cost account reproduction on copiers and duplicators.

In November, 1976 the company and Xerox Corp. settled claims against each other pertaining to alleged patent infringement and monopolistic practices. As part of the settlement, the company received a one-time payment of $8 million from Xerox.

DIVIDEND DATA

Quarterly dividends were resumed in April, 1978, following omission since June, 1974. A $0.10 special dividend was paid in 1977.

Amt. of Divd. $	Date Decl.	Ex-divd. Date	Stock of Record	Payment Date
0.10Spl.	Sep. 20	Sep. 27	Oct. 3	Nov. 9'77
0.05...	Feb. 21	Mar. 14	Mar. 20	Apr. 10'78
0.05...	May 22	Jun. 14	Jun. 20	Jul. 10'78
0.07...	Sep. 18	Sep. 21	Sep. 27	Oct. 10'78

[1]Listed N.Y.S.E.; also listed Midwest & Pacific S.Es. & traded Boston & Philadelphia S.Es.   [2]Indicated rate, excl. $0.10 special on Nov. 9, 1977.   [3]Reflects general adoption of LIFO acctg. aft. 1975-6; 1976-7 acctg. changes (capital leases) aft. 1974-5; & 1975-6 acctg. change for foreign currency translations in 1974-5.   [4]Incl. $0.07 from tax loss carryforward.   d Deficit.   *Based on latest 12 mos. earns.

STANDARD N.Y.S.E. STOCK REPORTS   **STANDARD & POOR'S CORP.**

© Copyright 1978 Standard & Poor's Corp.

Published at Ephrata, Pa. Editorial & Executive Offices, 345 Hudson St., New York, N.Y. 10014

[1]INCOME STATISTICS (Million $) AND PER SHARE ($) DATA

Year Ended July 31	Net Sales & Oper. Revs.	% Oper. Inc. of Sales	Oper. Inc.	[4]Depr. & Amort.	Net bef. Taxes	[3]Net Inc.	Common Share ($) Data: [3]Earns.	*Funds Generated	Divs. Paid	[3]Price Range	Price-Earns. Ratios HI LO
1979—	——	——	——	——	——	——	——	——	0.14	————	———
1978—	666.6	8.6	57.56	19.26	36.66	21.26	2.54	6.34	0.20	32⅞-13⅜	13- 5
1977—	596.3	6.8	40.45	23.62	d10.37	d14.00	d1.70	1.45	0.10	15⅞- 9⅞	———
1976—	572.9	6.4	36.66	18.21	16.65	6.43	0.80	2.82	Nil	13½- 7¾	17- 10
1975—	584.2	6.3	37.05	18.63	10.97	4.91	0.61	2.95	Nil	9½- 3¼	16- 5
1974—	540.8	4.6	24.92	17.83	2.60	0.31	0.04	2.04	0.45	11¾- 3	294- 75
1973—	489.8	8.3	40.60	14.95	5.42	3.23	0.40	1.94	0.60	34 -10⅝	85- 29
1972—	441.6	9.4	41.37	13.52	28.74	16.65	2.07	4.12	0.60	49½-31⅝	24- 15
1971—	412.3	10.3	42.35	14.36	8.79	4.99	0.62	2.58	0.80	49¼-23⅞	79- 39
1970—	420.5	11.2	47.21	16.66	29.58	15.68	1.95	4.07	1.40	62 -19½	32- 10
1969—	416.1	16.8	69.70	16.16	53.12	26.60	3.31	5.42	1.40	85 -59	26- 18

[1]PERTINENT BALANCE SHEET STATISTICS (Million $)

July 31	Gross Prop.	[2]Capital Expend.	Cash Items	Inven-tories	Receiv-ables	Current Assets	Current Liabs.	Net Workg. Cap.	Cur. Ratio	Long Term Debt	Share-hldrs. Equity	($) Book Val. Com. Sh.
1978—	237.46	30.74	43.12	147.8	120.9	354.30	170.09	184.21	2.1-1	72.76	218.39	25.92
1977—	252.65	30.59	56.31	145.2	112.0	332.73	182.57	150.16	1.8-1	89.45	198.42	23.72
1976—	228.38	20.90	41.78	130.6	113.6	300.96	132.99	167.98	2.3-1	77.14	217.74	26.69
1975—	230.01	27.07	15.62	147.0	124.5	304.34	153.41	150.93	2.0-1	78.47	209.26	25.60
1974—	223.06	35.06	5.99	164.3	132.8	317.67	169.00	148.77	1.9-1	87.61	204.35	24.84
1973—	213.72	38.47	21.57	139.7	130.3	309.61	140.74	168.87	2.2-1	85.62	207.66	25.41
1972—	191.89	19.61	34.66	112.8	116.5	275.64	85.47	190.16	3.2-1	83.42	208.01	25.74
1971—	186.52	19.01	34.23	108.5	109.3	264.68	80.55	184.13	3.3-1	85.43	196.18	24.21
1970—	180.82	21.93	20.23	139.9	112.0	288.16	88.51	199.65	3.3-1	100.77	200.21	24.61
1969—	169.58	15.74	26.11	111.1	115.9	258.81	86.58	172.23	3.0-1	72.85	195.21	23.91

[1]Data for 1973 & thereafter as originally reported; data for each yr. prior to 1973 as taken from subsequent yr.'s Annual Report; reflects acctg. change for capital leases and reflects general adoption of LIFO acctg. aft. 1976. [2]Net additions prior to 1970.. [3]Aft. $0.25 a sh. reduction from general adoption of LIFO acctg. in 1977 & $1.57 chge. for receivables & inventory adjustment in 1973 & $0.10 devaluation loss in 1968; bef. spec. cr. of $0.15 a sh. in 1973; bef. spec. chgs. of $0.64 a sh. in 1977, & $0.32 in 1971. [4]Incl. amort. of intangibles aft. 1970. d Deficit. *As computed by Standard & Poor's Corp.

Fundamental Position

Addressograph-Multigraph manufactures, sells and services equipment and supplies relating to reprographics and management systems. Reprographics accounted for 79% of total revenues in fiscal 1978, 99% of operating profit, and 74% of identifiable assets. Management systems contributed 21%, 1%, and 26%, respectively. Operations in Europe accounted for 22% of total revenues in fiscal 1978, 24% of operating profit, and 21% of identifiable assets.

Reprographic equipment includes duplicators (56% of total reprographic sales in fiscal 1978); engineering graphics (19%); data recording, repetitive writing and mail handling (14%); copiers (7%); and other equipment (4%). Duplicators are made in 10 models ranging from table-top models to larger units used by commercial printers and in-plant printing departments. Engineering graphics includes a line of diazo copying machines for the reproduction of engineering drawings. The company discontinued production of copiers in January, 1977. However, the existing installed base is being maintained to the extent of residual market demand, but installations and revenues are declining.

Management systems include composition and word processing systems (61% of management systems revenues in fiscal 1978), micrographics (24%), and management control systems (16%). Composition systems are electronic photocomposing machines which produce finished type copy for printing and include editing terminals, record-playback modules, off-line input stations, high-production video display phototypesetters and peripheral equipment, and related supplies and services. Word processing systems are software compatible with composition systems, thereby permiting documents prepared on word processors to be set in type without further text keyboarding. Micrographics products offered include microfiche duplicators, camera-processors, retrieval-display units, readers, reader-printers, and supplies. Management control systems include electronic point-of-sale systems for use primarily by fast-food managements and systems which monitor, control and cost account for the use of copy reproduction equipment.

Quarterly dividends were paid from 1935 until omission in June, 1974 and were resumed in April, 1978. Special dividends of $0.10 were paid in November, 1976 and 1977.

Employees: 18,500. Shareholders: 14,800.

Finances

During fiscal 1977 the company phased out certain copier, duplicating and electronic terminal products; estimated costs of this phaseout amounted to $1.36 a share.

Institutional Holdings

Institutions: 34. Shares: 1,095,000 (13% of the total outstanding).

CAPITALIZATION

LONG TERM DEBT: $72,755,000, incl. $11,650,000 4¾% debs., due 1988, conv. into com. at $80 a share.

COMMON STOCK: 8,400,431 shs. ($2.50 par).

Incorporated in Delaware in 1924. **Office**—1900 Ave. of the Stars, Los Angeles, Calif. 90067. **Tel**—(213) 556-9500. **Chrmn & Chief Exec Officer**—R. L. Ash. **Pres**—J. R. Mellor. **Secy**—T. B. Clark. **VP-Treas**—B. T. Swan. **Dirs**—R. L. Ash, J. P. Birkelund, F. R. Eckley, Jr., P. E. Gray, A. F. Kelly, H. Knowlton, Jr., J. R. Mellor, R. M. Paget. **Transfer Agents & Registrars**—Citibank, NYC; Bank of America, San Francisco; Harris Trust & Savings Bank, Chicago.

W.C.H.

CHAPTER 5

Understanding the Dow Theory

In order to make a profit in the retail business, all clothing merchandisers must buy at the right price. They must buy at wholesale to sell at retail. They must pick out merchandise which will be attractive to buyers so they can sell most of it at the height of the season and at the top price. As the season draws to a close they begin to reduce their prices. If it is summer merchandise, they must get rid of any left-over stock before the fall and winter things come in. This gives them the capital, increased by profits, to pay for the new merchandise. Again they sell most of the new winter things at the height of the season, reduce their price as the season wanes, and empty their stores of the winter merchandise by spring. And every year the cycle repeats itself.

The same is true in the buying of stocks, whether they are bought to keep as an investment for a few years or whether they are bought to sell as soon as the price goes up enough to insure a good profit. The buyers must buy at a "wholesale" price to sell at a "retail" price. In other words, they must buy when the price of the shares is low and wait until the price rises to sell. They must pick out stocks that are attractive to others so that there will be eager buyers to whom to sell. Ideally these shares should be sold at the height of the bull market season because as the advance wanes, the price received will be reduced. And by all means, they must be sold before they drop greatly during a bear market season, so there will be capital available to invest when the new bull market begins. Just as in the clothing business, the investment business has cycles too, and sometimes just as frequently.

In one way the merchandisers have a much easier time than the investors. They can go to the factory showrooms to buy at wholesale prices. They have no trouble knowing the seasons—the calendar tells them, even though at times the weather can trip them up. A cold, rainy summer can play havoc with the sale of beach clothes, and a warm, dry winter can ruin the sale of ski clothes.

The buyers of stocks have a much more difficult time. They have to learn on their own how to tell when stocks are at "wholesale" prices. This is vital to any investment plan. Whether they wish to be traders and sell the stocks when they rise in price, or whether they plan to keep them as a source of investment income, they still should buy stocks when their prices are low. Let's use American Telephone and Telegraph Company stock, known as a friend of widows and orphans, as an example of buying right. During 1976 the stock fluctuated from a low of $50.87 to a high of $64.75. If we add $80 for commission, a hundred shares of the stock would have cost from a low of $5,168 to a high of $6,555. The dividend paid during 1976 was $3.70 a share. Had you bought the stock at a lower price, your rate of return would have been 7.1 per cent ($370 divided by $5168 equals .071). Had you bought the stock at the higher price, the rate of return would have been 5.6 per cent ($370 divided by $6555 equals .056). If you were depending on this stock for income, the difference to you would be important.

The investors have no calendar to tell them when stocks will be low and when they will be high. They have no calendar which states that on this date a bull market will begin and that on this later date a bear market will begin. But they can study what many astute observers have written about the cycles of these markets and learn how they have made a "calendar" of sorts to predict those cycles. This "calendar" is called the Dow Theory.

Charles Dow was a newspaper editor who founded *The Wall Street Journal* in 1889. His daily editorials expounded a new view of the stock market in which he theorized about the importance of price movement, whether up or down, and its relationship to future events. At that time there were no laws mandating full disclosure on the part of corporations. Financial statements were either nonexistent or difficult to understand; yet there were investors who controlled pools of money who appeared to have "inside" information.

These groups of investors wielded enormous financial power and influence, usually to the detriment of the ill-informed public. As editor and financial writer, Dow monitored the activity of the stock market so that he could detect where the more-informed were investing their money.

After many years of observation, Dow concluded that the stock market could be equated to the ocean. Both had three movements: primary (tides), secondary (waves), and daily fluctuations (ripples). The major advances and declines of the market, like the tides, were a dominant force that lasted for recognizable periods of time. These long-term movements were subject to secondary reactions, the waves, that lasted for a shorter period of time and might temporarily seem to contradict the primary trend. And finally the waves themselves were broken down into daily reactions, the ripples. Dow felt strongly that no means of manipulation could divert the eventual course of a major primary move.

The discovery of the rhythmic movements of the market led to the formulation of the Dow-Jones Averages, named after the company which publishes *The Wall Street Journal*. Beginning in 1897, the newspaper began to publish two sets of averages—the industrials and the railroads, using 12 industrial companies and 20 railroads. Later the number was expanded to 20 companies for the industrials and then to 30, the present number. Charles Dow felt these two sectors of the market were interdependent. When industry was doing well, the railroads were kept busy transporting the products they produced. Whenever the price trends of the two averages did not move in the same direction, as when one rose while the other dropped, it meant that one sector was stronger or weaker than the other, and if this disparate movement continued, it would eventually result in a major reversal for the general stock market. And so, no price movement of the market—either up or down—is valid unless or until confirmed by both averages.

The railroad average continued to be used until the rise of the airline and trucking industries forced a change. In 1969 Dow Jones & Company revised the rail average to include the other two means of transportation. Today the Dow-Jones Transportation Average fills the original requirements of a balance between industrial firms and the transportation network.

The Dow-Jones Industrial Average has also reflected changes in our economy. Different companies have been substituted to keep the list representative as new financial giants emerged with the expansion of technology. Only General Electric from the original list remains, although it too was once dropped for a while. Also, changes in the number of shares, stock splits, stock dividends, have all forced changes in the way the averages are computed and has caused some distortion. This has given rise to new computations such as Standard & Poor's 500 Stock Index and the New York Stock Exchange Index. However, the Dow-Jones has been compared for many years with the other two and is found to follow them very closely, so it does not matter which of the three indexes you use. Because the Dow-Jones is the oldest, it is the one most widely reported and still remains the most popular.

Now that you know the historical background of the averages, let's discuss the Dow Theory. Of greatest importance in this theory is the primary movement, lasting for years. Like the incoming tide, the bull market advances, then partly recedes, then advances again, then recedes again, then advances to its peak. It usually consists of five movements: three advances and two reverses. Each advance usually rises higher than the previous high, and each time it recedes less than the previous low. After the peak has been reached, the process reverses. Like the outgoing tide, the bear market recedes, then partly advances, then recedes again, then partly advances again, then recedes to its lowest point. Like the bull market, it too usually has five movements, but these consist of three reversals and two advances. Each time it usually recedes farther than the previous low, and each time it advances less than the previous advance. When the tide is all the way out, when the Dow-Jones averages have dropped as far as they will go, the entire process begins all over again. This complete bull and bear cycle usually takes from 3½ to 4½ years from beginning to end.

The following chart illustrates these cycles. They can most easily be noted by marking the low points of the bear markets. These occurred in 1929, 1932, 1938, 1942, 1946, 1950, 1953, 1958, 1962, 1966, 1970, 1974, and 1978.

Notice how much more volatile the market has become since the 1950's, and how much farther apart are the highs and the lows of each cycle. It is believed the rise of the huge investment funds is responsible for this greater volatility.

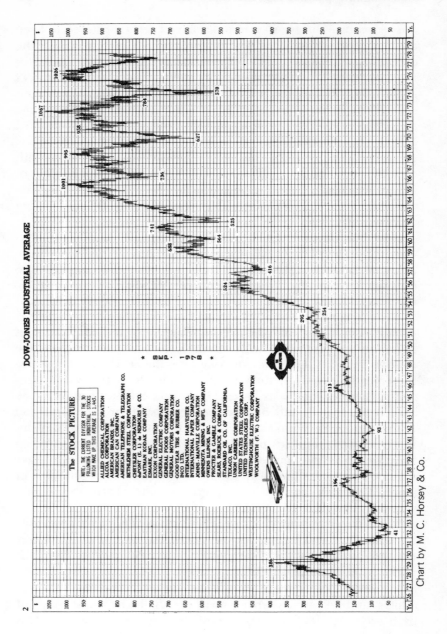

DOW-JONES INDUSTRIAL AVERAGE

The STOCK PICTURE

NOTE: THE CURRENT DIVISOR FOR THE 30
FOLLOWING LISTED INDUSTRIAL STOCKS
WHICH MAKE UP THIS AVERAGE IS 1.465.

ALLIED CHEMICAL CORPORATION
ALCOA CORPORATION
AMERICAN BRANDS, INC.
AMERICAN CAN COMPANY
AMERICAN TELEPHONE & TELEGRAPH CO.
BETHLEHEM STEEL CORPORATION
CHRYSLER CORPORATION
duPONT (E. I.) de NEMOURS & CO.
EASTMAN KODAK COMPANY
ESMARK, INC.
EXXON CORPORATION
GENERAL ELECTRIC COMPANY
GENERAL FOODS CORPORATION
GENERAL MOTORS CORPORATION
GOODYEAR TIRE & RUBBER CO.
INCO LTD.
INTERNATIONAL HARVESTER CO.
INTERNATIONAL PAPER COMPANY
JOHNS-MANVILLE CORPORATION
MINNESOTA MINING & MFG. COMPANY
OWENS ILLINOIS, INC.
PROCTER & GAMBLE COMPANY
SEARS, ROEBUCK & COMPANY
STANDARD OIL CO. OF CALIFORNIA
TEXACO, INC.
UNION CARBIDE CORPORATION
UNITED STATES STEEL CORPORATION
UNITED TECHNOLOGIES CORP.
WESTINGHOUSE ELECTRIC CORPORATION
WOOLWORTH (F. W.) COMPANY

Chart by M. C. Horsey & Co.

The following table will give you a clearer picture of the bull-bear timing cycles:

Bull Market Began	Bear Market Ended	Length of Cycle
June, 1949	Sept., 1953	4 yrs., 3 mos.
Sept., 1953	Oct., 1957	4yrs., 1 mo.
Oct., 1957	June, 1962	4 yrs., 8 mos.
June, 1962	Oct., 1966	4yrs., 4 mos.
Oct., 1966	Apr., 1970	3 yrs., 7 mos.
Apr., 1970	Oct., 1974	4 yrs., 5 mos.
Oct., 1974	Apr., 1978	3 yrs., 7 mos.

The secondary movements in the bull-bear cycles are the very important reactions when the Dow-Jones Industrial Average recedes in a bull market for one-third to two-thirds of its previous gain, or rises in a bear market the same amount from its previous loss. These are the waves within the tides.

Joseph E. Granville, in his book *New Strategy of Daily Stock Market Timing for Maximum Profit*, gives an excellent description of the timing of these secondary movements. He says the bull and bear cycle covers the 3½ to 4½ year period and within that time must be the three phases of the bull market and the three phases of the bear market. However, the timing of each phase is not precise. They are not like the four quarters of a football game covering 15 minutes each, or the two 20 minute halves of a basketball game. Rather they resemble the innings of a baseball game, in which some innings can last five minutes with three men coming up to bat and being put out in a few pitches, with other innings lasting 20 minutes with the whole team coming to bat and making many runs. So some phases of the cycle can be short and some longer, and some can show great changes while others show comparatively little change. And even at times, like a baseball game's going into extra innings, sometimes an extra advance or an extra reverse can crop up.

In the normal course of the market, however, there are two of these reverses in a bull market and another two reverses in a bear market. They each have their own particular characteristics:

1. The movement is more rapid in a reversal than in a primary trend. This means the price drops faster in a reversal of a bull market than it took to rise, and rises faster in a bear market reversal than it took to drop.

2. The reversal may last from three weeks to three months and typically retraces about 40 per cent to 50 per cent of the movement since the end of the last major reversal. An advance of 10 points will usually have a relapse of 4 points or more. A 20 point advance will decline about 8 to 10 points.

3. The length of time needed to complete this reversal is usually much shorter than the time of the previous movement it is reversing. If the first phase of the bull market, to use this as an example, takes seven months to reach its peak, the reversal time will be much shorter, perhaps three months. Then the second phase of the bull market should begin.

4. Secondary reactions are often followed by periods of extreme dullness before the major primary trend asserts itself. This period of dullness, which is a phase of backing and filling, is called a phase of consolidation. The length of this period of consolidation usually depends on the length of the reversal. In a bull market, if there is a minor downward movement in price, in most cases a small phase of consolidation will follow. If the downward adjustment is more severe, then the period of consolidation will usually be longer. In other words, in most cases the greater the drop, the longer the period of consolidation before the next rise.

5. One important point to be aware of is that the reaction between the first and second advances of the bull market and the first and second recedings of the bear market are usually the most severe. These usually do a greater degree of reversing than do the reversals between the second and third phases.

The weather calendar has its four seasons, with each one following in correct order. The stock market has a similar predictable cycle of bull and bear markets. Once a new bull market starts, the market must follow a pattern which takes it through the bull market and then into and through the bear market which follows, just as surely as spring follows winter.

If you will refer back to the previous chart, you can check the cycle between 1970 and 1974. Note the bull market began in April, 1970, at a low of 627 and the first phase peaked at 958. Then came the reversal, and, as I said just previously, it was the most severe reversal, to 791. The second phase went back up to 980; the second reversal dropped to 900. The third phase topped at 1067 and then the bear market began. The chart clearly shows the two reversals in the bear market.

To be able to read what time it is on this market "calendar" is the most important skill you need to learn. This ability to figure out the timing is considered to be an art rather than a science, because the market throws out many confusing clues, each one subject to a person's own interpretation. To develop this "feel" for the market, you need to study and understand the characteristics of each phase, even though there may be confusing overlapping of such characteristics. No matter how freezing cold and snowy March may be, there are signs of spring if we know where to look for them. So, too, can we read the signs of the market, if we know where to look for them.

The third movements in the Dow Theory are the ripples, the daily fluctuations, indicated by the daily high and low prices. These are of interest mostly to the day-to-day traders and to those who keep a record of the daily price ranges on their individual charts of the companies they follow. The daily closing price is the one most important to everyone else.

Once investors become knowledgeable about the timing of the primary trend, their chances of financial success are greatly enhanced. They can buy confidently near the bottom of a bear market, knowing that the beginning of a bull market is not far off. They can wait for relapses in a bull market or rallies in a bear market to buy their stocks for trading purposes. They can go counter to crowd psychology and buy when prices have dropped so much that people are fearful and are selling out. And they can sell out when stocks are near a market top when others are eager to buy. Now they are part of the "smart money" investors who rake in consistent profits.

CHAPTER 6

Timing—The Primary Tool

In the previous chapter I discussed the Dow Theory of the movements of the stock market. Since they are important, some major points about the movements need emphasizing:

1. The stock market has made a complete bull and bear cycle every 3½ to 4½ years.

2. Nothing that has happened in national or world events has affected these bull-bear cycles. Not the heart attack of one president, or the assassination of a second, or the resignation of a third, with all our emotional responses to these events, made a difference as far as the internal timing of the cycles were concerned. Neither did the outbreak of wars, nor the onset of peace. The Dow-Jones more than doubled in the World War II years; the Korean War did not affect the bull market then in its infancy; nor did the Viet Nam War prevent the three bull markets during its 12 year span.

3. The state of business and industry in our country has had no affect on the timing of the stock market cycles. In fact, business has its own cycles. Research has shown 28 up-cycles since 1854, with only one lasting less than a year, the average length being three years. Business cycles and stock market cycles have not matched 60 per cent of the time. So when business is good or bad, don't assume the stock market will be good or bad at the same time.

4. You need to have a starting place to figure your timing. Market bottoms are much more easily defined than market tops, so use that as a fixed point to begin your time calculations. Review again the chart in the previous chapter which shows the Dow-Jones Industrial Average line over the years and notice how much more clearly defined the bottoms are.

34

5. Once the latest bear bottom has been defined, you must take into your calculations that you have 3½ to 4½ years before the next bottom will occur. This time span will need to cover all six phases of the bull-bear cycle. The tools discussed in the next few chapters will enable you to follow these phases.

6. The bull and the bear phases are not equal in length. If the bull market lasts three years, then the bear market will last only 1 to 1½ years. If the bull market is shorter, as the last one was (from October 1974 through January 1977, a total of 28 months), then the bear market will probably last at least 16 months and perhaps more. (The 1974 bear market is considered to have ended in October because, although the Dow-Jones Industrial Average went lower, the transportation average did not confirm the industrial average.) When the bull market is a very long one, then the bear market will be very short. Conversely, a shorter bull market means a longer bear market. You must keep in mind the 3½ to 4½ year timing. Thirty months for a bull market is about average.

7. The first phase of a bull market can further help our timing. In the past the industrial average has regained at least half the points it had lost no later than six months after a bear market low. This confirms the first phase of a bull market. For example, our chart shows a low of 570 in December, 1974, a drop of 497 points from its 1973 high. It also shows a recovery to 889 in April, 1975, less than six months after the low.

8. In previous years, the early buyers who bought at the bottom would be selling from the sixth through the ninth month later in order to take advantage of the six-month capital gains law. However, the change of the law to a year for a long-term capital gain will surely affect the selling. Since this is a new situation, we will have to wait to see how the market reacts to this new law.

9. End-of-the-year sales of stocks in order to claim tax losses and lessen the tax burden will affect the market. December is a good month to look for bargains to be held for a short term as the market generally advances in January.

10. The second advance of the bull market usually takes about the same length of time as the first phase did. Many times the reaction between the first and second advances has been the more severe reaction between the advances, meaning the decline is usually greater in this first reversal. The change of the six-months capital

gains law may affect this also, as investors may tend to hold for the longer period of time.

11. Just as the first phase of the bull market is the one most easily defined, the third phase is the most difficult. It usually begins about 24 months after the major bottom, lasts about six months, but shows increasing deterioration in terms of technical indicators, which will be discussed later.

12. Sometimes the third phase is so weak it seems not to come at all. Then you need all the more to keep in mind the timing of the entire cycle so that you can sell before the bear market drops too far.

Additional Timing Techniques

A. *Years*

Of interest to investors are the statistics which have been compiled to show the years which have been favorable to the stock market and those which have not been favorable. It has been found that these follow patterns, just as the Dow Theory shows the market as a whole also follows patterns.

1. The most favorable year in each decade is the one ending in 5. Since 1885 the stock market has shown a strong advance in all years ending in 5, and 1975 was a good example.

2. The above strong advance carries over to the years ending in 6, and the market continues to rise. However, it begins to show some signs of impending weakness.

3. Years ending in 7 show a precipitous slide the second half of the year.

4. Years ending in 8 show a major market advance before the end of the year.

5. Presidential election years ending in 4 are very favorable ones. These have been 1904, 1924, 1944, and 1964. The other years ending in 4 have been involved in bear markets.

6. The other years are favorable or unfavorable, depending on whether they are in a bull or bear cycle.

B. *Months*

1. The January barometer: The action of the stock market in the month of January is very closely watched. January is considered to be the barometer for the rest of the year, and with good reason. Since 1950 the January performance has correctly forecast the

year's close in December for 24 out of 28 years. (For judging this we need to use the Standard & Poor's 500 Stock Index as it gives a broader market range than the Dow-Jones Industrial Average, which is based on only 30 giant companies.)

If the Standard & Poor's Index is higher at the end of January than it was four weeks earlier at the end of the previous December, then the year will probably close 11 months later even higher than it had been in January. Only once since 1950 has this not proved to be true. That year was 1966. The other 16 years this barometer has worked perfectly.

Conversely, if the Standard & Poor's Index is lower at the end of January than it was at the end of the previous December, then the year will probably close even lower. Of the 11 years which showed losses in January, eight following Decembers also showed losses. Only three years, 1956, 1968, and 1970 did not follow suit.

The following table will give you an idea of how this barometer works:

Year	Previous Year's Close	January Close	December Close	Change
1972	102.09	103.94	118.05	Both up
1973	118.05	116.03	97.55	Both down
1974	97.55	96.57	68.56	Both down
1975	68.56	76.98	90.19	Both up
1976	90.19	100.86	109.46	Both up
1977	107.46	102.03	95.10	Both down

2. Spring rallies: Another important point to note is about the 11 years during which the January barometers showed a decline. Ten of those declines were followed by a healthy spring rally, with 1973 the only exception. If a bull market is drawing to a close, during these rallies would be a good time to sell those stocks which you feel are apt to decline in the ensuing bear market. It is also a time to consider short selling (which is explained in Chapter 20.)

In these ten January declines, the lowest points occurred between the last week in January and the early part of March. The good rallies that followed each one reached their tops from four to fourteen weeks after the low point of the winter decline, with six or seven weeks as average. You might wish to make use of this in timing your sales.

3. Holiday rallies: Many financial writers speak of a summer rally, but this has not been a consistent stock market pattern since 1959. This rally which does occur, and has occurred rather consistently since 1954, is the Fourth of July rally. This can begin anywhere between two and eight trading days before the holiday and lasts about a week after the Fourth. Selling during this rally can be profitable.

Another holiday which seems to affect the market is Labor Day. Since 1961 the market has shown gains for the three days prior to the holiday. This four-day week acts in two ways:

a. Since 1960, except for two of the years, a decline those four days has meant a decline the rest of the month too, and suggests postponing your purchase for 30 days. A gain that week has shown a gain for the rest of the month, so any purchase should be made immediately. You could gauge your sales accordingly too.

b. The second way this four-day week acts is to predict the balance of the year. The four days following the holiday act as a barometer, but it is in reverse to the January one. If the Labor Day week shows a rise, and the rest of the month shows strength, the fourth quarter of the year usually shows a decline. If the Labor Day week shows weakness and the month itself does too, the market usually rises in the fourth quarter of the year.

4. Fall months. October is the best buying month of the year because it comes before the three most bullish months of the year—November, December, and January—and so is a good time to look for bargains. Five of the major bear markets have turned during this month: 1946, 1957, 1962, 1966, and 1974.

November is the second best month for buying stocks, with declines usually beginning in the first half of the month, but with the last five days showing a rise.

December is the season of tax-loss selling, especially the last few weeks. This last-minute liquidation may severely depress many stocks, but this is usually only a temporary condition. Bargain hunters look for those stocks that are making new lows, or are near their lows for the year, or are much below their yearly highs. These are the ones being sold the hardest to take tax losses. These are also the ones which will usually rally the strongest in the first few weeks in January. An alert trader can make a nice profit in just a few weeks.

Paradoxically, the best performing stocks may have a sharp rally during these last few weeks in December, as many of the sellers of the poor performers switch into what they consider to be better investments. This frequently leads to a decline in price for these good performers in January, as delayed profit-takers sell in order to have a full extra year before paying taxes on their profit.

CHAPTER 7

Keeping Track of the Stock Market

There are two approaches to investing in the stock market. The first is called the fundamentalist approach. In it investors carefully study the fundamentals of a company; they look over its balance sheet carefully, check its profit and loss statement to see how well it has been doing, and read the reports about the company to judge what its potential is for future growth. If they think the company is sound and that they will get a good return on their money from dividends and from an increase in the price of the shares, they then buy the stock. These investors plan to keep these shares for a long period of time and do not worry about the fluctuations of the market. They figure that if the price drops, it will always come back up, and meanwhile they will be getting their dividends.

The second approach to the market is called the technical approach and is the one usually used by those interested in trading for shorter terms rather than in investing and keeping the stock for long periods of time. These people are more interested in the price of the shares than in the fundamentals of the company. This is not to say that intelligent traders completely ignore the fundamentals of the company; they simply feel that other factors, such as the timing of the market, are more important. They relied on fundamentals when they chose their list of stocks to follow for possible investment; they used them as an initial screening device to narrow the potential list down to a manageable level. They also rely on fundamentals when they cull their list during bear markets with the idea of replacing their weakest stocks with those more likely to advance when a new bull market arrives. But during bull markets they feel it is possible to ignore fundamentals since the upward momentum will carry practically all stocks with it, and their own computations show them which stocks on their investment list are responding well.

But just as those who use the technical approach to the market need on occasion to use the fundamentals of a company, so too should the fundamentalists know and make use of such technical devices as timing. They can prevent losses by not buying at the tail end of a bull advance when prices are their highest. They can profit much more by buying near the beginning of a bull advance when prices had already dropped severely and are getting ready to rise.

Charles Dow devised his Dow-Jones averages as a technical tool to measure the movements of the market as a whole in order to determine the trend of prices. Other astute observers of the market have devised methods to keep track of these cycles more accurately. Two methods that you should use to help you learn the feel of the market are the moving average line and the advance-decline line. To do so you need to have only a pencil, paper, a small hand calculator and a Sunday newspaper which reports the weekly New York Stock Exchange prices.

On the following page is a copy of a Sunday newspaper stock market report for the week. You will be interested in only three parts: the Dow-Jones Stock Averages, the Standard & Poor's 500 Stock Index, and the New York Stock Exchange weekly statistics. Each will be discussed.

1. In column one are the Dow-Jones averages. You will use the closing price of the 30 industrials for your computations. The high-low figures are used only as stated in #17 at the end of this chapter. You do not use the 20 transportations, but note that this week the two averages diverge.

2. In the second column are the advances and declines for the week of the stocks on the New York Stock Exchange. This week 1039 stocks advanced in price and 778 declined. The next chapter will explain how you will use these figures.

3. In the last column is the Standard & Poor's 500 Stock Index. Many technicians feel this index is a more accurate picture of the market as a whole and they use this one in their computations instead of the Dow. However, since it takes so little extra time, you might profit from using both the index and the 30 industrials and keeping a record of the two.

Week in Review

DOW JONES STOCK AVERAGES

	Open	High	Low	Close	Chg
30 Indus	844.33	844.33	824.41	827.09	− 8.23
20 Trans	225.51	225.51	223.90	224.78	+ 0.20
15 Utils	108.45	108.45	105.01	105.85	− 0.51
65 Stocks	290.17	290.17	285.12	286.73	− 1.75

WEEK'S MOST ACTIVE NYSE COMP. STOCKS

	Sales	High	Low	Close	Chg
PnAm Air	2,857,000	7 1/2	6	7 3/8	+1 1/4
K martCp	1,696,400	27 1/4	23 7/8	24 7/8	−2 1/4
G T E Cp	1,475,600	30 3/4	29 1/8	29 1/4	−1 1/8
Carrier Cp	1,469,500	20 7/8	19 1/8	20 5/8	+1 3/8
Dow Chml	1,457,900	26 7/8	24	25 1/4	−1 5/8
Hercules	1,419,800	17 3/8	14 7/8	17	+2
Boeing Co	1,363,600	48 1/2	39 7/8	47 1/4	+7 1/2
Sears Roe	1,318,300	25 7/8	23 3/4	24 1/2	−1 3/8
Genl Mtrs	1,297,200	65 3/4	63 1/8	63 1/8	− 7/8
Am T&T	1,267,600	65 7/8	61 3/4	62 1/4	− 1/2
PepsiCo	1,237,200	30 3/8	28 5/8	30 1/4	+ 7/8
Brunswk	1,217,900	15 7/8	14 1/4	15 1/4	+ 7/8
Exxon Cp	1,214,600	48 7/8	46 5/8	48 5/8	+1 1/2
Eastrn Air	1,155,300	10 1/2	8 7/8	10	+1
East Kdk	1,155,100	54 1/2	50 5/8	52 1/4	+ 7/8
Technicr	1,110,000	14 1/8	11	12 7/8	+2 1/8
Gulf OilCp	1,073,900	24 1/2	23	23 7/8	− 3/8
Texaco	1,069,000	26	24 7/8	25 1/8	− 3/4
Am HmPr	1,046,900	30 1/4	28 1/4	30	+1 1/2
U A L Inc	1,022,500	28 3/8	25 7/8	28	+2 1/8

DOW JONES BOND AVERAGES

	Open	High	Low	Close	Chg.
20 Bds	88.95	89.06	88.85	88.90	− 0.11
Utils	92.36	92.60	92.36	92.47	+ 0.01

WEEK'S MOST ACTIVE AMEX COMP. STOCKS

	Sales	High	Low	Close	Chg
Houston Ol	1,002,100	26 3/8	22	25 1/2	+2 7/8
RelGrp wts	803,800	2 1/8	15-16	1 1/8	− 3/8
Shen OilCp	796,700	40 1/4	37 5/8	40 1/4	+5 7/8
Macrodyne	623,300	1 3/8	7/8	1 3/8	+ 1/2
LoewsT wts	597,100	14 5/8	10 5/8	13 7/8	+3 3/8

WHAT THE AMEX MARKET DID

Wk. Ended	High	Low	Adv	Dec	Unch
May 5, 1978	568	116	501	371	199
April 28, 1978	673	123	1123	748	252
May 6, 1977	229	118	1255	555	295

WHAT THE NYSE MARKET DID

Wk. ended	High	Low	Adv	Dec	Unch
May 5, 1978	259	28	1039	778	287
April 28, 1978	250	22	506	377	786
May 6, 1977	99	88	496	391	255

AMEX INDEX

	High	Low	Close	Chg
Market Value	139.93	137.24	139.89	+ 3.23

NYSE INDEXES

	High	Low	Close	Chg
Common	54.42	53.11	53.97	+ 0.07
Indust	58.93	57.32	58.43	+ 0.15
Transport	44.14	43.22	44.00	+ 0.51
Utils	39.96	39.46	39.54	− 0.35
Finance	57.89	56.48	57.28	+ 0.04

NYSE DAILY COMPOSITE VOLUME

	Past Wk.	Prev. Wk.
Monday	41,569,060	
Tuesday	46,759,040	62,036,750
Wednesday	42,944,710	49,821,530
Thursday	41,801,320	39,549,240
Friday	47,112,600	36,945,360
Total	220,186,730	226,687,800

STANDARD & POOR'S 500 STOCK INDEX

	High	Low	Close	Chg
400 Indust	107.92	105.92	106.64	− 0.30
20 Trans	14.09	13.94	14.02	− 0.03
40 Utils	52.36	51.85	51.85	− 0.27
40 Fincl	11.87	11.61	11.70	− 0.03
500 Stocks	97.67	95.93	96.53	− 0.30

WEEKLY SALES

	Past Wk.	Yr. Ago
NYSE Comp. Stk	220,186,730	124,061,500
NYSE Bond	$114,508,000	$91,571,000
AMEX Comp. Stk	27,416,790	13,455,780
AMEX Bond	$7,735,000	$5,837,000
Midwest Stock	9,185,000	6,311,000

The moving average line is the device used by technicians to measure the primary trend of the market, meaning is the market in a bull phase? or in a bear phase? or in a strong reversal of either? The moving average line used to determine this primary trend is the 200-day, or 40-week, computation of the Dow-Jones Industrial Average (or the Standard & Poor's Index, or both). Using this length of time, the weekly changes are small and are not likely to show false signals about the primary trend. To explain, if the 40-week moving average line is rising in a bull market, a short reversal of a week or two is not likely to turn the line down. It takes a large reversal in the Dow to change the trend of a moving average line.

The secondary movements of the markets, the reversals which occur between the phases of the bull and bear markets, can be kept track of by use of a 10-week moving average line. Some writers and some chart services use anywhere from a 5-week to a 30-week line also. Others divide the year by quarters and keep 13-week, 26-week, and 39-week lines. I feel two moving average lines to compute are enough, one longer one for the primary trend and a shorter one for the secondary movements.

The procedure for computing a moving average line in any time series is very simple, especially with the use of a calculator. For the sake of brevity, I will compute a 5-week moving average line. All the longer ones listed above follow the same pattern. (The x's in the second column indicate that those numbers have been checked off in the computation.)

Week	Closing Weekly Dow	5 Week Total	5 Week Average Line
1	800 x		
2	810 x		
3	825 x		
4	820 x	(Add the 5 weeks)	(Divide by 5)
5	840	4095	819
6	835	(Subtract week 1, check off, add week 6) 4130	(Divide by 5) 826
7	850	(Subtract week 2, check off, add week 7) 4170	(Divide by 5) 834
8	860	(Subtract week 3, check off, add week 8) 4205	(Divide by 5) 841
9	855	4240	848

Simple mathematics like this is all you ever need, but you can see why a calculator is such a time saver. Notice that I wrote down the closing figure (using round numbers to make it easy) for the Dow-Jones Industrial Average each week, and it was not until the sixth week that the computation began. For the longer average lines, you will need to list the closing Dow for the longer periods of time before you can begin to compute. You will then divide your total by this longer period of time.

To show you what information the moving average lines give, let's construct two to show what the market as a whole was doing from 1974 through 1977. The 40-week moving average line is for the long-term because it is less sensitive to change and eliminates many false signals from random variations, preventing investors from being "whipsawed" by buying and then selling too quickly to make a profit. The 10-week moving average line is for the short-term. The principal reason for using a 10-week line is that it is easy to compute mathematically. Just move the decimal point over one.

I am also including a line chart of the Dow-Jones Industrial Average. This will be helpful in giving you an all-over picture of the figures and will help you to understand them. The dates given are from the Sunday papers.

Following the tables and the chart are specific items that can be learned from study of the two moving average lines. You will need to refer back to them continuously to understand the information given in each item.

DOW-JONES INDUSTRIAL AVERAGE

1974		Price		10-Week Total	10-Week Average	40-Week Total	40-Week Average
Jan.	6	880.23	xx				
	13	841.48	xx				
	20	855.47	xx				
	27	859.39	xx				
Feb.	3	843.94	xx				
	10	820.40	xx				
	17	820.32	xx				
	24	855.99	xx				
Mar.	3	851.92	xx				
	10	878.05	xx	8507.19	850.71		
	17	887.83	xx	8514.79	851.47		
	24	878.13	xx	8551.44	855.14		
	31	846.68	xx	8542.65	854.26		
Apr.	7	847.54	xx	8530.80	853.08		
	14	844.81	xx	8531.67	853.16		
	21	859.90	xx	8571.17	857.11		
	28	834.64	xx	8585.49	858.54		
May	5	845.90	xx	8575.40	857.54		
	12	850.44	xx	8573.92	857.39		
	19	818.84	xx	8514.71	851.47		
	26	816.65	xx	8443.53	844.35		
Jun.	2	802.17	xx	8367.57	836.75		
	9	853.72	xx	8374.61	837.46		
	16	843.09	xx	8370.16	837.01		
	23	815.39	xx	8340.74	834.07		
	30	802.41	xx	8283.25	828.32		
Jul.	7	791.77	xx	8240.38	824.03		
	14	787.23	xx	8181.71	818.17		
	21	787.94	xx	8119.21	811.92		
	28	784.57	xx	8084.94	808.92		
Aug.	4	752.58	xx	8020.87	802.08		
	11	770.30	xx	7989.00	798.90		
	18	731.54	xx	7866.82	786.68		
	25	686.80	xx	7710.53	771.05		
Sep.	1	678.58	xx	7573.72	757.37		
	8	677.88	xx	7449.19	744.91		
	15	627.19	xx	7284.61	728.46		
	22	670.76	xx	7168.14	716.81		
	29	621.95	xx	7002.15	700.21		
Oct.	6	584.56	xx	6802.14	680.21	31908.98	797.72
	13	658.17	xx	6707.73	670.77	31686.92	792.17
	20	654.88	xx	6592.31	659.23	31500.32	787.50
	27	636.19	xx	6496.96	649.69	31281.04	782.02
Nov.	3	665.28	xx	6475.44	647.54	31086.93	777.17
	10	667.16	xx	6464.02	646.40	30910.15	772.75
	17	647.61	xx	6433.75	643.37	30737.36	768.43
	24	615.30	xx	6421.86	642.18	30532.34	763.30
Dec.	1	618.66	xx	6369.76	636.97	30295.01	757.37
	8	577.60	xx	6325.41	632.54	30020.69	750.51
	15	592.77	xx	6333.62	633.36	29735.41	743.38
	22	598.48	xx	6273.93	627.39	29446.06	736.15
	29	602.16	xx	6221.21	622.12	29170.09	729.25

1975		Price	10-Week Total	Average	40-Week Total	Average
Jan.	5	634.54 xx	6219.56	621.95	28957.95	723.94
	12	658.79 xx	6213.07	621.30	28769.20	719.23
	19	644.63 xx	6190.54	619.05	28569.02	714.22
	26	667.28 xx	6210.21	621.02	28376.40	709.41
Feb.	2	703.69 xx	6298.60	629.86	28245.45	706.13
	9	711.91 xx	6391.85	639.18	28111.46	702.78
	16	734.20 xx	6548.45	654.84	27995.22	699.88
	23	749.77 xx	6705.45	670.54	27926.15	698.15
Mar.	2	739.05 xx	6846.02	684.60	27848.55	696.21
	9	770.10 xx	7013.96	701.39	27816.48	695.41
	16	773.47 xx	7152.89	715.28	27736.23	693.40
	23	763.06 xx	7257.16	725.71	27656.20	691.40
	30	770.26 xx	7382.79	738.27	27611.07	690.27
Apr.	6	747.26 xx	7462.77	746.27	27555.92	688.89
	13	789.50 xx	7548.58	754.85	27553.65	688.84
	20	808.43 xx	7645.10	764.51	27574.85	689.37
	27	828.48 xx	7739.38	773.93	27615.39	690.38
May	4	848.48 xx	7838.09	783.80	27679.30	691.98
	11	850.13 xx	7949.17	794.91	27776.85	694.42
	18	837.61 xx	8016.68	801.66	27844.16	695.60
	25	831.90 xx	8075.11	807.51	27944.52	698.61
Jun.	1	832.29 xx	8144.34	814.43	28090.01	702.25
	8	839.64 xx	8213.72	821.37	28251.07	706.27
	15	824.47 xx	8290.93	829.09	28397.66	709.94
	22	855.44 xx	8356.87	835.68	28625.91	715.64
	29	873.12 xx	8421.56	842.15	28828.27	720.70
Jul.	6	871.79 xx	8464.87	846.48	29078.11	726.95
	13	871.09 xx	8487.48	848.74	29364.64	734.11
	20	862.41 xx	8499.76	849.97	29568.88	739.22
	27	834.09 xx	8496.24	849.62	29748.09	743.70
Aug.	3	826.50 xx	8490.84	849.08	29938.40	748.46
	10	817.74 xx	8476.29	847.62	30090.86	752.27
	17	825.64 xx	8462.29	846.22	30249.34	756.23
	24	804.76 xx	8442.58	844.25	30406.49	760.16
	31	835.34 xx	8422.48	842.24	30626.53	765.66
Sep.	7	835.97 xx	8385.33	835.53	30843.84	771.09
	14	809.29 xx	8322.83	832.28	31075.53	776.88
	21	829.79 xx	8281.53	828.15	31312.55	782.81
	28	818.60 xx	8237.72	823.77	31532.67	788.31
Oct.	5	813.21 xx	8216.84	821.68	31743.72	793.59
	12	823.91 xx	8214.25	821.42	31933.09	798.32
	19	832.18 xx	8228.69	822.86	32106.48	802.66
	26	840.52 xx	8243.57	824.35	32302.37	807.56
Nov.	2	836.04 xx	8274.85	827.48	32471.13	811.77
	9	835.80 xx	8275.31	827.53	32603.24	815.08
	16	853.67 xx	8293.01	829.30	32745.00	818.62
	23	840.76 xx	8324.48	832.44	32851.56	821.28
	30	860.67 xx	8355.36	835.53	32962.46	824.06
Dec.	7	818.80 xx	8355.56	835.55	33042.21	826.05
	14	832.81 xx	8375.16	837.51	33104.92	827.62
	21	844.38 xx	8395.63	839.56	33175.83	829.39
	28	859.81 xx	8423.26	842.32	33272.58	831.81

1976		Price		10-Week Total	10-Week Average	40-Week Total	40-Week Average
Jan.	4	858.71	xx	8441.45	844.14	33361.03	834.02
	11	911.13	xx	8516.54	851.65	33524.90	838.12
	18	929.63	xx	8610.37	861.03	33665.03	841.62
	25	953.95	xx	8710.65	871.06	33810.55	845.26
Feb.	1	975.28	xx	8845.17	884.51	33957.35	848.93
	8	954.90	xx	8939.40	893.94	34063.77	851.59
	15	958.36	xx	9078.96	907.89	34172.00	854.30
	22	987.80	xx	9233.95	923.39	34322.19	858.05
	29	972.61	xx	9362.18	936.21	34462.90	861.57
Mar.	7	972.92	xx	9475.29	947.52	34603.53	865.08
	14	987.64	xx	9604.22	960.42	34751.53	868.78
	21	979.85	xx	9672.94	967.29	34906.91	872.67
	28	1003.46	xx	9746.77	974.67	35054.93	876.37
Apr.	4	991.58	xx	9784.40	978.44	35173.39	879.33
	11	968.28	xx	9777.40	977.74	35269.88	881.74
	18	980.48	xx	9802.98	980.29	35379.27	884.48
	25	1000.71	xx	9845.33	984.53	35517.57	887.93
May	2	996.85	xx	9854.38	985.43	35680.33	892.00
	9	996.22	xx	9877.99	987.79	35850.05	896.25
	16	992.60	xx	9897.67	989.76	36024.91	900.62
	23	990.75	xx	9900.78	990.07	36190.02	904.75
	30	975.23	xx	9896.16	989.61	36360.49	909.01
Jun.	6	963.90	xx	9856.60	985.66	36489.05	912.22
	13	978.80	xx	9843.82	984.38	36631.88	915.79
	20	1001.88	xx	9877.42	987.74	36824.47	920.61
	27	999.84	xx	9896.78	989.67	36994.52	924.86
Jul.	4	999.84	xx	9895.91	989.59	37175.76	929.39
	11	1003.11	xx	9902.17	990.21	37365.66	934.14
	18	993.21	xx	9899.16	989.91	37534.96	938.37
	25	990.91	xx	9897.47	989.74	37693.69	942.34
Aug.	1	984.64	xx	9891.36	989.13	37837.81	945.94
	8	986.00	xx	9902.13	990.29	37987.77	949.69
	15	990.19	xx	9928.42	992.84	38142.16	953.55
	22	974.07	xx	9923.69	992.36	38262.56	956.56
	29	963.93	xx	9885.74	988.57	38385.73	959.64
Sep.	5	989.11	xx	9875.01	987.50	38514.17	962.85
	12	988.36	xx	9863.53	986.35	38683.73	967.09
	19	995.10	xx	9855.52	985.55	38846.02	971.15
	26	1009.31	xx	9871.62	987.16	39010.95	975.27
Oct.	3	979.89	xx	9860.60	986.06	39131.03	978.27
	10	952.38	xx	9828.34	982.83	39224.70	980.61
	17	937.00	xx	9779.34	977.93	39250.57	981.26
	24	938.75	xx	9727.90	972.79	39259.69	981.49
	31	964.93	xx	9718.76	971.87	39270.67	981.76
Nov.	7	943.07	xx	9697.90	969.79	39238.46	980.96
	14	927.69	xx	9636.48	963.64	39211.25	980.28
	21	948.80	xx	9596.92	959.69	39201.69	980.04
	28	956.62	xx	9558.44	955.84	39170.51	979.26
Dec.	5	950.55	xx	9499.68	949.96	39148.45	978.71
	12	973.15	xx	9492.94	949.29	39148.68	978.71
	19	979.06	xx	9519.62	951.96	39140.10	978.50
	26	985.62	xx	9568.24	956.82	39145.87	978.64

1977		Price		10-Week Total	10-Week Average	40-Week Total	40-Week Average
Jan.	2	1004.64	xx	9634.14	963.41	39147.05	978.67
	9	983.13	xx	9652.34	965.23	39138.60	978.46
	16	972.16	xx	9681.43	968.14	39142.48	978.56
	23	962.43	xx	9716.17	971.61	39124.44	978.11
	30	957.53	xx	9724.90	972.49	39081.26	977.03
Feb.	6	947.89	xx	9716.17	971.61	39032.30	975.80
	13	931.52	xx	9697.14	969.71	38967.61	974.19
	20	940.24	xx	9664.23	966.42	38915.24	972.88
	27	933.43	xx	9618.60	961.86	38857.92	971.44
Mar.	6	953.46	xx	9586.44	958.64	38836.15	970.90
	13	947.72	xx	9529.51	952.95	38819.97	970.49
	20	961.02	xx	9507.40	950.74	38802.19	970.05
	27	928.86	xx	9464.10	946.41	38729.17	968.22
Apr.	3	927.36	xx	9429.03	942.90	38656.69	966.41
	10	918.88	xx	9390.38	939.03	38575.73	964.39
	17	947.76	xx	9390.25	939.02	38520.38	963.00
	24	927.07	xx	9385.80	938.58	38454.24	961.35
May	1	926.90	xx	9372.46	937.24	38390.23	959.75
	8	936.74	xx	9375.77	937.57	38342.33	958.55
	15	928.34	xx	9350.65	935.06	38284.67	957.11
	22	930.46	xx	9333.39	933.33	38224.94	955.62
	29	898.83	x	9271.20	927.12	38149.70	953.74
Jun.	5	912.23	x	9254.57	925.45	38098.00	952.45
	12	910.00	x	9238.00	923.80	38019.68	950.49
	19	920.45	x	9239.57	923.95	37951.77	948.79
	26	929.70	x	9221.51	922.15	37886.37	947.15
Jul.	3	912.65	x	9207.09	920.70	37789.71	944.74
	10	907.99	x	9188.18	918.81	37717.81	942.94
	17	905.95	x	9157.39	915.73	37671.38	941.78
	24	923.42	x	9152.47	915.24	37657.80	941.44
	31	890.07	x	9112.08	911.20	37609.12	940.22
Aug.	7	888.69	x	9101.94	910.19	37532.88	938.32
	14	881.10	x	9070.81	907.08	37470.91	936.77
	21	863.48	x	9023.50	902.35	37406.70	935.16
	28	855.42	x	8958.47	895.84	37313.32	932.83
Sep.	4	872.31	x	8901.08	890.10	37229.01	930.72
	11	857.07	x	8845.50	884.55	37135.53	928.38
	18	856.81	x	8794.32	879.43	37019.19	925.47
	25	839.14	x	8727.51	872.75	36879.27	921.98
Oct.	2	847.11	x	8651.20	865.12	36740.76	918.51
	9	840.35	x	8601.48	860.14	36576.47	914.41
	16	821.64	x	8534.43	853.44	36414.98	910.37
	23	808.30		8461.63	846.16	36251.12	906.27
	30	822.68		8420.83	842.08	36111.36	902.78
Nov.	6	809.94		8375.35	837.53	35963.77	899.09
	13	845.89		8348.93	834.89	35861.77	896.54
	20	835.76		8327.62	832.76	35766.01	894.15
	27	844.42		8315.23	831.52	35670.19	891.75
Dec.	4	823.98		8300.07	830.00	35560.74	889.01
	11	815.23		8268.19	826.81	35422.51	885.56
	18	815.32		8243.16	824.31	35290.11	882.25
	25	829.87		8251.39	825.13	35158.96	878.97

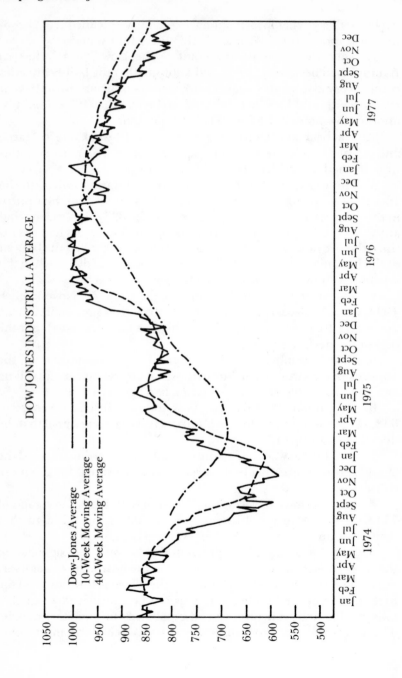

DOW JONES INDUSTRIAL AVERAGE

Dow-Jones Average
10-Week Moving Average
40-Week Moving Average

Now let's see what information we could have gleaned from keeping these moving average lines during these four years:

1. Since the previous low point in the Dow-Jones Industrial Average had been May, 1970, and knowing that the bull-bear cycles come every 3½ to 4½ years, with most coming in 4-to-4½-year cycles, we should have been alerted to the fact that 1974 should be another low point if the Dow Theory holds true.

2. The back-and-forth movement of the 10-week line in March and April of 1974 are shown by squiggly lines. The market at this time seemed undecided about which way to go.

3. The week of June 9, 1974, showed a summer rally with the 10-week line rising. But the rally was not sustained, and the upturn in the 10-week line lasted only one week—the 837.46 is circled. Had any traders bought into the rally thinking that four years had passed since the previous low and that this might have signalled the bottom of the bear market, they would have sold out at a small loss when the downturn showed the bottom had not yet been reached.

4. The next break in the long decline came on November 3, 1974, when the weekly Dow-Jones Industrial Average of 665.28 rose above the 10-week line of 647.54. This was the first signal that the end of the decline was nearing.

5. The December 15, 1974, break in the downtrend of the 10-week line was a signal to buy to those investors and traders willing again to take a chance that the bottom had been reached.

6. On January 5, 1975, the Dow-Jones Industrial Average of 634.54 rose above the 10-week line of 621.95, a strong signal that the decline had stopped.

7. The January 26, 1975, upturn in the 10-week line verified the change from a bear to a bull market and was a signal for the more conservative investors.

8. On February 9, 1975, the Dow-Jones Industrial Average of 711.91 rose above the 40-week line of 702.78 and gave further confirmation that the new bull market had begun.

9. The April 20, 1975, upturn in the 40-week line signalled to the most conservative of all investors that the bear market was over.

10. The July 20, 1975, downturn in the 10-week line signalled the first reverse in the bull market. This can be considered a signal to take profits and wait until the reversal ends to buy stocks again. These reversals last from three weeks to 13 weeks and most stocks

lose about 40 per cent to 50 per cent of their previous rise. This reversal lasted 12 weeks.

11. On October 19, 1975, the 10-week line again turned up as the second advance of the bull market began.

12. On April 11, 1976, the 10-week line again turned down, but the downturn lasted only one week. However, it should have alerted traders that the end of the advance was nearing. This was verified on May 30th. Yet this was not really a downturn. For the next four months the 10-week line moved back and forth within a five point range. During this time the Dow ranged above 1,000 three times, but each time the average fell back.

13. The second reversal began on October 3, 1976, as indicated by the 10-week line. Again this could be considered a signal to take profits if the individual stocks indicated a similar movement. This second reversal lasted 11 weeks.

14. On November 7, 1976, the 40-week line also turned down after having been rising for a year and a half. This indicated that the reversal was a severe one.

15. The 10-week line turned up for the third advance on December 19, 1976, but it was a very short one, lasting only seven weeks. This advance was so weak it was unable to turn the downward moving 40-week line around. Alert traders are aware that at times there is no clear-cut third phase of a bull market and watch for this possibility. This is one reason getting the feel of the market is considered an art rather than a science.

16. Beginning on January 30, 1977, the definite downturn of the 40-week line signalled the beginning of the bear market. This was verified by the 10-week line downturn on February 6th.

17. With the exception of the two weeks circled (May 8, 1977, and June 19, 1977), the Dow's 10-week line continued its bear market downward path until December 25, 1977. But this was an unusual bear cycle in that the stocks showing the greatest declines were the so-called "blue chips," those of the largest and most solid companies listed. Since 30 of these companies are the basis of the Dow-Jones Industrial Average, the 10-week line was unable to turn to show any rallies. But the stocks which declined very little were the so-called "secondary" stocks, and these are best reflected in the Standard & Poor's 500 Stock Index. This is one reason I suggested earlier that you keep track of both market indicators.

STANDARD & POOR'S 500 STOCK INDEX

1977	Price		Total	10-Week Average	Total	40-Week Average
Jan. 2	107.45	xx	1032.04	103.20	4127.21	103.17
9	105.01	xx	1034.15	103.41	4129.97	103.24
16	104.01	xx	1037.34	103.73	4133.63	103.33
23	103.32	xx	1041.42	104.14	4136.28	103.40
30	101.93	xx	1041.43	104.14	4135.92	103.39
Feb. 6	101.88	xx	1040.16	104.01	4136.18	103.40
13	100.22	xx	1037.62	103.76	4134.50	103.36
20	100.49	xx	1033.41	103.34	4133.65	103.34
27	99.48	xx	1028.63	102.86	4131.87	103.29
Mar. 6	101.20	xx	1024.99	102.49	4132.89	103.32
13	100.65	xx	1018.19	101.81	4134.39	103.35
20	101.86	xx	1015.04	101.50	4135.33	103.38
27	99.06	x	1010.09	101.00	4130.63	103.26
Apr. 3	99.21	x	1005.98	100.59	4126.12	103.15
10	98.35	x	1002.40	100.24	4120.36	103.00
17	101.04	x	1001.56	100.15	4116.42	102.90
24	98.44	x	999.78	99.97	4110.18	102.75
May 1	98.44	x	997.73	99.77	4104.56	102.61
8	99.49	x	997.74	99.77	4100.61	102.51
15	99.03	x	995.57	99.55	4095.85	102.39
22	99.45	x	994.37	99.43	4091.05	102.27
29	96.27	x	988.78	98.87	4084.95	102.12
Jun. 5	97.69	x	987.41	98.74	4081.16	102.02
12	98.46	x	986.66	98.66	4075.32	101.88
19	99.97	x	988.28	98.82	4070.64	101.76
26	101.19	x	988.43	98.84	4065.56	101.63
Jul. 3	100.10	x	990.09	99.00	4045.85	101.14
10	99.97	x	991.62	99.16	4041.65	101.04
17	100.18	x	992.31	99.23	4039.27	100.98
24	103.01	x	996.29	99.62	4041.40	101.03
31	98.95	x	995.79	99.57	4040.39	101.00
Aug. 7	98.76	x	998.28	99.82	4036.25	100.90
14	97.88	x	998.47	99.84	4033.31	100.83
21	97.51	x	997.52	99.75	4031.56	100.78
28	96.06	x	993.61	99.36	4025.72	100.64
Sep. 4	97.45	x	989.87	98.98	4020.02	100.49
11	96.37	x	986.14	98.61	4013.63	100.34
18	96.48	x	982.65	98.26	4005.41	100.13
25	95.04	x	977.51	97.75	3996.19	99.90
Oct. 2	96.53	x	971.03	97.10	3987.88	99.69
9	95.97	x	968.05	96.80	3976.40	99.40
16	93.56	x	962.85	96.28	3964.95	99.12
23	92.32		957.29	95.72	3953.26	98.83
30	92.61		952.39	95.23	3942.55	98.56
Nov. 6	91.58		947.91	94.79	3932.20	98.30
13	95.98		946.44	94.64	3926.30	98.15
20	95.33		945.40	94.54	3921.44	98.03
27	96.69		945.61	94.56	3917.61	97.93
Dec. 4	94.67		945.24	94.52	3912.80	97.81
11	93.65		942.36	94.23	3905.25	97.63
18	93.40		939.79	93.97	3898.00	97.44
25	94.69		940.92	94.09	3890.83	97.27

The 1977 Standard & Poor's 500 Stock Index 10-week and 40-week lines are also given so that you can see where the rallies in the bear market actually did occur. These are some comparisons for the year:

1. Like the Dow-Jones Industrial Average 10-week line, the Standard & Poor's 500 Stock Index shows the bull market ended on January 30, 1977. The 40-week line of the Index waited an extra two weeks before it began its downward plunge.

2. The Index 10-week line shows the first rally of the bear market began on June 19, 1977, and lasted nine weeks. This is the rally that does not show up on the Dow 10-week line because of the two-tier market in which the Dow companies' stocks remained depressed in price, but the secondaries of the Index turned up strongly enough to reverse the downward trend.

3. The second downturn of the bear market began on August 21st and lasted until the last week of the year.

4. The second rally on the Index seems to begin on December 25th. The Dow shows an upturn the same week.

These moving average lines must be kept up every week. It is essential that you try to find out at all times what the market is doing. True, there are times when the market tries to fool you, as evidenced by the times it shows no clear-cut trend. But by keeping track through the moving average lines, and by keeping in mind the timing of the Dow Theory, you will develop the necessary "feel" you need to succeed in your investment strategy.

CHAPTER 8

The Advance-Decline Line

Although the moving average lines of the Dow-Jones Industrial Average are given first as a technical tool to use in the timing of the stock market, many technicians consider the advance-decline line as more important. The industrial average deals with 30 industrial giants, and Standard & Poor's index deals with the price fluctuations of the stocks in the 500 largest industrial companies. But the total of smaller corporations far outnumber the large companies which dominate both the average and the index. And since the advance-decline line includes every company listed on the New York Stock Exchange, it represents the total market, over 1500 companies, not just a portion of it. Nor does the price of any of the shares make a difference.

As shown in the previous chapter, the Sunday newspapers list how many issues on the exchange have advanced, how many have declined, and how many are unchanged in price. The advance-decline line is based on the difference between the number of issues that have advanced and those that have declined. The unchanged ones are ignored.

The theory of the advance-decline line is that it is a breadth-of-the-market study which shows how strong or how weak the prevailing trend of the market is. There are times when the Dow-Jones Industrial Average may be rising, as in the final phases of a bull market, but the majority of the stocks on the exchange show a decline. This divergence exposes an underlying weakness in the market, and a reverse should be expected. The converse may also be

54

true. If the averages are falling but the advance-decline line is standing still or dropping much less, then the market is actually stronger than the averages show, and the investor should be alert for a change.

Therefore, the most important point to look for is a divergence between the Dow and the advance-decline line. In a bull market, when they are rising together, everything is fine. And when they are falling together in a bear market, the technician has no trouble following the market. It is when the advance-decline line is no longer in step with the Dow that a change in the pattern of the market is predicted. For example, when the Dow-Jones Industrial Average continues to fall but the advance-decline line begins to rise, the market will turn and will rise in the near future. Conversely, when the Dow-Jones Industrial Average is still rising but the advance-decline line reverses and falls, the market will fall soon too. At the bottom of some bear markets it is the industrial average which reverses first and signals the turn, but the importance lies in the divergence between the two, not which one reverses first.

The most useful function of the advance-decline line is to signal the tops in a bull market. If the advance-decline line fails to make a new peak when the Dow-Jones Industrial Average does, then the continuation of the bull trend is in doubt. The advance-decline line seldom rises through all three phases of the bull market, but usually tops out late in the second phase or early in the third phase. This divergence does not signal an immediate turn, but one in the near future.

Unfortunately, the advance-decline line is not as accurate in forecasting bottoms in a bear market and should be used in conjunction with other technical tools rather than be relied on as the sole one in a bear market to judge the bottom.

There are a number of ways to construct an advance-decline line. The simplest one is to put down the advances and declines in two columns, subtract the declines from the advances, which would give a plus or a minus difference in the third column, and lastly have a cumulative plus or minus total of the difference in the fourth column. The problem with this simple method is that it deals with a great many minuses, which is very confusing to a beginner. This is what these columns would look like in a bear market:

Date	Advance	Decline	Difference	Cumulative Difference
Apr. 7	594	1167	− 573	
14	605	1112	− 507	−1080
21	1006	701	+ 305	− 775
28	170	1670	−1500	−2275
May 2	531	1137	− 606	−2881
9	1562	247	+1315	−1566
16	554	1207	− 653	−2219

If we were to add another column, a 10-week moving average line of the cumulative difference, you can see that using more minuses would be even more confusing. To avoid all these minuses in the cumulative total and in the moving average line, I have taken the figure 20,000 as a selected constant. Any figure would do as long as it is high enough to eliminate the minuses.

Now let's construct a 1974 through 1977 advance-decline line and see what can be read into it. To clarify for you, the x's in the fifth column mean those numbers have been checked off.

These are the inferences we can make about the broad market from the advance-decline figures:

1. In 1974 the 10-week average, which we now call the 10-week line, reversed on March 31 and signalled a downturn in the bear market. This was an extremely severe one, and the 10-week line dropped about two-thirds of its previous advance.

2. On January 26, 1975, the 10-week advance decline line signalled a new bull market, the exact same time the Dow-Jones Industrial Average 10-week line also reversed.

3. This upward surge which had begun in January, 1975, continued for seven months until August, ending the first upward phase of the bull market. The reversal lasted 13 weeks.

4. In November, 1975, the advance-decline line again turned up and continued rising until April, 1976, when it reversed itself. This completed the second upward surge of the bull market. The reversal lasted ten weeks.

5. In July, 1976, the market started up for the third time, but it showed its weakness by going up from 16438 to 17059 and then falling back to 16499 again, practically where it had started from. The real surge began in December, 1976, and ended in February, 1977.

1974	Advance	Decline	Difference	Cumulative Difference	10-wk Cum. Diff. Total	10-week Average
Jan. 6	1647	247	+1400	21400 x		
13	599	1218	− 619	20781 x		
20	1216	538	+ 678	21459 x		
27	1017	757	+ 260	21719 x		
Feb. 3	812	947	− 135	21584 x		
10	537	1238	− 701	20883 x		
17	813	900	− 87	20796 x		
24	1321	427	+ 894	21690 x		
Mar. 3	1096	683	+ 413	22103 x		
10	1247	555	+ 692	22795 x	215210	21521
17	1084	656	+ 428	23223 x	217033	21703
24	440	1353	− 913	22310 x	218562	21856
31	284	1513	−1229	21081 x	218184	21814
Apr. 7	594	1167	− 573	20508 x	216973	21697
14	605	1112	− 507	20001 x	215390	21539
21	1006	701	+ 305	20306 x	214813	21481
28	170	1670	−1500	18806 x	212823	21282
May 5	738	967	− 229	18577 x	209710	20971
12	608	1125	− 517	18060 x	205667	20566
19	248	1549	−1301	16759 x	199631	19963
26	529	1204	− 675	16084 x	192492	19249
Jun. 2	531	1137	− 606	15478 x	185660	18566
9	1562	247	+1315	16793 x	181372	18137
16	554	1207	− 653	16140 x	177004	17700
23	213	1574	−1361	14779 x	171782	17178
30	396	1327	− 931	13848 x	165324	16532
Jul. 7	405	1286	− 881	12967 x	159485	15948
14	593	1141	− 548	12419 x	153327	15332
21	1045	678	+ 367	12786 x	148053	14805
28	911	799	+ 112	12898 x	144192	14419
Aug. 4	272	1483	−1211	11687 x	139795	13979
11	1337	416	+ 921	12608 x	136925	13692
18	229	1544	−1315	11293 x	131425	13142
25	247	1521	−1274	10019 x	125304	12530
Sep. 1	499	1260	− 761	9258 x	119783	11978
8	612	1095	− 483	8775 x	114710	11471
15	145	1707	−1562	7213 x	108956	10895
22	1416	361	+1055	8268 x	104805	10480
29	527	1188	− 661	7607 x	99626	9962
Oct. 6	487	1257	− 770	6837 x	93565	9356
13	1727	152	+1575	8412 x	90290	9029
20	1016	743	+ 273	8685 x	86367	8636
27	563	1207	− 644	8041 x	83115	8311
Nov. 3	1131	591	+ 540	8581 x	81677	8167
10	1191	571	+ 620	9201 x	81620	8162
17	580	1152	− 572	8629 x	81474	8147
24	274	1541	−1267	7362 x	81623	8162
Dec. 1	857	817	+ 40	7402 x	80754	8075
8	175	1692	−1517	5885 x	79035	7903
15	785	931	− 146	5739 x	77937	7793
22	683	1077	− 394	5345 x	74870	7487
29	844	831	+ 13	5358 x	71543	7154

1975	Advance	Decline	Difference	Cumulative Difference	10-W, Cum. Diff. Total	10-Week Average
Jan. 5	1688	206	+1482	6840 x	70342	7034
12	1668	242	+1426	8211 x	70027	7002
19	1063	734	+ 329	8595 x	69421	6942
26	1276	486	+ 790	9385 x	70177	7017
Feb. 2	1598	293	+1305	10690 x	73505	7350
9	1265	585	+ 680	11370 x	77473	7747
16	1172	634	+ 538	11908 x	83496	8349
23	962	773	+ 189	12097 x	89854	8985
Mar. 2	583	1177	− 594	11503 x	96012	9601
9	1405	416	+ 989	12492 x	103146	10314
16	1126	657	+ 469	12961 x	109267	10926
23	704	1055	− 351	12610 x	113611	11361
30	733	982	− 249	12361 x	117377	11737
Apr. 6	466	1342	− 876	11485 x	119477	11947
13	1056	678	+ 378	11863 x	120650	12065
20	1165	630	+ 535	12398 x	121678	12167
27	898	846	+ 52	12450 x	122220	12222
May 4	965	793	+ 172	12622 x	122745	12274
11	1165	645	+ 520	13142 x	124384	12438
18	935	827	+ 108	13250 x	125142	12514
25	824	939	− 115	13135 x	125316	12531
Jun. 1	985	721	+ 264	13399 x	126105	12610
8	1196	592	+ 604	14003 x	127747	12774
15	651	1142	− 491	13512 x	129774	12977
22	1234	555	+ 679	14191 x	132102	13210
29	1330	483	+ 847	15038 x	134742	13474
Jul. 6	878	879	− 1	15037 x	137329	13732
13	1104	689	+ 415	15452 x	140159	14015
20	901	925	− 24	15428 x	142445	14244
27	260	1612	−1352	14076 x	143271	14327
Aug. 3	474	1281	− 807	13269 x	143405	14340
10	301	1498	−1197	12072 x	142078	14207
17	687	1050	− 363	11709 x	139784	13978
24	351	1403	−1052	10657 x	136929	13692
31	1365	426	+ 939	11596 x	134334	13433
Sep. 7	556	1138	− 582	11014 x	130310	13031
14	384	1372	− 988	10026 x	125299	12529
21	1034	699	+ 335	10361 x	120208	12020
28	862	849	+ 13	10374 x	115154	11515
Oct. 5	582	1126	− 544	9830 x	110908	11090
12	1141	601	+ 540	10370 x	108009	10800
19	1057	666	+ 391	10761 x	106698	10669
Nov. 2	727	1049	− 322	11000 x	106654	10665
9	997	776	+ 221	11221 x	106279	10627
16	1210	575	+ 635	11856 x	107121	10712
23	657	1124	− 467	11389 x	108484	10848
30	1109	615	+ 494	11883 x	110006	11000
Dec. 7	235	1609	−1374	10509 x	110141	11014
14	754	975	− 221	10288 x	110599	11059
21	1135	608	+ 527	10815 x	111044	11104
28	1263	483	+ 780	11595 x	111878	11187

1976	Advance	Decline	Difference	Cumulative Difference	10-wk Cum. Diff. Total	10-Week Average
Jan. 4	1332	459	+ 873	12468 x	113024	11302
11	1790	176	+1614	14082 x	116106	11610
18	1465	426	+1039	15121 x	120006	12000
25	1441	426	+1015	16136 x	124286	12428
Feb. 1	1321	557	+ 764	16900 x	129797	12979
8	1046	846	+ 200	17100 x	135014	13501
15	1255	638	+ 617	17717 x	142222	14222
22	1362	506	+ 856	18573 x	150507	15050
29	611	1276	− 665	17908 x	157600	15760
Mar. 7	796	1042	− 246	17662 x	163667	16366
14	1024	807	+ 217	17879 x	169078	16907
21	697	1144	− 447	17432 x	172428	17242
28	1102	695	+ 407	17839 x	175146	17514
Apr. 4	701	1106	− 405	17434 x	176444	17644
11	535	1298	− 763	16671 x	176215	17621
18	849	919	− 70	16601 x	175716	17571
25	1282	555	+ 727	17328 x	175327	17532
May 2	745	1027	− 282	17046 x	173800	17380
9	799	989	− 190	16856 x	172748	17274
16	889	878	+ 11	16867 x	171953	17195
23	789	1009	− 220	16647 x	170721	17072
30	434	1376	− 942	15705 x	168994	16899
Jun. 6	661	1058	− 397	15308 x	166463	16646
13	1008	769	+ 239	15547 x	164576	16457
20	1376	453	+ 923	16470 x	164375	16437
27	978	835	+ 143	16613 x	164387	16438
Jul. 4	1106	705	+ 401	17014 x	164073	16407
11	1159	623	+ 536	17550 x	164577	16457
18	992	793	+ 199	17749 x	165470	16547
25	714	1092	− 378	17371 x	165974	16597
Aug. 1	627	1167	− 540	16831 x	166158	16615
8	1011	777	+ 234	17065 x	167518	16751
15	915	839	+ 76	17141 x	169351	16935
22	558	1266	− 708	16433 x	170237	17023
29	634	1138	− 504	15929 x	169696	16969
Sep. 5	1396	423	+ 973	16902 x	169985	16998
12	1013	769	+ 244	17146 x	170117	17011
19	1160	642	+ 518	17664 x	170231	17023
26	1126	677	+ 449	18113 x	170595	17059
Oct. 3	528	1319	− 791	17322 x	170546	17054
10	566	1242	− 676	16646 x	170361	17036
17	532	1294	− 762	15884 x	169180	16918
24	804	981	− 177	15707 x	167746	16774
31	1245	571	+ 674	16381 x	167694	16769
Nov. 7	834	926	− 92	16289 x	168054	16805
14	550	1273	− 723	15566 x	166718	16671
21	1391	476	+ 915	16481 x	166053	16605
28	1275	537	+ 738	17219 x	165608	16560
Dec. 5	1063	780	+ 283	17502 x	164997	16499
12	1487	441	+1046	18548 x	166223	16622
19	1048	833	+ 215	18763 x	168340	16834
26	896	908	− 12	18751 x	171207	17120

1977	Advance	Decline	Difference	Cumulative Difference	10-wk. Cum. Diff. Total	10-Week Average
Jan. 2	1586	334	+1252	20003 x	175503	17550
9	966	933	+ 33	20036 x	179158	17915
16	754	1094	− 340	19696 x	182565	18256
23	938	917	+ 21	19717 x	186716	18671
30	804	1056	− 252	19465 x	189700	18970
Feb. 6	883	938	− 55	19410 x	191891	19189
13	658	1201	− 543	18867 x	193256	19325
20	891	918	− 27	18840 x	193548	19354
27	558	1272	− 714	18126 x	192911	19291
Mar. 6	1204	636	+ 568	18694 x	192854	19285
13	839	947	− 108	18586 x	191437	19143
20	1137	707	+ 430	19016 x	190417	19041
27	515	1319	− 804	18212 x	188933	18893
Apr. 3	756	1024	− 268	17944 x	187160	18716
10	613	1137	− 524	17420 x	185115	18511
17	1439	392	+1047	18467 x	184172	18417
24	715	1149	− 434	18033 x	183338	18333
May 1	854	925	− 71	17962 x	182460	18246
8	1255	555	+ 700	18662 x	182996	18299
15	884	946	− 62	18600 x	182902	18290
22	1057	739	+ 318	18918 x	183234	18323
29	329	1578	−1249	17669 x	181887	18188
Jun. 5	1079	685	+ 394	18063 x	181738	18173
12	1114	713	+ 401	18461 x	182255	18225
19	1274	566	+ 708	19172 x	184007	18400
26	1319	545	+ 774	19946 x	185486	18548
Jul. 3	878	943	− 65	19881 x	187334	18733
10	1013	751	+ 262	20143 x	189515	18951
17	953	836	+ 117	20260 x	191113	19111
24	1181	661	+ 520	20780 x	193293	19329
31	416	1482	−1066	19714 x	194089	19408
Aug. 7	831	956	− 125	19589 x	196009	19600
14	687	1086	− 399	19190 x	197136	19713
21	703	1044	− 341	18849 x	197524	19752
28	606	1172	− 566	18283 x	196635	19663
Sep. 4	1145	638	+ 507	18790 x	195479	19547
11	690	1055	− 365	18425 x	194023	19402
18	824	933	− 109	18316 x	192196	19219
25	533	1288	− 755	17561 x	189497	18949
Oct. 2	1064	722	+ 342	17903 x	186620	18662
9	962	858	+ 104	18007 x	184913	18491
16	311	1561	−1250	16757 x	182081	18208
23	655	1176	− 521	16236	178127	17812
30	866	929	− 63	16173	176451	17645
Nov. 6	684	1106	− 422	15751	173919	17391
13	1648	265	+1383	17134	172263	17226
20	1063	782	+ 281	17415	171253	17125
27	1295	519	+ 776	18191	171128	17112
Dec. 4	719	1136	− 417	17774	171341	17134
11	539	1323	− 784	16990	170428	17042
18	839	986	− 147	16843	169264	16926
25	925	902	+ 23	16866	169373	16937

6. The first phase of the bear market began at the end of February, 1977, but did not go down very far. This indicated the strength of the broad market.

7. The first rally began in June, 1977, and ended in August of that year. It did not go up much, but note that at its peak on August 21st, the line was higher than at the peak of the third phase of the bull market. The technicians found this very confusing and wondered if the bull market had really ended in February.

8. The second phase of the bear market began on August 28, 1977, and continued downward until the end of the year. This was a much greater drop than the first phase had been.

9. The second rally in the bear market was signalled on December 25, 1977. This second rally usually does not reverse as much as the first one. It will be interesting to see if it follows the pattern.

During this year of 1977, when the advance-decline line dropped very little, the Dow-Jones Industrial Average dropped from just over 1000 to almost 800. The 30 industrial companies which make up the Dow-Jones Industrial Average were doing poorly, but the broad market was holding up very well. This showed the secondary stocks to be a much better investment at this time. This "two-tier" market is very unusual and is the reason the Dow-Jones Industrial Average could signal the first phase of the bear market, but the advance-decline line could not.

An important point to remember is that when both the Dow-Jones moving average lines and the advance-decline line are going in the same direction, then one can assume the existing trend will continue. When the moving averages and the advance-decline line rise together or fall together, then the established direction of the market should continue.

A change in the pattern of the market is signalled when one of the lines makes a reversal in its movement, but the other does not; for example, if the 40-week line of the Dow were to continue the same direction, but the advance-decline line were to change. This disparity means the movements are no longer "in gear," in the language of the technicians. The conservative investors wait until the moving average line and the advance-decline line again go in the same direction; the aggressive traders react at the first signal, since they are willing to take a small loss if they are wrong.

The most important thing to remember is not to rely totally on any one technical tool. A combination is essential to enable an investor to interpret the market from all angles.

CHAPTER 9

Keeping Track of Individual Stocks

A combination of fundamental analysis and technical analysis makes the most successful approach to the stock market and is probably the most frequently used by investors. The fundamental approach to the stock market is important in determining the long-term trend in investment profits. A solid company showing potential growth can be considered a safe and sound investment for dividend income, and hopefully for an increase in the price of shares. However, many investors use this fundamental approach to make short-term trading decisions, only to find themselves on the losing end of many of their transactions.

There should be a difference in approach to the market between an investor, one who plans to buy a stock and keep it for a few years, and a trader, one who buys a stock and plans to keep it for only a few weeks or months. For a short-term trader the risks are greater, but then the rewards are greater too. The investor can ignore the price fluctuations of his stock; the short-term trader plans to take advantage of them to make a profit.

A successful trader is wise enough to realize that there are short-term swings in prices in the stock market that cannot be predicted by fundamental analysis of the firm. He has studied the Dow Theory and is aware of the rhythmic pattern of change. So he has developed another way of measuring the movements that cause the short-term swings. He uses technical analysis to do so.

Technical analysis actually is the oldest form of security analysis known, dating back to the 1880's. At that time financial statements were not made public, and investors had to guess at the basic value of a company. So traders had to devise a method of improving their

63

timing of purchases and sales by tracing the price movement of individual stocks and their volume of trading. The Dow-Jones Industrial Average was developed by Charles Dow as a technical tool about then too to trace the price movement of the market as a whole by recording the combined action of 30 representative industrial stocks on the New York Stock Exchange.

The difference between fundamental analysis and technical analysis is that while the fundamentalists analyze the company, the technicians analyze the stock and its price. The technicians aim at assessing the strengths and weaknesses of the stock to determine the possible short-term direction of the price. They may use some of the same factors as the fundamentalists, such as the number of shares outstanding and available for trading, but they will use this information in a different manner. They will also ignore any news about the company because they will assume it has already manifested itself in the buy and sell orders. The pure technician is interested only in the price and volume action of the stock and learning to read these signals correctly to profit from them.

It is the belief of fundamentalists that the price of a stock reflects not only the basic value of the company, but also the future expectations of rising profits. In this sense the price of the stock can be looked upon as a barometer, and it is not unusual to see a stock price rising when news of the company continues to be bad, nor to see the price in a downtrend while earnings are continuing to be high. Maybe the company that had been in difficulty has now changed its management or has developed a new product, and a rising price reflects this despite the continued lack of profits. Maybe the company that had been doing well is now being affected by a downtrend in the business cycle. Whatever the cause, the change in price is anticipating a change in the expectations about the company. The fundamentalists are interested in such news, the technicians aren't. The latter figure the change in price is reflecting both the good and the bad news, and the price is all they need to watch.

The question has been posed many times whether technical analysis could possibly forecast stock market fluctuations with any reasonable degree of accuracy. Those who have studied the different devices for predicting the future course of the market have found the various indicators in the past have followed quite consistent, repetitive patterns which have much meaning for those who use them. There is no reason to believe the market will not continue to follow the same patterns in the future, and therefore, the technical approach can be considered invaluable for forecasting movements in the stock market.

But one must bear in mind that no one indicator is sufficient since some indicators perform better at various stages than others. A combination is advised for best results.

Alan R. Shaw, in *The Financial Analyst's Handbook*, writes that to be a successful technician there are three basic and necessary assumptions about technical analysis which must be taken into account.

1. The first assumption is that the market and/or individual stocks act as a barometer, not as a thermometer. (A barometer anticipates the future; the thermometer measures the present.) Events and their effect on prices have usually been anticipated, and the movements of the market and its stocks are the result of informed buyers and sellers at work. The price patterns that evolve due to their buying and selling are the result of both fundamentalists and short-term traders being convinced they will find their transactions profitable.

2. The second assumption deals with the law of supply and demand of the stock market. Although there is a buyer for every seller of stock, one force or the other is usually stronger or more influential, especially in the long run. If a large number of shares in a company is sold at a much lower price than the previous sale of shares (in stock market language, on a downtick) it is then considered that the seller was a stronger influence on the price than the buyer. Apparently the buyer, or buyers, were not too anxious to own the stock unless they could get it more cheaply than it had previously been priced. Had they really been eager to buy, the sale would have been with little change in price, or even on an increase (an uptick.) This major concession in price on a large number of shares is considered to be "distribution," meaning the stock is moving from strong to weak hands, in Wall Street terminology. It also means there is a supply of stock now available.

The opposite of distribution is called "accumulation." This occurs when a stock moves from weak to strong hands, or when buyers are willing to buy a stock and keep it, thus decreasing the amount of shares available, or even completely eliminating any.

The second assumption, according to Shaw, is that before a stock goes up in price, whether it is a minor or major mark-up, a period of accumulation usually will take place. In other words, the stock is being bought and its available supply is decreasing. Conversely, before a stock enters into a minor or major downtrend, a period of distribution will usually take place, meaning the stock is being sold and a good supply is now available. This supply and demand can be quite obvious at times; when the price is going up, people are buying and the demand is high. When the price is going down, people are reluctant to buy, and a large supply is available. However, accumulation or distribution can occur with little change in price, and it is when the price is in this neutral trading range that the technician is challenged to anticipate which is occuring, and, therefore, which way prices will go—up or down.

3. The third assumption deals with the relationship of the movements in the market to each other. The price of a stock does not go up and down like a yo-yo. Between movements there is a period of stock price consolidation, a phase of backing and filling until the price makes another move. If the consolidation period is short, the price movement following, either up or down, usually will also be short. A larger consolidation period can lead to a greater potential stock price move.

The converse is also true. A short decline in price should be followed by a short period of consolidation before the price moves up again. A greater decline calls for a longer period of consolidation.

The following paragraphs and figure, from Alan R. Shaw's handbook, illustrates the third assumption.

> In example A, the minor downward movement in price was followed by a short-term consolidation phase before the stock began to move up once again. In Example B, however, the downside adjustment was somewhat more severe than in the former case and thus the consolidation pattern was slightly longer in perspective. Example C is an extreme, reflecting a major downward trend. Simply stated, when the bulldozer, crane, and steel ball visited this scene, it took longer for the carpenters, electricians, and masons to accomplish their rebuilding procedure; the consolidation pattern was of longer duration.

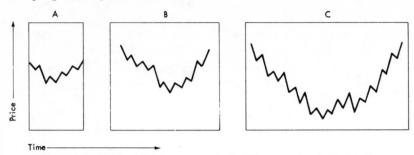

These are the three basic assumptions. They are simple and we hope logical to understand. But, they are often overlooked, even by more astute market students when attempting to understand technical stock market analysis. These assumptions, we hope, provide the framework for a clearer understanding of the methods that follow.

Just as the technicians keep track of the market as a whole through the methods illustrated in the previous chapters, so must they keep track of the individual stocks they are interested in. The phases in the bull and bear markets of the individual stocks do not always coincide with the market as a whole, and frequently not with other stocks. While the market as a whole may continue to rise to a bull market peak, perhaps as many as a third of the individual stocks have already begun their downturn. The more speculative stocks may still be showing rapid gains and some of the companies of the Dow-Jones may still be rising and so be holding up the averages, while many other stocks are now sliding slowly downward. The same is true in a bear market bottom. Many stocks anticipate the reversal and begin to rise before the Dow does. So it is at critical market tops and bottoms that investors need to keep an eye on their individual stocks.

The sole purpose of their keeping track of individual stocks is to improve the timing of buy and sell orders in order to increase their profits and to keep their losses small. Some methods of keeping track of individual stocks are simple, others quite complex. Let's begin with the most simple, using figures, and show you what keeping a list of the weekly prices of a stock can tell you.

I am using the statistics of the Addressograph Multigraph Company simply because it is the first alphabetically of those companies whose records I have kept. The dates are those of the Sunday papers I collect each week.

ADDRESSOGRAPH MULTIGRAPH COMPANY

1974	*Price*	*1975*	*Price*	*1976*	*Price*	*1977*	*Price*
Jan. 6	11¼	Jan. 5	3⅞	Jan. 4	7⅞	Jan. 2	13¼
13	9	12	4	11	8¼	9	13¾
20	9⅜	19	4⅛	18	8⅝	16	13¼
27	10¼	26	4¼	25	10	23	13⅜
Feb. 3	10	Feb. 2	5⅛	Feb. 1	10⅝	30	13¾
10	10	9	5¼	8	11⅝	Feb. 6	13¼
17	9⅞	16	5⅛	15	11½	13	13¾
24	9½	23	5⅞	22	13¼	20	13⅜
Mar. 3	10⅛	Mar. 2	5¾	29	9⅞	27	11½
10	10¾	9	6½	Mar. 7	11	Mar. 6	12
17	10	16	7½	14	10⅞	13	11½
24	10⅛	23	6⅞	21	10	20	12
31	9½	30	6¾	28	9¾	27	11⅜
Apr. 7	9	Apr. 6	6⅛	Apr. 4	9⅜	Apr. 3	10⅞
14	8½	13	6⅛	11	9¼	10	10½
21	8¼	20	7½	18	9⅜	17	11¼
26	7⅞	27	7½	25	9¾	24	10⅜
May 5	7½	May 4	7½	May 2	9½	May 1	10¼
12	6¾	11	8½	9	8¾	8	11⅛
19	6⅜	18	8⅛	16	9⅜	15	11⅞
26	6¾	25	8⅞	23	9¼	22	11½
Jun. 2	6¼	Jun. 1	8⅞	30	9⅛	29	12¼
9	5¾	8	8½	Jun. 6	8¾	Jun. 5	12¼
16	5½	15	7½	13	9¼	12	12⅝
23	5	22	8	20	9½	19	13¼
30	4¾	29	8¼	27	9⅜	26	13⅞
Jul. 7	5	Jul. 6	8¼	Jul. 4	9¾	Jul. 3	15
14	4⅞	13	8⅝	11	10⅜	10	13¾
21	5¾	20	8	18	11	17	13⅝
28	5¾	27	7	25	10½	24	14½
Aug. 4	5⅝	Aug. 3	6⅝	Aug. 1	9¾	31	13⅛
11	6⅜	10	6½	8	10	Aug. 7	12⅝
18	5½	17	6⅛	15	9⅜	14	13
25	5⅛	24	6¼	22	8⅞	21	13¼
Sep. 1	5	31	7	29	8⅞	28	13⅛
8	4⅞	Sep. 7	7⅜	Sep. 5	9	Sep. 4	14¼
15	4¼	14	7¼	12	8⅝	11	13⅝
22	4½	21	7⅝	19	9⅝	18	12⅞
29	4½	28	7½	26	11¼	25	13⅝
Oct. 6	3⅞	Oct. 5	7½	Oct. 3	10⅞	Oct. 2	13¾
13	4¾	12	7½	10	10⅜	9	13⅞
20	4⅝	19	8	17	9¾	16	13⅝
27	4	26	8¼	24	9¾	23	13
Nov. 3	4	Nov. 2	8	31	9⅞	30	12⅞
10	4⅝	9	7⅜	Nov. 7	10	Nov. 6	12⅝
17	4¼	16	8⅛	14	9⅞	13	14
24	4	23	8¼	21	10⅞	20	14⅞
Dec. 1	3⅞	30	8⅝	28	10½	27	15⅝
8	3⅜	Dec. 7	7½	Dec. 5	11⅜	Dec. 4	15
15	3	14	7⅛	12	11⅝	11	14⅝
22	3¼	21	7¾	19	11¾	18	14⅜
29	3¼	28	7	26	13	25	14¼

The following are some of the points you can read into the dates and prices.

1. Bottom of the bear market. Let's look at 1974 and see that the decline of Addressograph shares almost hit bottom in October, bounced up again and actually hit bottom in December. The stock market as a whole did the same thing, so analysts consider October as signalling the end of the bear market, meaning the end of the decline. An experienced trader would have been aware of the fact that October is a favorite month for bear markets to end.

2. End of the year. Traditionally stock prices decline in December because many people, wishing to show a loss for tax purposes, sell their losers that month. This is also the month in which many institutional funds get rid of their poorest holdings so they can show their investors a better portfolio of stocks. This accounts for the December, 1974, low point in prices, also for the 1975 decline in December. In 1976 the annual December decline was so publicized in the fall of the year that investors all clamored to get in early and the decline occurred in October and November. In 1977 Address-ograph was one of the two-tier secondary stocks doing much better than the Dow Jones Industrial average, and the price was showing only a slight decline.

3. Capital gains taxes. Let's see what effect the capital gains tax law had on the price of our stock. Investors were allowed a 50 per cent exemption from taxes of all profits made in buying and selling stock, provided they had kept the stock at least six months. Six months from the low of December, 1974, is the high of June, 1975, when short-term traders could sell their stock and pay less taxes. Then the stock retreated—remember the Dow Theory—and August, 1975, was the next low point. Six months from then was the high of February, 1976. The stock then retreated again to its most consistent low point, which was in August, 1976. With the change in capital gains tax law for 1977 to nine months instead of six, the rest of the year shows no definitive pattern. In 1978 the law for capital gains will be changed to holding the stock for a year, so you will need to study to see what effect this will have on prices.

4. Application of the Dow Theory. You recall the Dow Theory maintains that there are three rising waves in a bull market, with one-third to two-thirds reversals between the waves, mostly in the 40

percent to 50 percent range. Note how the theory has worked with this stock:

a. The Addressograph low in December, 1974, of 3 to the June, 1975, high of 8 equals a rise of 5⅞ points. The stock price then reversed to a low of 6⅛ in August, 1975, a loss of 2¾ points, or a reversal of 47 per cent. This completed the first phase of the bull market.

b. The next high was 13¼ in February, 1976, a rise of 7⅛ points. The stock then reversed to 8¾ in June of the same year, a loss of 4½ points. This is a reversal of 63 per cent and completed the second phase of the bull market.

c. The important thing to remember is that when reversals of the current trend do occur, they will be anywhere from one-third to two-thirds of the previous move. This can be highly profitable to a trader. Note that in 1977 the January high of 13¾ dropped to 10¼ in May, a reversal of 70 per cent of the previous rise. Also the high of 15 in July dropped to 12½ in August, a reversal of 47 per cent of the previous gain. In learning these moves of your favorite stocks, and in developing a "feel" of how they act, you can make money in the stock market.

Short-term traders would have found these changes in price very profitable. Without hitting the bottoms and the tops, if they had bought 100 shares at 4 in January, 1975, and sold at 8 in July, they would have doubled their money. If they had used the $800 and bought 123 shares at 6½ in August, 1975, and sold at 11½ in February, 1976, they would have made $615, a gain of 76 per cent in six months. If again they had used the $1415 received from the last sale and bought 157 shares at 9 in August, 1976, and sold at 13 in January, 1977, they would have made $629, a gain of 44 per cent in six months. In two years' time, from January, 1975, to January, 1977, their original $400 would now be $2044, a gain of $1644, an increase of 511 per cent. For the sake of comparison, I have not added in commissions nor deducted any income tax that might have been paid.

Fundamentalists buying at 4 in January, 1975, and holding for two years, then selling at 13 in January, 1977, would have increased their money by $900, a gain of 325 per cent. For the conservative investor this is a fine profit.

We must remember that the bear market of 1974 was one of the worst in the history of the stock exchange, so opportunity for such profits may not come again for a long time. But this certainly illustrates the difference in profit between investing for the long term and short-term trading. Keep in mind the risks are greater, but so too are the profits.

CHAPTER 10

Individual Stocks—Moving Averages

A second way of keeping track of individual stocks is by the use of moving average lines, similar to those used in computing the Dow-Jones Industrial Average lines. The purpose of these lines is to show longer-term trends in price of the individual stocks, which help technicians get a larger picture of the movement of the price of the stocks in which they are interested. The benefits of keeping these records is twofold: They feel these moving average lines signal turns in the market and so give clues about the proper time to buy and sell. They also can be used to indicate price levels at which to buy and sell these shares without risking too much of one's capital.

Analysts in the business of selling advice through stock brokerages or through advisory services are able, through the use of computers, to keep daily moving averages of their stocks. These may range from 10-day averages to 200-day averages. An individual at home could not possibly keep up with this, but could buy their services, though they are very expensive.

However, it is not necessary to keep that close a watch on stocks. Computing weekly averages is less time consuming, yet can give a sufficient picture for the trader. For the long-term trend a 40-week average, which most nearly equates the 200-day average, should be kept. The object of this longer time period is that it smoothes out fluctuating stock prices over a period of time. Its objective is to keep investors fully invested in any stock that has an extended bull market move, regardless of the length of that move. It is also designed to keep investors out of any stock during an extended bear market move.

72

The 40-week moving average can be said to represent the complete cycle of a stock as it goes through its own particular bull and bear markets, which may or may not coincide with the market as a whole. Its own bull market begins when its 40-week average line turns up, and it continues to grow as long as that moving average line is ascending. When the line flattens out and turns down, the bear market part of the cycle has begun. The angle of the moving average line shows the vigor of the price rise and the degree of the decline.

At least one short-term moving average should also be computed to enable you to clearly see the waves within the longer-term tides. This could be a 5-week average, a 10-week average, or a 15-week average. Because of its ease in computation and the saving of time, I have used a 10-week moving average in addition to the 40-week one.

The more meaningful of the two moving averages is the 40-week line. It is the more reliable and the more informative about the long-term movement of the price of a stock. This moving average can be used in conjunction with the price movement for profitable buy and sell signals. While the 40-week average line is advancing, the investment decisions most likely to prove profitable are those based on bullish assumptions. There are four situations the beginner should learn to recognize as potentially profitable buy signals:

1. In a bear market or in a reversal, if the 40-week line flattens out at the end of a decline or begins advancing, and the price of the stock rises above the average line, this signals a major buying opportunity.

2. If the price of the stock drops below the 40-week line during a reversal, but the average line is still rising, this is another buying signal.

3. If in a reversal the price of the stock declines toward the 40-week line but fails to drop below it and begins to rise again, this also is a buying signal.

4. For trading purposes, a stock which drops very rapidly below its declining 40-week average line may frequently rally back towards this line and can be bought for short-term profits.

When the 40-week average turns down, a cautious or bearish investment strategy is likely to be correct. There are also four sell signals the beginner needs to learn to recognize:

1. Following a bull market rise or a rally, if the 40-week average line flattens out or starts declining, and the price of the stock drops below this line, this comprises a major selling signal.

2. If in a rally the price of the stock rises above a 40-week moving average line which is still falling, this is another selling opportunity.

3. If a stock price falls below the 40-week average line, reverses and rises towards that line, does not penetrate the line but starts to turn down again, this is another selling signal.

4. A stock price which rises too rapidly above its advancing 40-week average line will frequently reverse itself back to the line and becomes a good candidate for a short sale.

The 40-week moving average is more meaningful than the 10-week moving average because it portrays more accurately the primary direction in which the stock is traveling. When this line has been moving down for six months or more, then flattens out and turns up, the stock price is likely to move up for at least the next six months. Then later when it flattens out again and turns down, the next primary direction in price is likely to be down. As a general rule, stocks should be bought only when this 40-week line turns up and may be held as long as it continues trending up. You should not own the stock once this 40-week line has reversed and has started to move down.

The second moving average is the 10-week moving average, which measures the intermediate trend of price moves. It has three purposes. One objective is to signal when a major change of direction has taken place at a point fairly close to the tops and bottoms of most major price movements. Another objective is to eliminate the very short changes of price direction which cause investors to buy stock and then a short time later sell out at little or no profit. A third objective is to limit the loss on any bad investment.

The chart for United Nuclear illustrates the use of the two moving averages. When the 10-week moving average line turned up in December, 1974, a trader could have bought the stock with the understanding that if this turned out to be only a brief rally, the stock would be sold. However, the following month the 10-week line crossed over the 40-week line and the 40-week line itself turned up, both indicating that the bear market for the stock was over and it was establishing a new bull market uptrend.

Let us look more closely at the United Nuclear chart and see what more we can read into it. Note that the week the 10-week line had turned up the stock was selling at 7¼. Note too that it had dropped from 11½ in November to 6 in October, but had never gone lower.

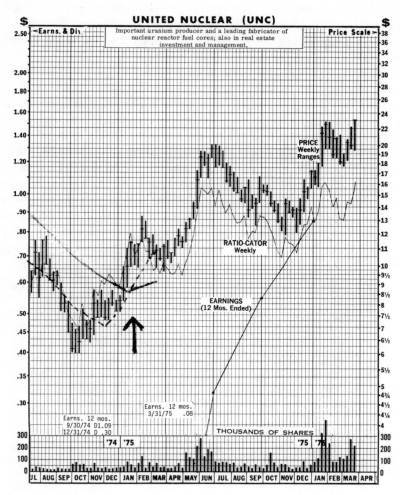

This 6 could be called a support area because the stock had tested that price three weeks in October but had never dropped below it.

A trader would have bought the stock at 7¼ and put in a stop-loss order at 5⅞, taking a chance on losing 1⅜ points on the transaction but optimistically expecting the price to go back up to at least the 11½ where it had been the previous August. This 11½ could be called a resistance area because you can see it had been there three times in August, but the price could not break out above that figure.

If the stock were to go back up to the resistance point, the profit would be 4¼ points. In other words, the trader takes a chance of losing 1⅜ points against profiting 4¼ points. In this case it would have been a good speculation.

There is one situation which needs to be warned against when using the 40-week average line to time the buying and selling of stocks. This is when a stock settles for a long period of time into a horizontal pattern where the price moves back and forth within a very narrow trading range. This is illustrated by the Del Monte chart. When this happens the trader risks being whipsawed back and forth as the average first indicates the stock is to be bought and then immediately afterward indicates it is to be sold. One way to avoid this is to choose for your list of companies to follow only those which show a tendency towards wide and regular price swings. The United Nuclear chart illustrates this type of company.

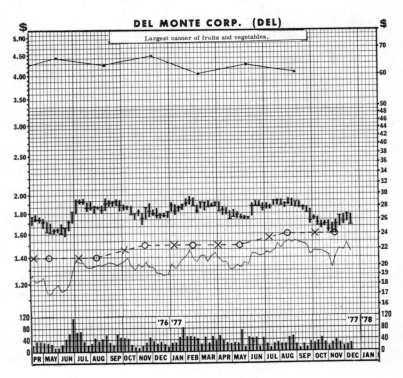

DEL MONTE CORP. (DEL)

Largest canner of fruits and vegetables.

I showed you the two preceding charts to give you a quick picture to illustrate a point, but all you need to keep are the moving averages to get the same information. The method of computing them is exactly the same as that used in the chapter on the moving average lines of the Dow-Jones Industrial Average. However, with the prices of stocks you must deal in fractions. It would be useful for you to learn the following decimals for your calculator to replace the fractions:

$$\frac{1}{8} = .125 \qquad \frac{5}{8} = .625$$
$$\frac{1}{4} = .25 \qquad \frac{3}{4} = .75$$
$$\frac{3}{8} = .375 \qquad \frac{7}{8} = .875$$
$$\frac{1}{2} = .5$$

I will again use the Addressograph Multigraph Company. First I will give you the mathematical computation of the two moving averages for 1974 through 1977. Then I have made a chart to further clarify the picture for you. On the chart I have drawn the weekly price of the shares and the two moving average lines. This is not to say you need to draw any charts yourself. They take too much time because you would need to compute the moving averages anyway. The time would better be spent studying the figures until you become very familiar with the usual behavior of that particular stock. Charts are very pretty, but some writers say that chartists become so involved in their drawings that they have little time to study what the charts reveal.

These are some of the things we might read into the moving averages for Addressograph Multigraph Company stock prices. This is going to require some study on your part, and you will need to constantly refer back to the figures, or the chart, or both.

1. The 40-week average line begins in October, 1974. Since the 10-week line is below the 40-week line and is in a downward trend, you would not consider owning the stock.

2. The upturn of the 40-week moving average indicates a turn in the primary trend of the price of the stock. It indicates the change from the bear market to the bull market for this particular stock. This occurred in February, 1975. As long as this moving average trends upward, the stock should be held by an investor. You can see clearly that the line did not actually turn down enough to warrant being sold from 1975 through 1977.

ADDRESSOGRAPH MULTIGRAPH

1974		Price		10-Week Total	10-Week Average	40-Week Total	40-Week Average
Jan.	6	11¼	x x				
	13	9	x x				
	20	9⅜	x x				
	27	10¼	x x				
Feb.	3	10	x x				
	10	10	x x				
	17	9⅞	x x				
	24	9½	x x				
Mar.	3	10⅛	x x				
	10	10¾	x x	100⅛	$10.01		
	17	10	x x	98⅞	9.88		
	24	10⅛	x x	100	10.00		
	31	9⅝	x x	100¼	10.02		
Apr.	7	9	x x	99	9.90		
	14	8⅝	x x	97⅝	9.76		
	21	8¼	x x	95⅞	9.58		
	28	7⅞	x x	93⅞	9.38		
May	5	7⅝	x x	92	9.20		
	12	6¾	x x	88⅝	8.86		
	19	6⅜	x x	84¼	8.42		
	26	6¾	x x	81	8.10		
Jun.	2	6¼	x x	77⅛	7.71		
	9	5¾	x x	73¼	7.32		
	16	5⅝	x x	69⅞	6.98		
	23	5	x x	66¼	6.62		
	30	4¾	x x	62¾	6.27		
Jul.	7	5	x x	59⅞	5.98		
	14	4⅞	x x	57⅛	5.71		
	21	5½	x x	55⅞	5.58		
	28	5¾	x x	55¼	5.52		
Aug.	4	5⅝	x x	54⅛	5:4G		
	11	6⅜	x x	54¼	5.42		
	18	5½	x x	54	5.40		
	25	5⅛	x x	53½	5.35		
Sep.	1	5	x x	53½	5.35		
	8	4⅞	x x	53⅝	5.36		
	15	4¼	x x	52⅞	5.28		
	22	4½	x x	52½	5.25		
	29	4½	x x	51½	5.15		
Oct.	6	3⅞	x x	49⅝	4.96	289¼	$ 7.23
	13	4¾	x x	48¾	4.87	282¾	7.06
	20	4⅝	x x	47	4.70	278⅜	6.95
	27	4	x x	45½	4.55	273	6.82
Nov.	3	4	x x	44⅜	4.43	266¾	6.66
	10	4⅝	x x	44	4.40	261⅜	6.53
	17	4¼	x x	43⅜	4.33	255⅝	6.39
	24	4	x x	43⅛	4.31	249¾	6.24
Dec.	1	3⅞	x x	42½	4.25	244⅛	6.10
	8	3⅜	x x	41⅜	4.13	237⅜	5.93
	15	3	x x	40½	4.05	229⅝	5.74
	22	3¼	x x	39	3.90	222⅞	5.57
	29	3¼	x x	37⅝	3.76	216	5.40

	1975	Price		10-Week Total	10-Week Average	40-Week Total	40-Week Average
Jan.	5	3⅞	x x	37½	$ 3.75	210¼	$ 5.25
	12	4	x x	37½	3.75	205¼	5.13
	19	4⅛	x x	37	3.70	200¾	5.01
	26	4¼	x x	37	3.70	196¾	4.91
Feb.	2	5⅛	x x	38⅛	3.81	194	4.85
	9	5¼	x x	39½	3.95	191½	4.79
	16	5⅛	x x	41¼	4.12	190	4.75
	23	5⅞	x x	44⅛	4.41	189½	4.73
Mar.	2	5¾	x x	46⅝	4.66	188½	4.71
	9	6½	x x	49⅞	4.98	188¾	4.72
	16	7½	x x	53½	5.35	190½	4.76
	23	6⅞	x x	53½	5.35	190½	4.76
	30	6¾	x x	59	5.90	193½	4.84
Apr.	6	6⅛	x x	60⅞	6.08	195⅝	4.87
	13	6¼	x x	62	6.20	196⅛	4.90
	20	7½	x x	64¼	6.42	198¾	4.97
	27	7⅝	x x	66¾	6.67	200⅞	5.02
May	4	7⅝	x x	68½	6.85	202¾	5.07
	11	8⅝	x x	71⅜	7.13	205¾	5.15
	18	8⅛	x x	73	7.30	207½	5.19
	25	8⅞	x x	74⅜	7.43	210⅞	5.27
Jun.	1	8⅞	x x	76⅜	7.63	214⅝	5.37
	8	8½	x x	78⅛	7.81	218⅛	5.45
	15	7⅝	x x	79⅝	7.96	220⅞	5.52
	22	8	x x	81⅜	8.13	224⅝	5.62
	29	8⅛	x x	82	8.20	228¼	5.71
Jul.	6	8¼	x x	82⅝	8.26	232	5.80
	13	8⅝	x x	83⅝	8.36	236¾	5.92
	20	8	x x	83	8.30	240	6.00
	27	7	x x	81⅞	8.18	242⅜	6.06
Aug.	3	6⅝	x x	79⅝	7.96	245	6.13
	10	6½	x x	77¼	7.72	247½	6.19
	17	6⅛	x x	74⅞	7.48	249	6.23
	24	6¼	x x	73½	7.35	251	6.27
	31	7	x x	72½	7.25	254	6.35
Sep.	7	7⅜	x x	71¾	7.17	257½	6.43
	14	7¼	x x	70¾	7.07	261⅜	6.53
	21	7⅝	x x	69¾	6.97	266	6.65
	28	7½	x x	69¼	6.92	270¼	6.75
Oct.	5	7½	x x	69¾	6.97	274½	6.86
	12	7½	x x	70½	7.06	278⅛	6.95
	19	8	x x	72⅛	7.21	282⅛	7.05
	26	8¼	x x	74¼	7.42	286¼	7.15
Nov.	2	8	x x	76	7.60	290	7.25
	9	7⅜	x x	76⅜	7.63	292¼	7.30
	16	8⅛	x x	77⅛	7.71	295⅛	7.37
	23	8¼	x x	78⅛	7.81	298¼	7.45
	30	8⅝	x x	79⅛	7.91	301	7.52
Dec.	7	7⅝	x x	79⅛	7.91	302¾	7.56
	14	7⅜	x x	79	7.90	303⅝	7.59
	21	7⅛	x x	78⅝	7.58	303¼	7.58
	28	7¾	x x	78⅜	7.83	304⅛	7.60

1976		Price		10-Week Total	10-Week Average	40-Week Total	40-Week Average
Jan.	4	7⅞	x x	78	$ 7.80	305¼	$ 7.63
	11	8¼	x x	78¼	7.82	307⅜	7.68
	18	8⅝	x x	79½	7.95	309¾	7.74
	25	10	x x	81⅜	8.13	312¼	7.80
Feb.	1	10⅝	x x	83¾	8.37	315½	7.88
	8	11⅝	x x	86¾	8.67	319¼	7.98
	15	11½	x x	90¾	9.07	322⅛	8.05
	22	13¼	x x	96½	9.66	327¼	8.18
	29	9⅞	x x	99⅜	9.93	328¼	8.21
Mar.	7	11	x x	102⅝	10.26	330⅜	8.26
	14	10⅞	x x	105⅝	10.56	332¾	8.32
	21	10	x x	107⅜	10.73	335⅛	8.38
	28	9¾	x x	108½	10.85	336⅞	8.42
Apr.	4	9⅜	x x	107⅞	10.78	338⅛	8.45
	11	9½	x x	106¾	10.67	339⅜	8.48
	18	9⅜	x x	104½	10.45	340⅛	8.50
	25	9¾	x x	102¾	10.27	341⅞	8.55
May	2	9½	x x	99	9.90	344⅜	8.61
	9	8¾	x x	97⅞	9.78	346½	8.66
	16	9⅜	x x	96¼	9.62	349⅜	8.73
	23	9¼	x x	94⅝	9.46	352½	8.81
	30	9⅛	x x	93¾	9.37	355⅜	8.88
Jun.	6	8¾	x x	92¾	9.27	357⅛	8.92
	13	9¼	x x	92⅝	9.26	359	8.97
	20	9½	x x	92⅝	9.26	361¼	9.03
	27	9⅜	x x	92⅝	9.26	363	9.07
Jul.	4	9¾	x x	92⅝	9.26	365¼	9.13
	11	10⅜	x x	93½	9.35	368⅛	9.20
	18	11	x x	95¾	9.57	371⅝	9.29
	25	10½	x x	96⅞	9.68	374⅛	9.35
Aug.	1	9¾	x x	97⅜	9.73	375⅝	9.39
	8	10	x x	98¼	9.82	377⅝	9.44
	15	9⅜	x x	98⅞	9.88	379⅝	9.49
	22	8⅞	x x	98½	9.85	380⅜	9.51
	29	8⅞	x x	97⅞	9.78	381	9.52
Sep.	5	9	x x	97½	9.75	381⅜	9.52
	12	8⅝	x x	96⅜	9.63	382½	9.56
	19	9⅝	x x	95⅝	9.56	384¾	9.61
	26	11¼	x x	95⅞	9.58	388⅞	9.72
Oct.	3	10⅞	x x	96¼	9.62	392	9.80
	10	10⅜	x x	96⅞	9.68	394½	9.80
	17	9¾	x x	96⅝	9.66	396	9.90
	24	9¾	x x	97	9.70	397⅛	9.92
	31	9⅞	x x	98	9.80	397	9.92
Nov.	7	10	x x	99⅛	9.91	396⅜	9.91
	14	9⅞	x x	100	10.00	394⅝	9.86
	21	10⅞	x x	102¼	10.22	394	9.85
	28	10½	x x	103⅛	10.31	391¼	9.78
Dec.	5	11⅜	x x	103¼	10.32	392¾	9.81
	12	11⅝	x x	104	10.40	393⅜	9.83
	19	11¾	x x	105⅜	10.53	394¼	9.85
	26	13	x x	108⅝	10.86	397¼	9.93

1977	Price			Total	10-Week Average	Total	40-Week Average
Jan. 2	13¼	x	x	112⅛	$11.21	400¾	$10.01
9	13¾	x	x	116	11.60	405⅛	10.12
16	13¼	x	x	119¼	11.92	408⅞	10.22
23	13⅜	x	x	122¾	12.27	412⅞	10.32
30	13¾	x	x	125⅝	12.56	416⅞	10.42
Feb. 6	13¼	x		128⅜	12.83	420⅝	10.42
13	13¾	x		130¾	13.07	425⅝	10.64
20	13⅜	x		132½	13.25	429½	10.74
27	11½	x		132¼	13.22	431⅞	10.78
Mar. 6	12	x		131¼	13.12	434¾	10.86
13	11½	x		129½	12.95	436½	10.91
20	12	x		127¾	12.77	439¼	10.99
27	11⅜	x		125⅞	12.58	441⅛	11.04
Apr. 3	10⅞	x		123⅜	12.33	443⅝	11.07
10	10½	x		120⅛	12.01	444⅜	11.10
17	11¼	x		118⅛	11.81	445¼	11.13
24	10⅜	x		114¾	11.47	444⅝	111.11
May 1	10¼	x		111⅝	11.16	444⅜	11.10
8	11⅛	x		111¼	11.12	445¾	11.14
15	10⅞	x		110⅛	11.01	446⅝	11.16
22	11⅞	x		110½	11.05	449⅛	11.22
29	11½	x		110	11.00	451¾	11.29
Jun. 5	12¼	x		110⅞	11.08	455⅛	11.37
12	12⅝	x		112⅝	11.26	458¾	11.41
19	13¼	x		115⅜	11.53	463⅜	11.58
26	13⅞	x		118	11.80	467⅝	11.69
Jul. 3	15	x		122⅝	12.26	471⅜	11.78
10	13¾	x		126⅛	12.61	474¼	11.85
17	13⅝	x		128⅝	12.86	477½	11.93
24	14½	x		132¼	13.22	482¼	12.05
31	13⅛	x		133½	13.35	485⅝	12.13
Aug. 7	12⅝	x		134⅝	13.46	488⅜	12.20
14	13	x		135⅜	13.53	491⅜	12.28
21	13¼	x		136	13.60	494¾	12.34
28	13⅛	x		135⅞	13.58	497	12.42
Sep. 4	14¼	x		136¼	13.62	500¾	12.51
11	13⅝	x		134⅞	13.48	503	12.57
18	12⅞	x		134	13.40	504¼	12.65
25	13⅝	x		134	13.40	506⅛	12.65
Oct. 2	13¾	x		133¼	13.32	506⅞	12.67
9	13⅞	x		134	13.40	507½	12.68
16	13⅝	x		135	13.50	507⅜	12.68
23	13			135	13.50	507⅛	12.67
30	12⅞			134⅝	13.46	506⅝	12.65
Nov. 6	12⅝			134⅛	13.41	505½	12.63
13	14			133⅞	13.38	506¼	12.65
20	14⅞			135⅛	13.51	507⅜	12.68
27	15⅝			137⅞	13.78	509⅝	12.74
Dec. 4	15			139¼	13.92	513⅛	12.82
11	14⅝			140⅛	14.01	515¾	12.89
18	14⅜			140⅝	14.06	518⅝	12.96
25	14¼			141¼	14.12	520⅞	13.02

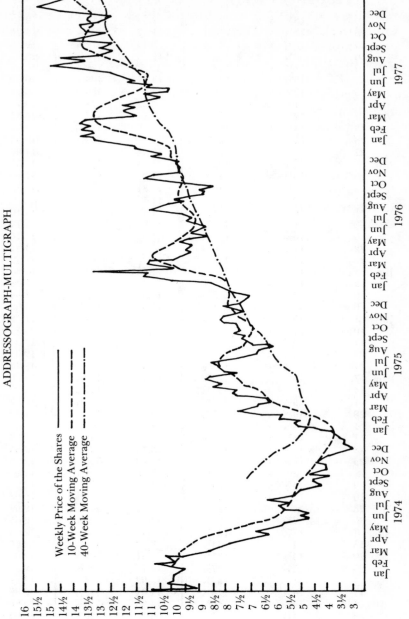

ADDRESSOGRAPH-MULTIGRAPH

Weekly Price of the Shares
10-Week Moving Average
40-Week Moving Average

3. An aggressive investor would have bought in January, 1975, when the price of a share rose above the 10-week moving average for several weeks in a row. This is the time to anticipate the turn to a bull market and be willing to take a small loss if you are wrong. If you will check the 1974 prices you will see that in October, 1974, and December, 1974, the stock's lowest price was 3. This then is a resistance point, and had you bought in January, your loss would not be much more than one point were the price to turn down again.

4. Another buy signal was given when the price of a share rose above the 40-week moving average. This was on February 2, 1975, when the price was 5⅛ and the 40-week moving average was $4.85.

5. Yet another buy signal was given on March 9, 1975, when the 10-week moving average rose above the 40-week moving average. However, it was not necessary to wait that long. The 10-week average was clearly rising, and it could be anticipated to go above the 40-week average in a short period of time.

6. For the traders who knew that July would bring a downturn because of those traders who would take profits when the six month short-term profit period ended, the July drop of prices below the 10-week moving average signalled a time for short selling. This strategy is explained in a later chapter.

7. Those who missed the earlier signals, or who had sold their stock at the July high, were given another buy signal on August 17, 1975, when the price of the stock fell below the rising 40-week moving average. Another buy signal came again in December of the same year when the price again fell below the rising 40-week average. This is the time to buy the stock, on the reverses in a bull market, not at the tops.

8. A sell signal came for traders in February, 1976, when the price of the stock jumped from 11½ to 13¼ in one week. This large jump in price is called a gap, and prices usually fall back to fill the empty space on the chart. Notice how far back the price fell the next week, to 9⅞, although it quickly went back up to 11, which is where a gap would normally be filled. Another gap occurred in September, 1976, and another reverse followed immediately. In July, 1977, the same maneuver of gap and reversal occurred again.

9. In May, 1976, a buy signal was given when the price of the stock fell almost to the still rising 40-week average. This was repeated in June and again in August when the price did fall below the 40-week

moving average. October gave a buy signal also when prices again dropped to the moving averages.

10. In May, 1977, there was another buy signal. The 40-week moving average was still now rising although the Dow-Jones Industrial Average moving line was now dropping. The individual stocks do not follow the Dow-Jones exactly; almost a third top out earlier, about a third coincide, and usually another third top out after the Dow-Jones has already started its downward trend. The Addressograph Multigraph average did not turn down until October, 1977, nine months after the Dow-Jones did.

11. Using the two moving averages is much better for buying stock, but not nearly as good for pinpointing when the stock should be sold. The first real sell signal came in October, 1977, when the 40-week moving average line turned down. However, this downturn lasted only a short time as Addressograph Multigraph is one of the strong stocks of the two-tier market mentioned previously which prevailed in 1977.

12. When a 40-week moving average line turns down, investors need to reassess their positions. The line first turned down in October and November of 1976. However, no one indicator is sufficient for a decision. It was necessary to reexamine the Dow Theory and the timing of the market as a whole to see where it stood. Our time check told us that there had been only two advances and two retreats in the bull market, (two legs, in Wall Street terminology) and that a third advance was still expected, so the stock would not have been sold immediately but watched. Also, only two years had passed since the bull market had begun. Study of the cycles has shown that the length of time it takes for a complete bull market is longer than for a complete bear market; so investors should know there should be at least six months more left of the bull market. In December the average turned up again and stayed up until October, 1977. Since the stock market timing told us we were now in a bear market, this would be the time to think about selling. However, the October-November reversal was so minor, the stock should not have been sold until there was certainty. The 40-week average quickly resumed its upward movement.

13. The 10-week moving average more clearly shows the phases of the bull market and of the bear market. An outline will help you see this more clearly:

a. The first bull phase started in February, 1975, and the 10-week moving average continued rising until its reversal began in July of the same year.

b. The second bull market phase began in October, 1975, and was interrupted slightly by the frequent December downturn, when investors sell their stock to take losses for income tax purposes. The 10-week moving average continued rising until its reversal began in April, 1976.

c. The third bull market phase in this stock had difficulty just like the market as a whole. After struggling to get off the ground for 15 weeks, it finally began in October, 1976, and lasted until February, 1977, when the bear market began.

d. The first complete phase of the bear market began in February, 1977, and reversed in May. The rise lasted 14 weeks.

e. The second phase of the bear market should have begun in August, 1977, but as has been said earlier, this stock showed greater strength than the market as a whole, and it did not really seem to want to drop to a great extent. Instead the 10-week moving average line seemed to be almost horizontal.

f. The second bear market reversal (an upturn) began in November and continued until the end of the year and into 1978.

g. Remember, there should be one more phase of the bear market before the bull market begins again, although sometimes, like the third phase of the bull market, it hardly shows.

CHAPTER 11

Keeping Track
of Stocks Through Charts

A third technique of keeping track of individual stocks is through charts. Charting is undoubtedly the most widely accepted system of technical analysis for the short-term trader and is practiced by thousands around the world. A chart is a picture representation of the price of the stock in the past. Just looking at a chart does not enable investors to judge what future patterns will evolve. The chartists must do their own interpreting of what the stock is likely to do, and many will disagree with each other. Since chart reading is so dependent upon the person doing the reading, most writers consider it an art, not a science.

The purpose of keeping charts is to get a picture of the movement of the price of a stock in the market. Some charts also keep track of the volume of shares changing hands, others do not. Pure chartists ignore the fundamentals of a company. They maintain that the price of the stock plus the volume takes into account every possible bit of necessary information about a company. They also claim to be able to forecast future stock price action solely on the basis of what price and volume have done in the past.

What these chartists actually are doing is studying their charts to discover any important changes in the balance of supply and demand of a stock. These changes may show up first as an increase in volume and then as a significant change in price. These chartists also keep close watch on the trend of a stock to see if demand is high and prices are rising, or if supply is ample and prices are falling, or if the stock is faltering in a sidewise movement with no clear trend. Then they are on the lookout for the first clues which would indicate the start of a new trend.

Chartists feel that their method of keeping track of stocks has many advantages. One important claim is that timing for buying and selling is improved considerably by the use of charts. Their charts may not tell them that a company is sound and therefore its stock should move up in price; what the charts do tell them is what stocks are moving up and how far they are likely to move in the short term.

One problem with buying stocks on fundamental analysis of a company can be that although the company may show a profit with every quarter report it issues, the price of the stock may remain in a narrow trading range. Then after the shares are sold because the price is going nowhere, the stock decides to make its big upward move. Chartists claim to avoid this situation by insisting that a stock should not be bought until it does begin to make its move. Hopefully, the chart will signal this upward swing at the beginning.

A second important claim is that charting can disclose significant news about a company before the public learns of it. Inside buying or selling may show up on the chart in a change of volume and price, and a skillful chartist may discover this and take advantage of it long before a person studying the company can.

Charts can be a valuable trading aid. They show areas of support and resistance and so offer a logical point for the proper placement of a protective stop order to prevent too great a loss when you buy a stock and also a helpful resistance point for selling at a profit.

The final advantage of charts is that even beginners can gain a great amount of useful information from even a brief study of a chart. They can tell if the pattern of behavior is cyclical with wide swings or if it usually trades in only a narrow horizontal pattern unsuitable for trading. Also they can see immediately the present trend of the stock price as well as the long-term price and volume history of the stock. Without a chart it would take a great deal of time and effort to ferret out the same information.

There are three basic types of charts: the line chart, the bar chart, and the point and figure chart. The line chart is used to show only one statistic, such as price, and is the one most frequently used to show how well or how poorly industry groups are doing. Or it may be used to show the pattern of the weekly closing prices for a single stock. In earlier chapters I have already shown you two line charts. One shows the Dow-Jones Industrial Average weekly figures and has a 10-week and a 40-week moving average line drawn in also. The

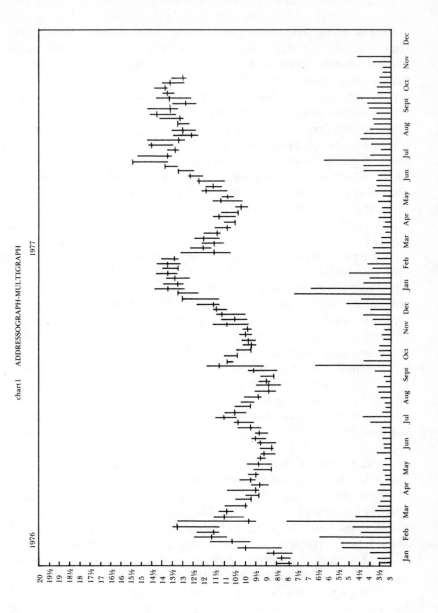

chart 1   ADDRESSOGRAPH-MULTIGRAPH

second chart does the same for Addressograph Multigraph Company.

The most commonly used of the three charts is the bar chart. This chart is one which may give a daily, weekly, or monthly record of the price performance of a stock. A vertical line is drawn showing the high and low ranges of the price (the numbers of which are indicated on the side) for the stock for the stated period, a week in our case. The bar drawn horizontally through the vertical line is the closing price for that week. At the bottom are vertical lines indicating the volume of shares changing hands. Below that are the dates. Chart 1 is a bar chart for Addressograph Multigraph Company for 1976 and 1977. This is what your chart would look like if you were to keep a weekly chart of the company.

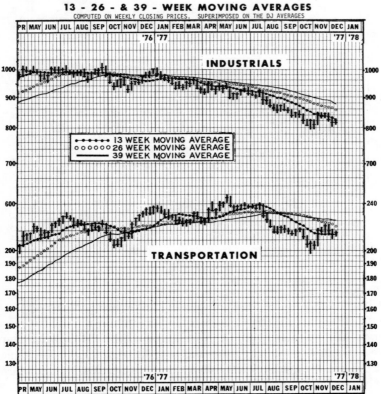

chart 2

Charts indicate what the stock market on a whole is doing. You can see at a glance by Chart 2, which has the three moving averages this chart service uses superimposed on the Dow-Jones Averages, that the Industrials have been in a decline for most of 1977 but that Transportation has not shared in all of the decline. This reinforces what has been discussed in earlier chapters about the two-tier market.

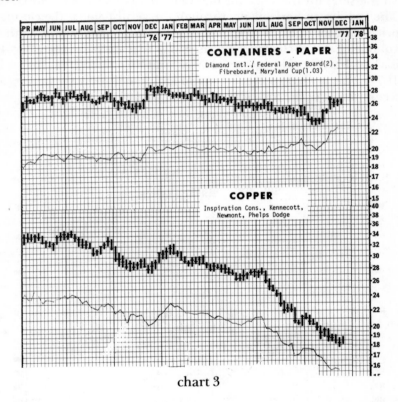

chart 3

Charts are also helpful in showing what industry groups are doing. Chart 3 measures investors' preference as well as price trends. It is of interest to investors to see what the following chart shows: that the paper container industry has remained quite stable, but the copper industry has fallen upon hard times, at least where the price of their stocks and investor interest is concerned.

Charts are most helpful in indicating what individual stocks have done in the past. Stock prices tend to move in trends, meaning they continue to move in a given direction until a reaction sets in or until a period of consolidation takes place. A major, or long-term, trend may last from one year to several years; a secondary, or inter-mediate, trend may last from a few months to a year or more; and a minor, or short-term trend, may last from a few days to a few weeks. Technicians take it for granted that these trends continue over sufficient time to be measured and that within these trends the same price patterns will recur many times. They base their forecasts of the future movement of the price of the stock upon these patterns.

When a stock is in a bull uptrend, it will regularly move to new highs; and each time the price reverses, it will stop at a higher level than the previous decline. This uptrend is then measured by con-necting the lows and extending the line. On chart 4, showing Archer-Daniels-Midland, the major trend is drawn in by the solid

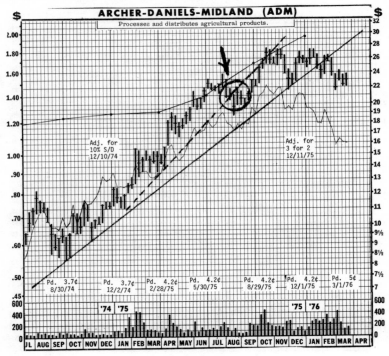

chart 4

line and the intermediate trend by the broken line. When the intermediate line was penetrated in August, 1975, this would have
alerted the trader. However, with the major trend still being upward, this did not necessarily call for the sale of the stock. The
penetration of the major trend in February, 1976, would call for a
sale on the next upswing. Interestingly, the stock rose several points
higher in July of that year and then began a long decline.

A downtrend is exactly opposite to the uptrend, with each new low
point being lower than the last, and with each rally failing to achieve
the previous surge. The downtrend is then measured by connecting
the highs. The bear market is in force until an upward penetration
of the downtrend lines signals a possible reversal can be anticipated.
Chart 5, the Zenith Radio Corp. chart, shows the major downtrend
solid line and the broken intermediate line. These show that the
stock should not be purchased at all during this period. A trader
would consider it a good candidate for a short sale.

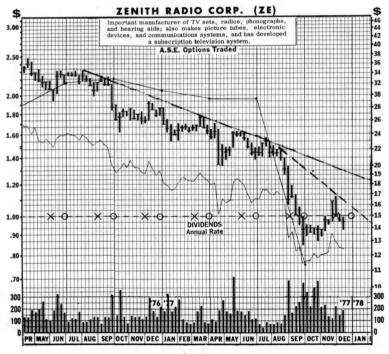

chart 5

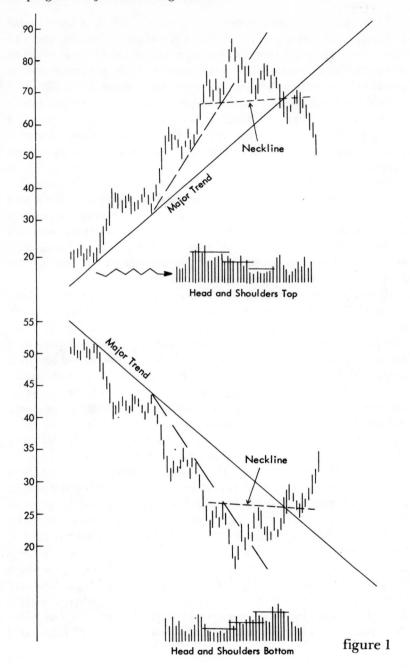

Head and Shoulders Top

Head and Shoulders Bottom

figure 1

There are many price patterns on charts which have been found to occur over and over again in the same shape. The movement of the price of the stock that follows these patterns have been observed to be consistent enough for the experienced chartists to be able to predict the direction the price will take and so trade profitably.

One of the most common reversal patterns is called the head-and-shoulders configuration. It is called this because it vaguely resembles that part of the human anatomy. In Figure 1 are examples of this reversal, with the trend lines drawn in to show how they have been reversed.

Another common reversal pattern is the double top found at the end of a long major uptrend, or the double bottom found at the end of a long major decline. The triple top and bottom is another variation of a reversal. Both the double and the triple top and bottom patterns are broad patterns that form over many months and so are found only at the end of a long major advance or decline. Examples of these formations are shown in Figure 2.

Before continuing farther, I feel it necessary to review a point made about technical analysis. In an earlier chapter I wrote of the three assumptions that successful technicians must make. The second of these stated that before a stock goes up in price, a period of accumulation usually takes place; and before a downtrend sets in, a period of distribution takes place. These periods of consolidation, when stocks seem to be moving sideways and resting, are known as areas of congestion. These periods of congestion, when prices seem to be moving up and down within a narrow price range, are important in that they frequently offer support to keep a price from falling below this area, or resistance to keep a price from rising above it.

The terms "support" and "resistance" are frequently used. You might read about a stock that is selling at 28, that it has support at 22–24 and resistance at 36–39. This means that before the price of the shares rose to 28, there was a period of consolidation when the price moved sideways between 22 and 24 for a fairly long period of time. Then the price took an upward surge above 24 (this is known as a breakout) and rose to its present price of 28. Now the question traders might ask is how high the price might possibly go. On their charts they can see another period of consolidation when the price moved sideways for a time between 36 and 39. They feel that when the upward price movement reaches that level, it will meet with

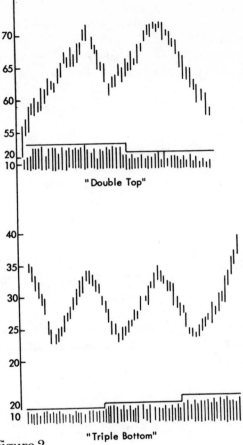

figure 2

resistance and will again move sideways in a period of consolidation. Then they must wait to see if it again breaks out above 39 or reverses and drops. Not all stocks show this pattern, but many do with great regularity. Figures 3 and 4 illustrate support and resistance levels.

The configurations of these periods of consolidation on a bar chart are carefully studied by chartists. There are a number of different kinds that they look for, as illustrated by Figure 5. The first kind of configuration is the triangle, of which there are three kinds most common. These are the "symmetrical," the "ascending," and the "descending," as illustrated in the next figures. The ascending

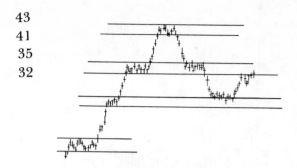

Figure 3. Support Areas

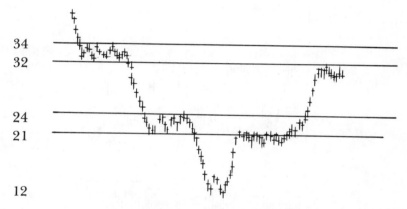

Figure 4. Resistance Areas

and descending triangles have predictive value, but the symmetrical triangle is neutral.

In the ascending triangle, you can see by the illustration that the top of the triangle is flat, but note the higher lows at the bottom. This kind of consolidation is most often found in an upward price trend and usually indicates the same trend will continue.

Conversely, the descending triangle has a flat bottom and descending highs. This configuration is mostly found in a major downtrend in price and usually predicts the price will continue to drop.

The symmetrical triangle is neutral because it gives no indication of which way the breakout might go. It may be presumed that the price will continue in the same direction it had previously been going, but this kind of triangle also can signal a reversal. Chartists watch these carefully.

Triangles

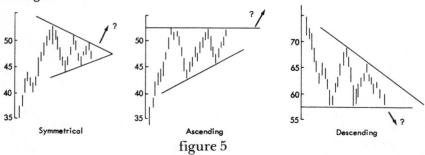

| Symmetrical | Ascending | Descending |

figure 5

Besides the triangles, there are a number of other consolidation patterns that occur frequently. These are illustrated by Figure 6. The "wedge", also known as the rectangle, is similar to the triangles, except both the bottom lines and the top lines move in the same direction. When both lines are parallel they give a neutral signal like the symmetrical triangle. When the lines slant, the slant is almost always against the trend: A falling wedge will be found in an up-trend; an upward slanting wedge is found in a declining stock.

In a high-velocity stock can be found the short-term patterns called the "flag" and the "pennant". They appear in rapidly moving stocks that do not pause long enough to complete longer consolidation patterns. They are preceded by sharp moves in price which form the pole and are accompanied by a large increase in volume. Like the wedge, these too slant against the trend. Both the flag and the pennant are significant as measuring devices. Traders consider them to be the half-way point of a large move, either on the upside or the downside. They use this information in placing their stop-loss orders or in their short sales decisions.

These are some of the more important patterns found in a bar chart. Not that I advocate your using these charts to make your investment decisions, but the study of a chart book can be very valuable. Besides, if you are to become a knowledgeable investor in

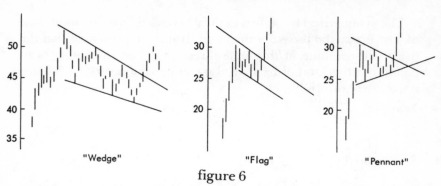

figure 6

stocks, you need to learn how others approach their investment strategy.

The third type of chart is the point and figure chart. This kind seems to be the most difficult to master. The point and figure chart shows neither time not volume elements as such, only as they are incorporated in the movement of the price. And these movements are not recorded until the stock moves up or down one full point, or three points, or five points, depending on the type of point and figure chart used. For low-priced stocks these points might be halved or quartered. For daily charting of prices, the one-point chart is the most popular, but for the weekly price changes we keep, the three-point reversal would be sufficient. Since the three-point reversal reveals only those movements of three points or more in each direction, this eliminates the minor fluctuations. Figure 7 shows what the same stock would look like in all three kinds of point and figure charts.

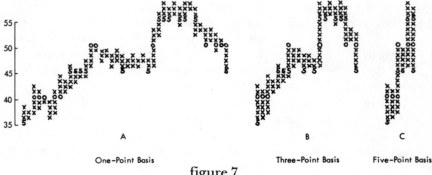

figure 7

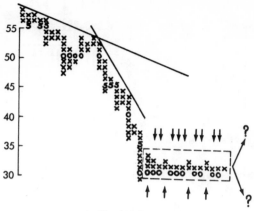

figure 8

Like bar charts, point and figure charting affords the opportunity to analyze stock price trends as well as support and resistance levels. In addition, such technical price configurations as head and shoulder reversals, double and triple tops and bottoms can also be observed. And as with bar charts, the length of the periods of consolidation can give clues as to the possible trend of the breakout and how high or how low the price move could go.

Following are some examples from Alan R. Shaw's handbook which illustrate trends of prices and periods of consolidation which might give some indication of the direction of the breakout. Figure 8 shows a stock which was in a significant downward move prior to entering a period of consolidation. The important question facing chartists is which way prices will go when the period of congestion is over. You can see by counting the arrows that the price dropped nine times to 30 but failed to go lower. Also it rose four times to 32 without rising above that figure. Since the bottom of 30 was tested so many more times without being penetrated, a point and figure chartist would assume this shows strength, and the breakout would come on the upside.

Figure 9 shows a stock in an upward trend which has reached a period of consolidation. Note by the arrows pointing upward that the price tried ten times to go above 70 and was unable to do so. Since the top was tested so many more times than the bottom, this congestion period is likely to end in a reversal. The breakout would probably be on the downside.

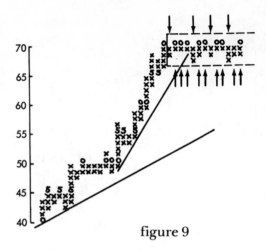

figure 9

Charting does not obviate the need for timing as the primary tool in your investment strategy. Remember that being in a bull or in a bear market plays an important role in the price trends on your charts. You can project probable higher upward movements and upside breakouts in a bull market, particularly in the first two phases, and downside calculations in a bear market. And you can look for reversals when your timing tells you these should be coming about soon.

The most important benefit of charting is in their assistance in finding support and resistance areas. This will improve the timing of your commitments and will help you set your profit objectives more effectively. You should also be able to place your stop loss orders in a more logical manner. In short, charts are most helpful for short-term trading in assisting you to make your decisions about when to get in, how much profit to expect, when to get out, and where to place the stop loss orders.

Should you decide to do charting, you need to be aware of some of its limitations:

1. One of the problems with charts is that they are subject to their worst misinterpretations at the tops in a bull market and at the bottoms of a bear market. They look as if they will be going up and up, or going down and down, and they fail to signal the turns. Their best uses are during the long middle periods of the bull and bear markets. And they are particularly helpful in pointing out the stock's

pattern during market fluctuations to help determine whether the stock is one of growth, or cyclical, or one likely to offer a good yield.

2. Another problem to be avoided is to become so involved in charting that you slavishly follow them in making all your investment decisions. Both fundamental analysis and common sense are important in decisions too.

3. A danger lies in that with so many chartists using the same charts, they tend to bring about the very price action they are trying to predict. Then they all could possibly buy or sell at the same time. This could lead to swift reactions.

4. Remember that simple is better. Some chart systems become so elaborate that these chartists spend all their time making charts rather than studying them and mapping out their strategy.

5. A beginner should not go overboard and be fooled by the seemingly scientific nature of charting and, therefore, expect too much in the way of scientific consistency. Charting is still an art and not a science, despite the impressive appearance of many charting systems.

6. Charts are not the complete answer. You cannot drop fundamental analysis of a company completely. You need to know that the company is solid, at least potentially profitable, and is capable of growth.

Now that you know many of the problems with charting, here are some of the good points:

1. Charting is a valuable weapon for short-term trading, but it must be properly used. It should be used with fundamentals as a foundation. A beginner should gradually work charts into the trading plan by picking out the companies based on fundamentals and using the charts to time the buying and the selling.

2. Chartists claim their timing is improved with the use of charts. Fundamental analysis tells you which stocks are good and therefore should rise in price. But this does not mean they do rise. The chartists wait until their charts show when they begin to move, so they can buy at the beginning of the rise and so catch more of the profit.

3. Charts give a lot of useful information from a brief study. You can get an instant picture of the stock's trading behavior and price swings, and whether it is a candidate for investment, or for trading, or neither.

4. Charts are helpful for analysis of the trend of stock price movements, whether in an uptrend or a downtrend, or moving laterally in price. It is even more helpful to be alerted to the possibility of a trend reversal or a change in the slope of the trendline.

5. Support and resistance areas can be more quickly found on charts and can aid traders to determine their strategy. Also price objectives for the stock can many times be calculated through analysis of the chart.

After you have gained experience in both keeping track of the market as a whole and keeping track of individual stocks through moving average lines and the advance-decline line, you might want to try your hand at some charting. My advice would be to buy a chart book, one of the ones whose charts illustrate this book, and study it thoroughly. Then you can add this to what you are already doing rather than to replace the moving average lines with charts. Charts are just another tool, and no one tool should be used exclusively. However, added to what tools you are already using, charts can enhance your market investment strategy.

CHAPTER 12

Making Your Investment List

When a beginner opens the newspaper to the financial page and sees the 1600 or so stocks listed on the New York Stock Exchange, learning about them seems to be an impossible task—and it is. What needs to be done is to bring the task down to size, and the way this is done is to concentrate your efforts. This calls for some decision making on your part.

One important decision you need to make is whether you wish to become an investor or a trader. Do you wish to invest in stocks with the idea of keeping them for years and collect dividends? Or do you plan to buy and sell for the short-term and profit by the swings in price? Or would you like to be both until you have gained enough experience to make a more intelligent decision? No matter which you have decided you wish to be—an investor or a trader—an important problem is for you to decide in which companies to become interested.

If you want to become an investor and want stocks that pay good dividends and are safe, then you will need to look for those that do not go up too much in bull markets or drop too far in bear markets. You will look for those which have a pattern similar to Standard Brands shown on chart 6. Yet even here timing is important. Note that despite rising earnings and rising dividends, the stock still fluctuated and made a much more attractive investment at the lower levels. There is no reason why a stock like this one can't be bought during a bear market when it has dropped, sold at a peak during the third phase of a bull market, and bought back again during the next bear market. Then you have both safety and most of the dividends and also an increase in shares, provided you invest back all the money you received in the sale.

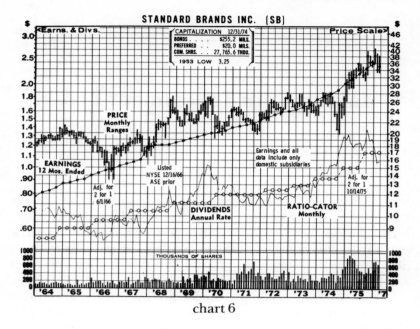

chart 6

Another stock pattern the investor should be interested in is that of the growth company which shows consistently better-than-average market performance. It has rising profits and rising dividends and shows good long-term growth. But even the best of these companies are subject to market cycles. Note the Carnation Company as shown on chart 7. Despite the rapidly rising dividends, the price of the shares still dropped to less than half during the bear market of 1974. This stock too could have been sold and then bought back later with great profit to the investor.

If you are interested in learning to be a trader, then you will look for stocks which are cyclical in nature. This means they fluctuate widely, not only in price, but frequently also in earnings and dividends. Many traders look for quick moves that give them a 10 per cent to 20 per cent profit in a few weeks or a few months. The chart of American Broadcasting Company, chart 8, shows such a cyclical company, with earnings and price showing wide fluctuations, but with dividends holding up nicely. (So does Chart 9, Brunswick Corporation).

Another kind of stock of interest to the trader is the recessive stock

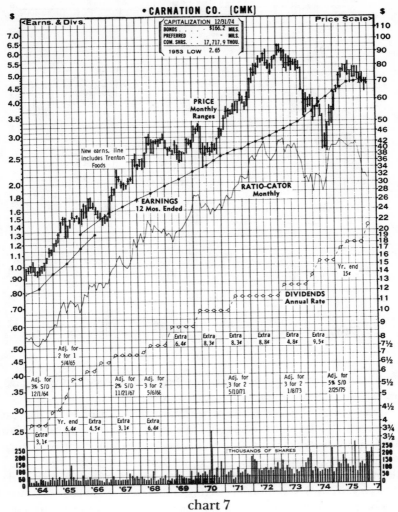

chart 7

with a declining pattern. It does not go down in a straight line, but rallies like all others in bull markets. However, the trend is persistently down, perhaps because management is weak, or the industry is declining, or it has obsolete products which resulted in a loss of competitive ability. Therefore, profits and dividends are declining or nonexistent. This type of company appeals to bargain hunters who think there is a possibility the situation will turn about

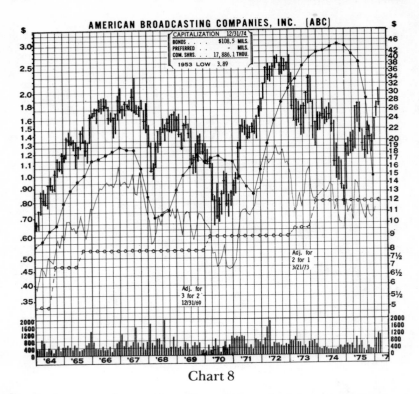

Chart 8

for the better and a good profit can be made. The chart for Lock-heed Aircraft, Chart 10, shows such a stock.

Once you have clarified in your mind what your objective is, you will need to select a list of possible candidates for investment. You don't want to make the mistake of reviewing too many stocks because you will find it very confusing when buying opportunities come along. Also you will spend so much time maintaining your records that you will have no time left to digest their significance.

The most intelligent way to go about investing is to narrow your efforts to where they will do the most good. You want to have time to study not only the market as a whole, but also to keep track of a limited number of companies. This will enable you to keep your investment strategy simple.

You need to decide how much time you are willing to spend each week on your investments. This will determine how many stocks you will be able to review each week. A list of 50 to 100 companies will

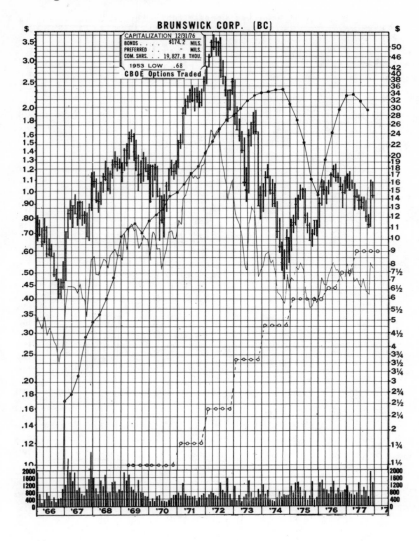

chart 9

take no more than about two or three hours a week for computation so that you don't tire or get too bored with the record-keeping, then about another hour to study the records and think over their significance and make any decisions that may be necessary. But if you are

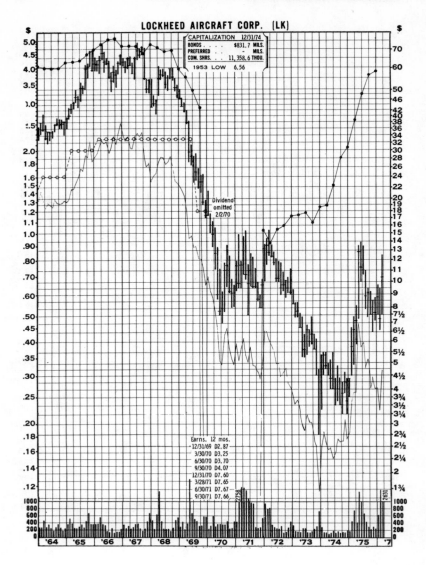

chart 10

to get the feel of the market, you must make this a regular routine. You can't skip weeks and double up weeks without losing the rhythm of the market, and as a result not performing as well as you might.

Since you are going to follow a comparative small number of stocks, you must eliminate from consideration any stocks that are unacceptable to you. If you would not feel comfortable owning stocks in liquor or tobacco companies, or if you are concerned with social issues or pollution, you should exclude from your list any stocks from these areas. You should not waste your time on any stocks you are not willing to own.

Of the stocks that you do follow, it is most essential that you cover as many different industry groups as possible. There is a tendency for individual stock prices to move up and down in harmony with the market as a whole and also in sympathy with other stocks in their industry groups. During each new bull market a few industry groups will out-perform the market as a whole. Virtually every stock in the group will move up in price much more than stocks in other groups. Also, each new bull market has its own super-stars. The groups that become the strongest performers of a new bull market are generally different from the industry groups that performed best during the previous bull market. Therefore, in order to assure yourself of some representation in whatever group is going to be the leader at any particular time, you should make an effort to diversify your interest among as many stocks as is practical for you and to select these stocks from as many different industries as possible.

To make it easier for you to start your record-keeping, I have gone through a number of group lists, combined some, expanded some, and have come up with 52 industry groups which cover most of American business. In addition, I have listed companies in each group and have given you their price highs and lows for the past three years. This will give you some basis for additional research to pick out the one firm you will follow in each category. I am also listing some alternate companies you might prefer.

How should you go about picking the company in each industrial category? There are a number of things to consider:

1. You may already be familiar with the company and pleased with its product.

2. The price of the shares might influence you. There is a differ-

ence of opinion about high-priced stocks and low-priced ones. One writer claims to have made a lot of money trading IBM, which is usually priced over $200 a share, while others claim the greatest percentage of profit can be made trading low-priced stocks. A third strategy is to buy low-priced stocks in the first phase of a bull market and to switch to higher priced ones in the later phases.

3. If you are interested in investing and not trading, the dividends paid would be of primary interest to you. You will find this information in the *Stock Guide*.

4. You could follow the institutional funds. There is a difference of opinion here too. Some writers maintain that the funds have paid for research and therefore know which companies are the best to invest in. Also, since they have difficulty unloading large numbers of shares, they tend to stabilize the price of their stocks more than the average. And when a price reaction does set in, they are hampered by their sheer size in making changes in their portfolios, while the small investor can move in and out of the same stocks with ease. The Standard & Poor's *Stock Guide* also lists how many institutions own stock in the company and how many shares they have.

5. If you are interested in trading, the cyclical stocks are of greater interest to you. This means you should compare the range between the highs and lows in price for the year. A stock which is volatile and moves both up and down more widely than the average can yield greater profits for the trader. You should then look at stocks that have a high for the year that is perhaps twice that of the low, or that at least has enough of a range to allow you good profits without hitting the very bottom or the very top. A study made by a brokerage house a few years ago showed that the average stock price moves in a 30 per cent range during the year. You, as a trader, should then look for stocks which have a range much higher than the 30 per cent average.

6. Another way of finding the kind of stocks you wish is to purchase a book of charts and look for stocks which follow the four patterns previously illustrated. You may look for the patterns of your choice: the income and growth for investing, and the cyclical and recessive for trading. One publication, *Cycli-Graphs* from Securities Research Company, 208 Newbury Street, Boston, Mass. 02116, shows a twelve year history of over 1100 stocks, including their prices, earnings, and dividends. Another long-term chart

book, *The Stock Picture,* is published by M. C. Horsey & Company, Inc., Salisbury, Maryland 21801, and covers over 1900 stocks.

7. Keeping a list of 52 stocks should not be such a burdensome chore that you will not have time to plan your strategy. You might, however, not have the time nor the inclination to follow that many, which is fine. Then pick out at least 25 of the 52 groups listed and keep track of a stock in each of them. After all, the specialist units which operate on the floor of the exchange usually handle no more than 30 or 40 stocks, and each man within this unit is responsible for only five or six of these. Even with this limited number, each special-ist finds trading his stocks highly profitable. And of those 25 you choose, you might concentrate on perhaps ten or so and get to know them so thoroughly, that these are all you need for trading. This should not mean you drop the others. Remember that leaders in the market change and those stocks which do best in one bull market are not usually the ones which lead in the next. Should you not find keeping a list of 52 stocks burdensome—and I urge you to try this many if you can—you may wish to keep a list of more than just 52. Many traders may choose more than one company in a category if they like their price patterns. They may choose the leading company in the category and also one of the secondary firms. Or they may choose a high-priced stock and a low-priced stock of the same group to follow.

8. The list given is only representative. If you would want additional companies, write to the New York Stock Exchange, 11 Wall Street, New York, New York 10005, for their booklet *Common Stocks Listed.* It lists all their stocks in alphabetical order and gives the industry area to which they belong.

Here is my list to give you a start:

Industry Groups

	1975		1976		1977	
	High	*Low*	*High*	*Low*	*High*	*Low*
1. Aerospace and Aircraft						
Boeing Co.	31⅞	15½	46¼	24⅜	29¾	23¼*
Lockheed	13⅞	5½	12½	6⅝	19⅛	8⅞
Martin Marietta	19½	13⅛	26⅜	16⅛	29¼	22⅛
McDonnell Douglas	18	8¼	25	14¾	27⅝	19⅜
United Tech.	62⅛	31¼	39⅜	23¼	41¼	33

Others: Curtis Wright, General Dynamics, Gruman

*stock split

	1975		1976		1977	
	High	*Low*	*High*	*Low*	*High*	*Low*
2. Air Transport						
American Air.	10⅛	5⅛	16⅜	8⅝	14¾	8
Delta Air.	41⅜	25⅜	45⅞	34½	40⅛	30
Pan-Am World Air.	5¾	2	7⅞	4¼	6½	3⅝
Trans World Air.	12½	5¼	15⅜	7½	12½	7¾
UAL, Inc.	28	13¾	29⅞	21⅛	27½	16¼
Others: Eastern, National Airlines, Northwest						
3. Automobile						
American Motors	7¼	3⅜	7¾	3⅝	5¼	3⅝
Chrysler	14½	7⅜	22⅜	10⅜	22	12⅜
Ford	45¼	32⅜	61⅞	43⅝	47⅜	41⅜
General Motors	59⅛	31¼	78⅞	57⅜	78½	61⅛
Others: Honda						
4. Automobile Equipment						
Borg Warner	21⅜	13⅛	30⅝	19⅞	33⅞	25¼
Budd. Co.	10⅝	7⅛	21¼	9⅞	24⅞	18½
Dana Corp.	19⅞	7¾	29½	19⅜	29¾	22
Eaton	30¼	19⅝	44¾	29½	45⅝	35
Libby-Owens-Ford	22¾	13⅞	37⅜	21⅞	37⅜	25⅜
Timken	42⅝	24¾	59⅜	36¾	55½	42¾
Others: Champion Spark Plug, Fruehauf, White Motor						
5. Banks						
Chase Manhatten	38¾	24¾	32¼	26⅜	34⅞	27⅜
Citicorp	39	24¾	37⅝	27¾	34	20⅜
Crocker National	26⅜	14⅞	28¾	21⅝	29	24
Morgan (J.P.)	71	44⅝	64⅜	50	56¾	39⅞
Wells-Fargo	20½	12⅞	27	15⅝	28⅞	24⅛
Others: Cleveland Trust, First Chicago, Rep. of Texas, Security Pacific						
6. Beverages—Brewers & Distillers						
Heilman	13⅜	6⅝	16½	9	25⅜	15⅝
Nat'l Distillers	17⅞	13⅝	27½	16⅛	25⅞	20⅜
Schlitz	30⅛	15½	24	15⅝	18½	10¾
Seagram Ltd	37	25	31⅝	19⅜	24	19¼
(Hiram) Walker	44	25⅞	33¾	24	28⅞	22⅞
Others: Heublein, Schaefer						
7. Beverages—Soft Drinks						
Coca Cola	93½	53¼	95¼	73⅜	40⅞	35½*
Dr. Pepper	15⅛	7	16¾	11	17¼	11
Pepsico	74¼	40⅞	87½	69½	28⅝	22¼*
Royal Crown	19¼	8⅞	23⅜	14¼	21½	14⅝

	1975		1976		1977	
	High	*Low*	*High*	*Low*	*High*	*Low*
8. Broadcasting						
Am. Broadcast.	27⅜	13⅛	40¼	19⅞	47¼	36
Capital Cities	43½	22	56⅜	42¼	61	44¼
C.B.S.	54	28⅞	61	46¾	62¼	46⅜
Metromedia	16⅞	5¼	30⅛	15	36	24⅜
Taft	28½	11⅝	32⅛	23¼	34¼	24
Others: Cowles, Cox, N.B.C.						
9. Building Materials & Equipment						
Am. Standard	17	8⅛	30⅛	16¾	39¼	25¾
Crane Co.	52½	26½	39	22¾	36	25
Johns Manville	26¾	19	35⅞	23	38¼	27⅜
Lone Star Ind.	19½	9⅜	22¾	15	23⅝	16¾
U.S. Gypsum	21¼	14⅛	28	16¾	26⅜	21⅝
Others:Carrier, Copeland, Flintkote, General Portland, Lehigh Portland, Marquette, Masonite, Nat. Gypsum, Penn Dixie, Jim Walter.						
10. Chemicals						
Allied Chemical	42	27	44⅞	33⅜	51⅜	38¾
Am. Cyanamid	30⅞	20⅝	28⅛	23½	29¾	23
Hercules	34¾	21½	38⅞	24	28½	14¾
Olin Corp.	30¾	14⅝	45⅛	30¼	20¼	16⅝*
Union Carbide	66½	40⅛	76¾	55⅝	62⅜	40
Others: Dow, duPont, Monsanto						
11. Communications						
Am. T. & T.	52	44¾	64¾	50⅞	65⅝	58⅜
Comm. Satellite	46½	23	33½	23⅞	37⅜	28⅜
Gen. Tele & Elec.	26	16⅞	31⅞	23¼	33½	28¼
United Telecomm.	16	12½	20⅛	14	21½	17⅞
Western Union	17⅛	9⅛	20⅞	15¾	20½	16⅞
12. Containers—Metal, Glass, Paper						
Brown Co.	9⅜	6⅞	13½	7¼	10½	8⅜
Continental Gr.	29⅝	22⅝	34⅜	26¾	37⅜	30¼
Crown Cork	23⅛	14⅝	22⅛	16⅞	25⅜	19¾
Diamond Int.	37¼	24⅜	42½	33⅝	39⅞	32⅛
Maryland Cup	18¾	11⅝	28	16½	31	23
Owens-Illinois	52⅛	32	63¼	50	29⅜	21⅝*
Others: American Can, Ball, Federal Paper, Fibreboard, Hoerner Waldorf, National Can						

	1975 High	1975 Low	1976 High	1976 Low	1977 High	1977 Low
13. Cosmetics						
Alberto Culver	8⅜	4⅝	8⅝	5¾	8⅛	6
Avon	51¼	27⅞	50¼	32¾	52⅛	43¼
Chesebrough-Pond	67	37⅛	32½	22½*	26⅞	20
Faberge	7⅞	4½	9½	5½	11⅞	7⅝
Helene Curtis	8	2¼	9⅜	5	9⅜	4¾
Revlon	81½	47⅜	45	34⅞*	46	36⅛
14. Drugs						
Abbott Lab.	42¾	32⅝	55¼	37¾	57¼	38⅞
American Home	43¼	27¾	37¾	28½	32⅛	24⅞
Bristol Myers	73¾	46½	83¾	61¼	35⅞	28¾*
Merck	85¾	57½	81½	62⅝	68½	50
Searle	25¾	13½	18	10¾	13¾	10⅞
Sterling Drug	25½	15¼	21	15	17	13⅛
Others: Foremost-McKesson, Lilly, Pfizer, Schering-Plough, Warner Lambert						
15. Electrical Equipment						
Ampex	7⅜	2⅝	9⅝	4¾	11¼	7⅜
Black & Decker	36¾	20⅛	28¾	15¾	20⅜	14⅝
Cutler-Hammer	33⅛	18	40¾	26⅝	36	27
Emerson Elec.	40¾	23½	41½	31⅝	36	31¼
General Elec.	52⅞	32⅜	58¾	46	57¼	47⅜
Square D	23½	14¾	29⅞	20¾	29⅝	23½
Others: McGraw Edison, Maytag, Otis Elevator						
16. Electronics						
AMP	40⅞	23⅛	35⅝	26	30⅜	24¼
Bunker Ramo	8	3¼	9¾	4⅜	12⅞	8
Control Data	23½	10⅝	27⅛	17⅝	29⅛	19⅜
Motorola	57⅞	33¾	59	41¼	56⅞	33⅝
Raytheon	59¾	25¼	67⅜	44¾	35⅛	28*
Others: Avnet, Perken-Elmer, Tektronix, Texas Instruments, Thomas & Botts						
17. Finance & Small Loan						
Aristar	4⅛	1¾	3½	1⅞	6¾	2⅝
Beneficial	21¾	14⅛	27⅝	17⅜	27	20⅜
CIT Financial	37½	26	40¾	28⅝	40¼	31¼
Heller	31½	21	29¾	18½	22⅞	16¼
Household	18½	11⅞	22⅛	15¾	21¾	18
Others: Ahmanson, Am. Invest., Credithrift Fin., Reynolds Sec. Talcott						
18. Foods—Canned						
Campbell	36	27⅜	39⅜	29¾	39⅝	33¼
Del Monte	27¾	20⅝	29½	22⅜	29⅝	24
General Foods	29⅜	18⅜	34⅜	26⅛	36⅛	29
Green Giant	19⅞	13⅝	18½	15¼	22⅜	16⅝
Heinz	57	38½	34½	26½*	37¼	28

	1975 High	1975 Low	1976 High	1976 Low	1977 High	1977 Low
Stokely-Van Camp	22¾	13⅞	28¼	18⅛	23⅝	19⅛
Others: Smucker, Tropicana						
19. Foods—Dairy & Meat						
Beatrice Foods	24⅞	14¼	28½	21½	28⅜	22½
Borden	28⅝	20½	34	26	36⅜	29⅛
Esmark	32¼	19⅞	42	30¼	35⅞	29
Iowa Beef	34⅜	12¼	25¼	15¾	32⅛	19¾
Kraft	45⅝	34¼	47½	40⅝	51	43⅜
Mayer (Oscar)	26⅛	14⅞	22½	16¼	26	22½
Others: Detter Intern'l, Fairmont Foods, Tobin Packing						
20. Food—Packaged						
General Foods	29⅜	18⅜	34¾	26⅛	36⅛	29
General Mills	30½	20⅝	35⅜	26⅝	34⅞	26¼
Gerber	28¾	12⅛	26⅜	19½	39½	24⅜
Kellogg	23⅜	14	28¼	20	27⅞	20¾
Standard Brands	29¾	26¼	40⅝	27	31⅛	24¼
Others: Archer-Daniels-Midland, Holly Sugar, Nabisco, Norton Simon, Pillsbury, Quaker Oats, Ralston-Purina						
21. Forest Products						
Boise Cascade	27¼	10½	33¾	23½	33¾	24⅛
Champion Int'l	18⅜	10½	28½	18	27⅜	17¾
Evans Products	7¼	2⅞	13¾	5	18	11⅜
Georgia Pacific	46⅛	24¼	38⅛	26⅞	38½	25¼
Weyerhaeuser	43¼	27⅝	49⅝	37	46½	25⅛
Others: Koppers Co., Louisiana-Pacific, Potlatch Corp.						
22. Gold Mining						
ASA Limited	47¾	26	33	12⅝	23⅝	17
Campbell Red lake	36¾	17½	27½	16½	35½	23
Dome Mines	56½	30	46	32½	64½	42½
Homestake Mining	55½	31½	44⅛	24⅞	43⅞	34½
23. Hotel-Motel						
Hilton	34⅝	11⅜	23¼	15	26	17
Holiday Inns	16½	5⅛	20	10⅝	16⅛	11⅛
Marriot	17¼	6⅜	18⅝	12¼	14	8¾
Ramada Inns	5⅞	2⅛	6⅝	3⅛	4½	3
Sonesta Int'l	4⅛	1⅞	6⅛	2⅝	7⅝	2⅞
Other: United Inns						
24. Insurance						
Aetna Life & Cas.	29⅜	17¼	36¼	22½	38⅜	28⅜
Continental Corp.	45¼	32⅛	57½	41⅝	64½	52½
INA Corp.	40⅜	28	47¾	34½	47¼	39⅛
Travelers	28½	19⅛	38⅛	25	37	28⅞
U.S. Fidelity	36¾	25½	55	32½	39⅝	29*
Other: American General, American National, CNA Financial, Continental Corp.						

	1975		1976		1977	
	High	*Low*	*High*	*Low*	*High*	*Low*
25. Leisure Time						
Brunswick	15¾	9	18¾	11	17⅝	11
Chris-Craft	6¾	2⅛	9⅜	4½	10	4⅜
Handleman	7⅞	3⅛	7⅝	3⅞	11⅞	4¼
Outboard Marine	29¾	11	36½	21⅜	27¾	19
Shakespeare Co.	7⅛	3¾	10⅞	5⅛	11½	7¾
Tandycrafts	16	10	21¾	11½	16	9⅝
Others: Coleco Ind., Ideal Toy, Lionel, Mattel, Winnebago						
26. Machine Tools						
Acme Cleveland	10⅜	7	10¼	8⅛	13⅞	9½
Chicago Pneumatic	31½	23¼	35¾	24¾	31⅜	21½
Cincinnati Mila.	25½	16⅜	•35½	18¾	42¾	30
Giddings & Lewis	7⅞	3	11½	5⅝	12⅞	8¾
Warner & Swasey	22¾	13⅝	30½	16⅛	32¼	19
Others: Brown & Sharp, Monarch						
27. Machinery—Agricultural						
Allis Chalmers	12¾	6⅝	30	11⅞	33¾	22¾
Deere	52	34½	36⅞	25⅞*	33½	24
Int'l Harvester	30½	19¾	33	22⅜	37⅞	26
Massey Ferguson	20¾	13½	32¼	16⅛	23⅛	12⅝
28. Machinery—Industrial						
Ametek, Inc.	21¾	10⅜	29⅝	19¼	35	27
Briggs & Stratton	50¾	36½	33⅜	22⅛*	33¼	23½
Cooper, Ind.	58½	23⅞	42¾	22⅞*	49¼	38⅜
Gardner-Denver	29¾	17¾	31	16¼	22⅞	14½
Ingersol Rand	84⅜	61⅛	95½	68⅝	78	55¾
Others: Chicago Pneumatic, Joy Mfg.						
29. Machinery—heavy						
Ex-Cello Corp	17	10	27⅜	14⅛	29⅛	23⅜
Foster Wheeler	34	15½	20⅞	10¼*	32⅜	19½*
Harnischfeger	32¾	22	22⅞	14*	24⅛	15
Mesta Machine	22	14½	30⅛	16⅞	29⅝	22¼
Wean United	7⅞	3⅛	7	4	6⅝	4⅝
Others: American Hoist, Colt, Combustion Engineering						
30. Machinery—Construction & Oil Well						
Bucyrus-Erie	25⅝	14	30¼	18	27⅜	18⅛
Caterpillar	75⅞	48	62¼	46⅜*	59½	48¾
Clark Equipment	34¼	22⅜	46½	25⅛	43¼	28⅝
Hughes Tool Co.	52⅜	30⅞	52½	34	43¾	29½
Schlumberger Ltd.	90½	60¾	68¾	46¾	74	56*
Others: Baker Oil Tools, Dresser, Ind., Halliburton, Koehring, Rexnord						

	1975		1976		1977	
	High	*Low*	*High*	*Low*	*High*	*Low*

31. Miscellaneous Products

Bausch & Lomb	39½	21⅝	39¼	25	45¼	28¼
Bulova Watch	9⅜	4⅞	11	6	8⅜	4⅞
Corning Glass	55⅜	28⅞	80	43⅝	71½	50½
Insilco	9¾	5⅞	14⅞	8⅜	16½	12⅝
Kroehler Co.	13¼	8⅛	15¼	10	14⅝	8⅞
Parker Pen	19⅜	6⅛	16⅞	11¾	21¼	15¾
Polaroid	43½	15	45⅛	31¼	38⅝	25

Others: D.H. Baldwin, Bell & Howell, Clorox Co., Eastman Kodak, Jewelcor, Kirsch, Lenox, Oneida

32. Motion Pictures

Columbia	9⅝	2⅜	7⅞	4½	20⅞	7⅜
Disney	55¾	21¼	61⅛	39⅞*	47⅝	32⅛*
MCA	89½	27¾	40¾	25*	44¼	31*
20th Century-Fox	15½	5⅛	15	8¾	26⅝	9⅞
Warner Comm.	22⅞	8¼	27	17½	34	25½
Others: MGM						

33. Non-Ferrous Metals

Alcan Aluminum	26⅜	18⅝	30⅜	19¾	29½	21¼
Ascaro	19¾	12	20	13⅛	23⅜	13
Kaiser Aluminum	34⅜	12⅝	40⅛	27½	40⅛	27⅝
Kennecott	41	27⅛	36⅞	25¼	30⅞	18⅝
Reynolds Metals	24¼	14⅝	42⅝	22⅛	44⅞	28¼

Others: Alcoa, Cerro, Inspiration Copper, Newmont, Phelps Dodge, St. Joe Mineral

34. Office & Business Equipment

Addressograph	9½	3¼	13½	7¾	15⅞	9
Burroughs	110¾	61⅛	108½	83⅛	91¾	54½
I.B.M.	227⅜	157¼	228½	223⅛	286⅛	244½
NCR	39⅜	14½	38	23⅝	47¼	32
SCM	14¾	9	22⅞	11½	25⅛	17⅞
Sperry Rand	48⅝	25⅝	51¾	38⅞	43⅛	29⅜

Others: Control Data, Digital Equip., Pitney Bowes, Xerox

35. Oil

Continental Oil	75	40⅝	40⅞	29⅞*	38	27
Exxon	94	65	56⅞	42⅝*	55¾	44⅞
Mobil	48⅞	34⅛	65	47½	71	58¼
Standard Oil Cal.	33	22⅛	41	29⅛	45½	37½
Texaco	28⅜	21⅛	28¾	23⅜	30⅝	25¾

Others: Atlantic Richfield, Getty, Gulf, Phillips, Shell, Union

	1975		1976		1977	
	High	*Low*	*High*	*Low*	*High*	*Low*
36. Paper						
Crown Zellerbach	40⅝	24⅛	49	35⅝	45⅛	32
Int'l Paper	61½	34⅝	79¾	57⅝	69⅝	39
Kimberley Clark	37⅜	24¼	47⅛	36¼	48¼	36⅞
Mead Corp.	18¾	13⅛	23	12	24	18⅛
Simplicity Patt.	18⅞	8	23½	11⅜	16⅝	10
Others: St. Regis, Scott, Union Camp, Westvaco						
37. Pollution Control						
American Air Filter	22	7⅜	21¼	13¾	24	16
Browning Ferris	9½	5	8¾	5¾	11	7½
Envirotech	27½	8¾	37⅛	17¾	42⅝	27
Wheelabrator-Frye	23⅜	10⅛	25¾	18	32½	24
Zurn Industries	12¾	4½	14⅝	9⅛	17⅜	13
Others: Peabody International						
38. Printing & Publishing						
Harcourt Brace	29¾	14⅜	34⅛	21⅛	35⅜	29
McGraw Hill	13¾	6	17⅛	12¾	20	15⅝
McMillan	6¾	3⅜	9⅜	4¼	12	7¾
Meredith	13½	8⅜	19	10¼	29¼	17¼
Scott Foresman	17¼	8¼	23	13⅛	33⅛	21¼
Time	63	24¾	39¾	28⅞*	39½	31⅜
Others: Arcata National, Times Mirror						
39. Railroad Equipment						
ACF Industries	47¾	33¼	36⅜	25⅜	39⅜	31⅝
Amsted	70¼	35¼	54½	28⅝*	59⅝	44
General Signal	42⅜	23⅞	56⅞	34¼	29½	22¾*
Portec	18⅜	12⅜	20¼	13⅝	26⅛	15⅛
Pullman	34	23	38⅞	27⅞	35⅝	26¾
Others: GATX						
40. Real Estate						
Amrep Corp.	4⅜	1⅜	3⅛	1¼	2⅝	1½
City Investing	9¼	4¾	14¼	7	16¼	11⅞
Gen. Development	6½	2¾	6⅞	3¾	7½	4½
Kaufman & Broad	10¾	3	11¼	6½	8¾	5⅛
Tishman Realty	13⅞	8⅝	16⅛	9½	18⅞	7¾
U.S. Home	7⅞	2⅜	10⅛	5¼	8⅜	6⅜
Others: Bush Universal, Deltona Corp, Webb (Del E.) Corp						
41. Restaurants						
Denny's	20¾	6⅜	25¼	18⅛	29¼	18⅝
Gino's	12½	4¾	18	7¾	9⅞	6⅝
Host Intn'l	13⅞	5⅞	16	8¼	14¼	9⅜
Howard Johnson	16	4½	17⅜	9⅝	12½	9⅛
McDonalds	60½	26¾	66	48¾	55⅜	37¾
Others: Church's Fried Chicken, Sambo's						

	1975		1976		1977	
	High	*Low*	*High*	*Low*	*High*	*Low*

42. Retail Stores—Department

Allied Stores	48⅛	15⅞	59¼	40¾	24⅛	19⅝*
Federated	56½	25⅞	60	42	49⅛	33
Macy (R.H.)	27¾	12⅜	38½	26⅝	40	31⅝
Marshall Field	26⅜	15⅝	25⅜	15¾	33	17⅜
Penney	63¼	36½	60¾	47¾	52¾	32⅛

Others: Associated, Carter Hawley, May Co., Mercantile, Zayre

43. Retail Stores—Food

American Stores	30⅝	16½	33	26¼	36⅜	27½
Great A & P	13⅜	7½	15⅝	10½	14¾	7½
Jewel	25⅞	16⅞	24½	19¼	26½	18
Kroger	24⅛	15¾	25¼	17⅝	29¼	23¼
Safeway	52⅝	34⅛	50¼	39¼	50⅜	39

Others: Food Fair, Lucky Stores, Stop & Shop, Winn-Dixie

44. Retail Stores—Mail Order & Variety

Gamble-Skogmo	25¼	19¼	29½	21⅜	39¼	22
K Mart	35⅜	20⅜	43¾	31¼	40⅞	25¾
Murphy C.G.	17½	10¼	23⅜	16¾	20½	16
Sears Roebuck	74⅜	48⅜	79¼	61½	32¾	27*
Woolworth	22¾	9⅜	27⅛	20¼	26¾	17⅞

45. Rubber

Firestone	23¾	13⅝	26	21¼	23¾	15
Goodrich	20¼	13¾	29⅝	18	33⅜	18¾
Goodyear	23⅛	12¾	25¼	20⅛	23⅞	16¾
Uniroyal	10	6⅜	10¾	7½	11¼	8
Rubbermaid	27¾	14	29⅜	22½	27½	21½

Others: Bandag, Dayco

46. Services

ARA Services	60⅝	32¼	60⅝	44⅝	50¾	33
Baker Industries	11⅜	4½	12¼	7⅞	20¼	8¾
Block, H. & R.	17½	10⅝	24½	14⅞	25⅝	18
Dun & Bradstreet	30⅞	18¾	33¾	24⅜	31½	25¾
Hosp. Corp. of Am.	26¾	8⅝	28½	20¼	27⅛	22¼
Nat'l Services	11¾	6⅝	15	9⅝	15½	12¼
Sperry Hutchinson	13¼	6⅞	16½	10	20⅝	15½

Others: American Express, Avis, Greyhound Corp., A. C. Nielson, Ryder System

47. Steel & Iron

Armco Steel	34	23	35½	26¾	32⅝	22⅜
Bethlehem Steel	40¼	24¾	48	33	40⅜	18¼
National Steel	45⅛	32¾	52¼	37⅜	45⅝	30⅞
Republic Steel	35⅞	22⅞	40⅜	27⅛	34⅞	21¾
U.S. Steel	71⅜	38¼	59⅜	43⅜*	50	27

Others: Inland, Interlake, Lykes-Youngstown, Mesabi Trust, Wheeling Pittsburg

	1975 High	1975 Low	1976 High	1976 Low	1977 High	1977 Low
48. Television						
General Instr.	14¼	5	20⅝	8⅛	23⅛	17¼
General Telev.	26	16⅞	31⅞	23¾	33½	28⅛
Oak Industries	11½	5½	12¼	7¼	20⅞	9⅝
Sony	13¼	5	10⅛	7¼	10⅝	6⅝
Zenith	28⅝	10	40⅝	23⅝	28	12¾
49. Textiles—Apparel						
Bluebell	39½	12½	29⅜	11⅞	31⅜	20
Cluett Peabody	8	3¼	11⅞	7⅝	11½	8⅝
Genesco	6¼	2⅞	9	4⅞	6¾	3⅜
Hanes	16⅜	6¼	28½	14⅜	29	22½
Munsingwear	17¾	11	20	14¾	19¼	16
Others: Jonathan Logan, Warnaco, Jack Winter						
50. Textiles—Products						
Burlington Indus.	29¾	14⅞	34	23⅞	30⅜	20⅜
Celanese	47½	25⅞	58	41¾	53	40
Spring Mills	11⅞	8⅝	15¼	10¼	15	12
J.P. Stevens	19⅛	10⅞	26⅝	17⅜	19⅞	14⅝
West Pt.-Pepperell	39	18¾	42⅜	33½	41	32½
Others: Cone, Granitville, Lowenstein, Opelika, Reeves						
51. Tobacco & Cigarettes						
American Brands	43⅝	30½	46	38⅛	48⅛	41⅛
Culbro Corp.	15⅝	10½	21¼	13⅝	23⅝	19½
Liggett & Myers	34	25⅝	36¼	29½	35½	26¼
Phillip Morris	59¼	40⅞	63¼	49¾	64⅞	51½
R. J. Reynolds	61½	49½	68¼	55	70⅝	58
52. Utilities						
Columbia Gas Sys.	28¼	21¾	30½	22¾	32¾	28
Commonwealth Edison	31⅞	22⅝	32¾	26¼	32¼	27⅞
Consolidated Edison	15	7½	21	15	25¾	20¾
Fla. Power & Light	27⅜	15¾	28⅞	20¾	34¼	28⅝
Northern Nat'l Gas	38⅛	25¾	53	33⅜	48¼	37⅛
Peoples Gas	37¼	30¼	48⅞	34¾	40½	33¼
Others: Detroit Edison, El Paso Co., Houston Industries, Pacific Gas & Electric						

There is yet another system for keeping an investment list which has its advocates. This one calls for working with only the 30 companies which make up the Dow-Jones Industrial Average. Benjamin Graham, an eminent author on the stock market and a respected investment counselor, suggested investing in those Dow-Jones companies which were going through a period of unpopularity. He suggested buying those companies with the lowest price-earnings ratios—this is discussed in the chapter on fundamental analysis—and switching each year.

This is a very conservative approach to investing. Another way, which could bring you more profits, would be to choose those Dow-Jones companies which have fallen the farthest in a reversal in a bull market and either keep the stock for investment purposes or trade it when it peaks in the next advance.

Should this method of choosing stocks to follow appeal to you, a list of the 30 Dow-Jones stocks follows:

Allied Chemical
Aluminum Company of America (Alcoa)
American Brands
American Can
American Telephone & Telegraph
Bethlehem Steel
Chrysler
Du Pont
Eastman Kodak
Esmark, Inc.
Exxon Corporation
General Electric
General Foods
General Motors
Goodyear Tire & Rubber
International Harvester
International Nickel
International Paper
Johns-Manville
Minnesota Mining & Manufacturing
Owens Illinois
Proctor & Gamble
Sears Roebuck
Standard Oil of California
Texaco, Inc.
Union Carbide
U.S. Steel
United Technologies
Westinghouse Electric
Woolworth

Making this investment list will require time and perseverance on your part. But you will receive encouragement from almost the beginning when you see the patterns of the price rhythms unfolding as you write them down, and you can see how most of them rise and fall together in response to the broad market. Don't be impatient; allow yourself plenty of time to set up your system. Once you have it done, you need not make frequent changes. You can add a company when you hear of one that sounds promising, or drop one that seems disappointing, but you will keep most of what you originally decided on. During bear markets is a good time to review the companies on your list and make any necessary changes.

Remember the most important part is learning the feel of the market. This comes only from faithfully keeping your weekly records, both on the market as a whole and all your individual stocks. This is a business you are entering into, not a hobby, and like all new businesses, it requires nurturing and devotion from you.

CHAPTER 13

HOW TO EVALUATE A COMPANY THROUGH FUNDAMENTAL ANALYSIS

Unless you are one of those persons who love to pore over figures, you might find the material in these next two chapters inherently dry. I wish there were some way to be clever about presenting this to you, but, alas, this material has never been amusing.

In an earlier chapter I wrote that there are two approaches to investing in the stock market: the fundamental approach and the technical approach. Yet neither is completely divorced from the other. The fundamentalist should consider technical tools to determine proper timing for the purchase and sale of stocks in order to receive a maximum return on the investments. The technician should consider the fundamentals of a company in setting up the list of stocks to follow and in culling this list from time to time as other stocks appear more favorable.

Whether you become an investor or a trader, you should learn how to evaluate a company. We can assume you will not bother with such companies as the giants of American industry, such as those which make up the Dow-Jones Industrial Average and others of like standing; but there will no doubt be a time when you will need to investigate a company to make sure buying the stock would be a safe investment. Should this happen, you need to know how to go about doing your checking.

Facts about any company in which you are interested are available from many sources. Brokerage firms have research bulletins; annual reports are available from the companies themselves; or you can look over the stock reports from Moody or from Standard & Poor.

If you are like most people, you did not learn in school how to read such things as balance sheets and profit and loss statements. But, actually, they are not difficult to understand. A balance sheet shows in detail a company's financial condition at a given time. You can draw up a balance sheet to show your own family's financial position at a given time, too. Let's pretend the following balance sheet is yours:

Current Assets (easily converted to cash)			**Current Liabilities** (short term debts)		
Cash	$ 800		Charge Accts.	$ 600	
Bonds	1,500		Car loan	3,500	
Stocks	1,200		Total		4,100
Total		$ 3,500	Mortgage on house		41,000
Fixed Assets (not easily converted to cash)			Total		$45,100
2 automobiles					
Cost	13,000		**Net worth**		
Less Depreciation	6,000		(Assets minus liabilities)		$32,400
Total		7,000			
House		60,000			
Furnishings	12,000				
Less Depreciation	5,000				
Total		7,000			
			Total Liabilities		
Total Assets		$77,500	plus net worth		$77,500

Notice that the last line in both columns have the same figure. This is the reason this financial report is known as a balance sheet. It is simply a way of keeping books.

The only question you might have is what is meant by depreciation. This is an important item to take into consideration. Many things that you buy and take home, a car for example, are immediately worth less because they are now considered to be "used" items. Therefore the original cost is no longer the value of your asset. You must consider what it is worth today if you were to sell it and subtract this depreciation in value when adding up your assets.

Now let's look at depreciation and see how it works. Say you have bought a new car for $6,000 and you plan to keep it for five years before you will trade it in for another new car at approximately the same price. You think you will be given $1,200 for yours as a trade-in. This means your car will depreciate $4,800 over the five year period you will use it. At the end of that time you will need to come up with that much money to buy the new car. The $4,800 divided by five means you will have to save $960 each year to end up with the necessary money. This is called "straight line" depreciation, and your bank account will look like this:

Years in Use	Depreciation	Savings Account
1	$960	$ 960
2	960	1920
3	960	2880
4	960	3840
5	960	4800

This is the ideal way to do it. You assume that, in addition to gas and oil and repairs, the car will cost you another $960 a year for the five years you will use it for you to be financially able to buy a new car to replace it; so you set the money aside. (But you will probably be like the rest of us humans and borrow the money at a bank or loan company.) But during this five-year period you figure your assets by deducting $960 from the cost of your car for depreciation for each year you have had it.

There is another way of figuring depreciation. As you may know, the value of a car drops the sharpest the first year you own it and least the last year before you trade it in. So you can figure your depreciation in this way:

Years in Use	Trade-in Value	Depreciation	Savings Acct.
1	$4000	$2000	$2000
2	2800	1200	3200
3	2000	800	4000
4	1500	500	4500
5	1200	300	4800

This second way of figuring is called "accelerated" depreciation. Notice the difference in the savings account column on how much money you put in each year. You might say, what difference does it make? You won't put money aside anyway. You are going to borrow from the bank like you always do. True, in that case it makes no difference as far as you are concerned. But it makes a tremendous difference in the world of business because it affects the amount of profit a company shows. For example, say a company bought fifty new cars for their salesmen in one year. If they were the $6,000 cars we have used in our examples of depreciation, then the company could set aside out of profits $48,000 in straight line depreciation or $100,000 in accelerated depreciation. This makes quite a difference in how much profit the company shows for the year.

Whenever you investigate a company, you look over its balance sheet carefully. In order to show you the information found in one, I have drawn up a balance sheet from a mythical company. You will find it on the double page. Refer to it as we examine some of the items on this company balance sheet which did not appear on the family balance sheet.

1. "Marketable securities" are such things as stocks and bonds bought as an investment, which can be immediately converted into cash if an emergency arises. These are usually listed on the balance sheet at cost, even though they may have changed in value.

2. The "accounts receivable" are goods that have been sold but which have not as yet been paid for at the time this balance sheet was

MYTHICAL MANUFACTURING COMPANY
Balance Sheet   December 31, 1978

ASSETS		
Current Assets		
Cash		$ 2,300,000
Marketable Securities		1,725,000
Accounts Receivable	$5,125,000	
Less Provision for		
Bad Debts	150,000	
Total		4,975,000
Inventories		3,350,000
Total Current Assets		$12,350,000
Fixed Assets		
Land	$ 400,000	
Plant and Equipment	8,750,000	
Total	$9,150,000	
Less reserve for		
Depreciation	3,975,000	
Total Fixed Assets		5,175,000
Prepaid Expenses & Deferred Charges		325,000
Patents & Goodwill		100,000
TOTAL ASSETS		$17,950,000

drawn up. Also we must realistically realize that there are people in this world who do not pay their bills, so we have allowed money for bad debts.

3. "Inventories" is the next item. For a manufacturer these are the goods that have already been manufactured but not as yet sold, plus all the unfinished products, plus all the raw materials stored in warehouses but not yet used. For a retailer this is all the goods that have been bought but not yet sold. These are current assets because they can be sold and thus converted to cash.

4. Next come the "fixed assets." Some companies lump them all together as one category; others may divide them into three or four categories. These are the items for which you deduct depreciation. In addition, you may also take a "depletion allowance" if your asset is an oil well or a mine. And some companies reserve funds for "obsolescence" if they feel there are better machines coming on the market all the time and it would pay them to replace what they now have some day, even though what they have is still useful.

5. "Prepaid expenses" are such things as insurance, which may be

LIABILITIES AND NET WORTH
Current Liabilities

Accounts Payable	$2,725,000	
Notes Payable	1,250,000	
Accrued Wages, taxes, expenses	1,400,000	
Total Current Liabilities		$ 5,375,000
Long Term Debt		
First Mortgage Bonds, 7% Interest, due 1991		2,900,000
Total Liabilities		$ 8,275,000
NET WORTH		
Capital Stock		
Preferred Stock, 5% Cumulative, $100 Par Value, Outstanding 10,000 Shares	$1,000,000	
Common Stock, $1 Par Value, Outstanding 3,500,000 Shares	3,500,000	
Capital Surplus	1,750,000	
Retained Earnings	3,425,000	
Total Net Worth		9,675,000
TOTAL LIABILITIES AND NET WORTH		$17,950,000

paid for three years in advance. "Deferred charges" could be investing money in a new product which may be profitable in the future.

6. "Patents and goodwill" are a very intangible item, and it is hard to put a value on them. A very conservative company may value them at $1. An extremely large amount carried for these two items would be highly questionable and calls for additional study on your part as to the complete honesty of the value of the total assets.

7. Now let's look at depreciation again. This is an item which needs study because the figures can be manipulated. To make things simple, if the plant and equipment, which on our balance sheet are valued at $8,750,000, were depreciated over a period of ten years, this would mean $875,000 would be set aside each year in straight line depreciation. At the end of three years there would then be $2,525,000 in the reserve fund. But the balance sheet shows the sum of $3,975,000, so we can assume the company has used accelerated depreciation. Suppose the company has had a bad fourth year but wants to show a better statement of current assets. They could change their accounting system that fourth year from accelerated to straight line depreciation and put the $1,450,000 difference into their cash account. It is necessary, therefore, to be wary of any indication that the accounting methods have been changed from those of previous years. The Moody and Standard & Poor reports will give this information, as will the company's annual report.

One reason outside accountants are required by the government to certify the accuracy of all corporation balance sheets is that in the past there has been misinformation in the use of these figures. The treasurer of the company might put down a large sum for depreciation, but use the money for something else. Or he might put down a large sum one year and nothing the next. Or nothing might have been set aside for depreciation and the company forced to go out of business because it had made no provisions for replacement of worn-out machinery. At least now, with the Internal Revenue Service looking over their shoulders, the outside accountants make certain the balance sheets are reasonably accurate and that they abide by acceptable bookkeeping practices.

Now let's go to the second page of the balance sheet:

1. "Accounts payable" are the bills the company owes.
2. "Notes payable" are the promissory notes, possibly owed to the

bank, which must be repaid within a year of the date of the balance sheet.

3. "Accrued wages, taxes, expense" are monies to be paid out in cash very shortly for wages and salaries, special fees, and, of course, income and property taxes.

4. "Long term debt" is borrowed money when it has more than a year to run before being repaid.

Understanding the terms in a balance sheet is important because they must be used to figure out something even more important: Does the company have enough money to function? Wall Street analysts have worked out a simple test, which they call "Current Ratio," to decide if the company has the needed funds. They agree that if the total current assets are at least twice the total current liabilities, the company is doing well. For our mythical company we would compute:

$$\$12,350,000 \text{ divided by } \$5,375,000 \text{ equals } \$2.29.$$

This means there is $2.29 available for every dollar the company must pay out this year, so we know the company is doing well.

As we said, as a general rule a company able to pay its bills would have a current ratio of 2 to 1 or better. However, the ratio will vary from industry to industry. A gas, electric, or telephone company need not have more than a 1 to 1 ratio because of the monthly cash it receives from its customers. In contrast, a company which does mostly seasonal business and which needs to build up inventories for seasonal sales will need a higher current ratio than 2 to 1.

Besides current ratio, another important item to look for in a balance sheet is to see what portion of the company's current assets consists of cash items. Too large a portion of inventories is not good in that it is uncertain at what price these same inventories might be sold. They might have to be discounted greatly at the time of sale.

The total assets minus the total liabilities are the net worth of the company. This net worth consists of:

5. "Preferred stock" is stock which carries a specific dividend every year which must be paid before any dividends can be paid to common-stock holders. It also assures the owners of this stock a prior claim to all assets of the company after all debts had been taken care of, should it be necessary to ever dissolve the company.

6. "Common stock", also known as just "stock," are shares in a

company that are sold to provide capital. All the shareholders own the company in common. They are entitled to attend the annual meeting or sign a proxy asking officers or directors to vote for them. If the company makes a profit and declares a dividend, they receive this payment.

7. "Capital Surplus" is that part of the earnings which the directors may pay out in dividends to the holders of common stock.

8. "Retained Earnings" are that part of the earnings which the directors may keep in a special fund to plow back into the company for production or research.

Before you buy any stock in this mythical company, you want to know if you will get any dividends. A quick glance at the right-hand side of the balance sheet will let you know. You know that the interest on bonds and the dividends on the preferred shares must be paid first, so you add those two together:

First Mortgage Bonds	$2,900,000
Preferred Stock	1,000,000
Total	$3,900,000

Then you add together the rest of the net worth:

Common stock	$3,500,000
Capital surplus	1,750,000
Retained earnings	3,425,000
Total	$8,675,000

Since the debt of the company is $3,900,000 and the rest of the net worth is $8,675,000, the holder of common stock should be able to expect to receive dividends on the common stock.

If you are researching a company, a background fact you should be interested in is the amount of borrowed money the company is using. Heavy borrowing entails risk because the interest charges must be paid regardless of how well or how poorly the company may be doing financially. But it also entails rewards because it enables a company to borrow for expansion and so greatly enhance its percentage of profit on the investment. This going into debt to enable the company to get a greater return on its own investment is called "leveraging."

The kind of leverage a company has, which is the amount of money it has borrowed, has meaning only when you relate it to the amount of total capital the company has. A $2,000,000 debt to a company with $25,000,000 in assets is only 8 per cent, but the same debt to a company with $5,000,000 in assets constitutes 40 per cent of the capital. Leverage over 25 per cent might require additional study by an interested investor.

To figure out how much leverage a company has is simple. The only additional fact you need to know besides what is on the right side of our balance sheet is the price of the stock. Let's assume our mythical company shares are now selling for $10 a share, and we want to find out how heavily leveraged the company is.

Long term debt	$ 2,900,000	Long term debt	$2,900,000
Preferred stock	1,000,000	Preferred stock	1,000,000
Common stock (at		Total	$3,900,000
$10 a share)	35,000,000		
Total	$38,000,000		

$3,900,000 divided by $38,000,000 equals 10.2 per cent.

We now know our mythical company is not leveraged too heavily.

Some investors are interested in what is called "book value." This means that in the event the company were liquidated, how much would each share be worth. This book value is arrived at by dividing the net worth figure by the number of common shares outstanding. For our mythical company this would be:

$9,675,000 divided by 3,500,000 shares = $2.76 a share.

Benjamin Graham, the father of modern security analysis, believed book value is important because it indicates the assets standing behind a stock. Others believe book value knowledge is unimportant unless there is a chance the company might merge with another company in the future.

Par value is the price the company put on each share when they first sold them and has little bearing on the present-day value of a stock. As you can see, our mythical company par value is one dollar a share, but the present value is ten dollars a share. Many companies put no par value on their stock. This is one item which can be ignored in your research.

If this chapter seems difficult to you as you read it, do not become discouraged. After you have followed its guidelines a few times, you will be pleased at how simple it will be to evaluate a company through a quick review of its balance sheet.

CHAPTER 14

Analyzing the Profit and Loss Statement

We have now studied the balance sheet thoroughly, but we still have not answered one important question: How much money is the company earning?

Prices of stock on Wall Street are based not only on the present earnings of a company, but on the future earnings as well. Both these earnings depend on a well-run operation. The more profit a company makes, the more we can assume it is well-run. Following is the profit and loss statement of our mythical company. Do look it over for a few minutes before you study what use should be made of it.

MYTHICAL COMPANY
Statement of Earnings for the Year Ended December 31, 1977

Net Sales		$120,000,000
Less:		
Cost of goods sold	$80,000,000	
Selling, General and		
Administrative Expense	18,000,000	
Depreciation	1,000,000	
Total		99,000,000
Operating Profit		$ 21,000,000
Less Interest Charges		200,000
Net Profit before taxes		$ 20,800,000
Less Provision for Taxes		10,000,000
Net Income		$ 10,800,000

There are two standard tests of earnings. The first is the relation of net income to sales. This is a quick and easy test for you to use with your pocket calculator. Take the bottom line, the net income, and divide it by the top line, the net sales to give you a very quick answer to what per cent the company is earning. In our Mythical Company it would be:

$$\$10,800,000 \text{ divided by } \$120,000,000 = 9\%$$

In deciding how profitable the company is and therefore how good an investment it would make, you must remember that average net income to sales varies considerably among different industries. For example, grocery chains earn less than 2 cents on each sales dollar, whereas the recent average in manufacturing is about 6 cents.

Although our Mythical Company seems to be highly profitable, we can measure how well it is doing by comparing its efficiency with other companies in the same industry. If another company making the same kind of products is earning 7 cents on each sales dollar, we know our company is doing well. However, if they are earning 11 cents, then we can assume something is wrong. Maybe the management of our company is not as efficient as it should be, maybe the company is being handicapped by too large an overhead, or it has old equipment, or perhaps patent problems. We may not know the reason, but we know our company is not doing as well as it should.

Another point to remember in judging a company is that although an increase in profits each year is desirable, most companies find some years better than others. Five and ten year trends are more meaningful than making a decision based on just one year.

A second important piece of knowledge to be gained from the statement of earnings is the net income per share of common stock. To arrive at this amount we must deduct the preferred stock dividends from the net income first. Not all companies have preferred stock, but our Mythical Company has 10,000 shares. The income balance is then available for common stocks, of which there are 3,500,000 shares. This also is simple to do with your pocket calculator and can show you immediately if any money might be available for dividends. For our Mythical Company we would compute as follows:

Net Income	$10,800,000
Less 5% interest on 10,000 shares preferred stock, $100 par value	50,000
Balance	$10,750,000

$10,750,000 divided by 3,500,000 = $3.07 per share

Earnings per share is perhaps the most significant financial statistic to investors, who are, after all, primarily interested in earnings power as it relates to the price of the stock. This relationship of price to earnings, called P/E ratio, is of such interest that newspapers have added it to the information included in the daily stock table. This price/earnings ratio is arrived at by dividing the listed price of the shares by the earnings per share. For our Mythical Company let's assume it is now a bull market and our stock is selling at $15 a share. To simplify the arithmetic, we will round out the earnings at $3. We now calculate:

$15 divided by $3 = 5

This would be shown in the newspaper as P/E 5. Remember that the P/E changes every time the price of the stock goes up or down.

What does the P/E ratio tell you? It actually means how many years a company will take to earn the money to recoup the investment when you buy their stock if their earnings remain the same in the future. Our Mythical Company with a P/E ratio of 5 would take five years to earn the price of their shares. If the stock were selling at $30, then the P/E ratio would be 10 and it would take 10 years to earn back the investment. The lower the P/E ratio, the greater the value the shares would have.

Does this automatically make a company with a P/E ratio of 5 a better buy than one with a P/E ratio of 10? Not necessarily, though to an inexperienced investor, it would seem so. If all companies earned the same profits each year, then the lower P/E ratio would automatically be better. But companies do not stand still and continue to earn the same profits year after year, so using the P/E ratio is not enough.

The future expectations of profits a company will earn are just as important as the present P/E ratio. To show you what a great difference there can be between a company standing still, or expanding slowly, and one whose future earnings can be expected to rise rapidly, let's compare our Mythical Company if it stood still, if it made a 10 per cent growth in profits each year, if it made a 20 per cent growth in profits, or if it became a super-growth company and made 30 per cent. Notice that a super-growth company earns more than twice as much as a static company in the five-year span shown below. Couldn't you also expect the shares to increase in value just as much?

Year	No Change	10%	20%	30%
Base	$ 3.00	$ 3.00	$ 3.00	$ 3.00
1st yr.	3.00	3.30	3.60	3.90
2nd yr.	3.00	3.63	4.32	5.07
3rd yr.	3.00	3.99	5.18	6.59
4th yr.	3.00	4.38	6.21	8.56
5th yr.	3.00	4.81	7.45	11.13
Total	$15.00	$20.11	$26.76	$35.25

With the difference in earnings over the five-year span, you can see why you should be willing to pay much more for a super-growth company than for a company whose profits stand still. If there were little expectations of a change in profits, the P/E ratio of our Mythical Company would probably continue to be low because no one would pay much more than the present $15 price for the stock. The higher the expectations for profit, the higher the P/E ratio should be. In the super-growth company, the P/E ratio could easily be 30. Investors would not hesitate to pay $90 a share for a stock in a company earning only $3.00 today if they believe it will increase its profits 30 per cent a year. In 10 years it would be earning $41.31 a share!

Your Sunday paper gives you the current P/E ratio, but for more information you need to refer to a stock report. If you will turn back to the chapter on where to get information about stocks and look at the back of the Standard & Poor's stock report of Addressograph Multigraph, you will notice at the top to the right is the column marked "Price-Earnings Ratio-Hi-Lo." This gives you the P/E ratio range for the company for the last ten years. Note that Addressograph Multigraph did not make any money in 1977, the deficit was $1.70 a share, so there was no P/E ratio for that year. In the stock report the column to the left of the P/E ratio is the "Price Range." Note also that the two columns fluctuated similarly most of the years.

There are some important points you need to know about P/E ratio when you use it as an investment tool. The first is that most stocks in a given industry tend to have about the same P/E ratio. All the automobile companies, for instance, have a low ratio because this is a cyclical industry, and when prices change because of a bull or bear market, all the P/E ratios in that industry move up and down together to reflect the price changes. These cyclical stocks are not necessarily good buys because their P/E ratios are low. Market timing is important here, because in a bear market their prices will drop too and the P/E ratios will go even lower.

Companies in growth industries tend to have a much higher P/E ratio because of the expectation of higher profits, and deservedly so, as the previous chart shows. Those that become overly high may be members of a favored group which is expected to grow very rapidly. These are the so-called "glamour" stocks. If the glamours live up to the confidence shown in them, the investor is richly rewarded; but many of these stocks can plummet even faster than they rose if they fall out of favor.

One way to use P/E ratios as an investment tool is to look at its high-low range. If a company in which you are interested has never gone below 8 and is now hovering in that range, you could probably consider it a safe investment. It has great potential for rising on a modest increase in earnings. However, if its high is about 24 and the P/E ratio is now near that point, your risk is much greater because unless it achieves a sharp increase in earnings in the future, the price is likely to fall. If you are conservative, you would probably be the safest if you bought when the P/E ratio is about the average for several years. But your best bet would be to buy stocks which are selling at their low P/E ratios and which are heading for an increased growth in earnings.

In comparing different companies in the same industry, the "cash flow" per share can be an important item. This is because of the two different kinds of depreciation discussed earlier. A company using accelerated depreciation will have a much higher current depreciation expense the first few years after a new investment and a correspondingly lower reported earnings than a company using the straight-line method. This difference might amount to millions of dollars on a new factory, for instance. To provide for this difference and to compare the companies more fairly, investors should use what is known as cash flow per share, which can be easily computed on your pocket calculator. Just add the total of net income after taxes have been deducted with the depreciation and divide the total by the number of shares the company has issued. For Mythical Company for 1977, this would be:

Net Income	$10,800,000
Plus Depreciation	1,000,000
Total Cash Flow	$11,000,000

$11,800,000 divided by 3,500,000 shares = $3.37 per share

Financial analysts always rate "good management" as a crucial element in the evaluation of a company. The problem here is that good management is difficult to evaluate. Too often a company is considered to have good management when its stock is rising in price and bad management when it is falling in price. However, there are some criteria you can use to help you decide about how good the management is. First ask you broker for whatever material he can get about the company. Then look at the annual report for some help in evaluating management. Some answers to look for would be in their strong emphasis on research and on any new and successful products they may have recently introduced. You might also ask if the company is diversified, or does it depend solely on one product? Has it developed a unique method of merchandising? And finally, does the management have a personal stake in the business so that the interests of the company is their own as well as the other stockholders?

CHAPTER 15

Volume—An Additional Technical Tool

Volume is the number of shares bought and sold on the New York Stock Exchange over a given period of time, like a day or a week or a month, depending on the statistics kept. With the rise of the institutional large block transactions this figure has risen tremendously, and twenty million shares a day now indicate a rather slow market.

There seems to be a difference of opinion among experts about the use of the figures of the volume statistics in keeping track of one's own stocks and of the stock market as a whole. Some maintain volume is important; others feel these figures make no difference. The bar chartists feel volume is an important part of their record keeping; the point-and-figure chartists completely ignore it. Some moving average advocates feel keeping track of volume is very important; others feel it unnecessary.

Keeping track of the volume of your stocks will impose an additional burden on you. If you do not have the time, or if you feel it too much of a burden, do not bother with this indicator. If you study the stocks in your own portfolio until you know their moves well, there is no reason you should feel keeping track of volume is a necessity.

But if you do have the inclination, you could try keeping these statistics. Or you can go back and check on volume figures if you are in the process of making a decision about buying or selling a particular stock. You need go back no further than the previous few months. This might be an added reinforcement to your decision.

This chapter will show you how to use this tool in case you should want to make use of this indicator. It can be used as a point of reference if you want to know more about how to use volume.

One of the technical tests of the strength or weakness of the stock market is the volume of trading on the New York Stock Exchange. Since price and volume usually tend to go in the same direction, high volume is a characteristic of rising prices and low volume is characteristic of falling prices.

Volume goes up when prices are rising simply because more people are encouraged to invest as they become more and more optimistic about making a profit. Similarly, there are fewer buyers in a falling market, so volume drops. These are normal conditions and nothing can be read into them. It is when these normal conditions change that they predict a turnabout in the market.

When prices rise on low volume, the alert traders look for a change to come about. The same holds true when volume remains high but prices do not advance. Both are a signal that a possible reversal is in the making.

At the beginning of a bear market, volume usually remains high but prices begin dropping. Investors and traders are still active because they are not convinced that a turnabout has taken place. As long as the volume remains high, the prediction is that the bottom of the bear market reversal has not yet been reached and that prices will continue to drop. Most bear markets drop to their lowest prices on low volume. Towards the very end, while prices are still dropping, there is usually a great burst of volume. This is a signal that the reversal is near at hand and a new bull market is approaching.

Timing is very important in the consideration of volume. You must be aware of the phase of a bull or bear market in which this volume takes place. Extra high volume in the third phase of a bull market is a danger signal that prices may reverse and fall. Extra high volume in the third phase of a bear market is a signal that the end is near and prices will soon rise.

Another point to remember is that neither extremely high volume nor extremely low volume is normal. When either condition dominates the market for an extended period, a change in the direction of the trend of the market should be looked for.

Interestingly enough, investors usually have the incorrect belief about volume in a bear market. They usually consider it an ominous signal when stock prices decline on heavy volume, but consider the decline to be temporary when it is on light volume. The opposite actually is the truth. Heavy volume indicates great interest in a stock and foreshadows a price rise; light volume indicates lack of buyers and therefore a further decline in price.

Statistics about the volume of shares bought and sold on the New York Stock Exchange are among the oldest technical tools in existence. An easy way to use this tool is to compute moving averages. Since you will already be keeping a ten-week and a forty-week moving average line for the Dow-Jones Industrial Average, you might also, if you wish to take the time, compute the same thing for the weekly volume figure. These may then be compared. You may also wish to do the same for some individual stocks in which you are particularly interested.

Remember that about 70 per cent of the time the two kinds of moving averages will be going in the same direction. This is normal. However, when the volume moving average line declines while the price line continues to advance, or when the reverse occurs and the volume line continues to advance but the price line begins to decline, it is a warning of weakness. Divergence of the two, when volume goes in one direction and the Dow in another, is always a signal that a reversal is in the making.

Historically volume peaks have preceded price peaks. But with the tremendous present-day increase in volume, due in large part to block institutional buying and selling, the two peaks will now coincide or the price peak will be reached before the volume peak. It is wise to be aware of this and make use of it in your trading strategy.

Another way of computing volume is through an on-balance method using price fluctuations as a base as advocated by Granville. He maintains this is superior to moving averages because it enables you to know whether stocks are being accumulated or being distributed, being bought or being sold. He feels that when the "smart money" crowd is selling a stock, it is no time for you to be buying; and when those who are reading the market correctly are buying, it is no time for you to be selling.

Granville uses as an example of the superiority of the on-balance method of computing volume by showing the bottoming of the bear market in 1974. October 4, 1974, is considered to be the bottom of the market because, although Dow-Jones Industrial Average dropped even lower on December 6, 1974, the Dow-Jones Transportation Average began to diverge after the October low and never confirmed the December low. The advance-decline line did continue to drop along with the Dow-Jones Industrial Average, but the divergence of the Industrial with the Transportation is considered the important signal.

But while the industrial and the advance-decline lines continued falling, the on-balance volume figures for the number of shares sold on the New York Stock Exchange told a different story. The last date this column showed a minus figure was September 13, 1974. The October 4th low showed an accumulation of 19 million shares, and on December 6th, the very bottom of the Dow-Jones Industrial Average, the on-balance volume showed an accumulation of 124 million shares. The "smart money" crowd was buying stocks when everyone else was sure the bottom was falling out of the market.

This on-balance method of computing volume is very simple. It can be used for the market as a whole or for individual stocks. Although Granville uses daily figures, you can do very well with weekly ones. There are three points to remember:

1. Whenever the weekly closing price has increased over the previous week, *add* the volume figure to your previous total.
2. Whenever the weekly closing price has decreased below the previous week, *subtract* the volume figure from your previous total.
3. Whenever there is no change in price, make no change in the total.

This on-balance volume method of checking accumulation and distribution lends itself very well to individual stocks. Here is the computation for Addressograph Multigraph for 1976 and 1977. The volume is given in hundreds to save time and space and to enable you to simplify your calculations.

1976	Price	Volume (in hundreds)	On-Balance Volume (in hundreds)
Jan. 4	7⅞	487	
11	8¼	+815	1302
18	8⅝	+1093	2395
25	10	+2806	5201
Feb. 1	10⅝	+2852	8053
8	11⅝	+3975	12028
15	11½	−1422	10606
22	13¼	+2145	12751
29	9⅞	−5316	7435
Mar. 7	11	+2074	9509
14	10⅞	−801	8708

1976	Price	Volume (in hundreds)	On-Balance Volume (in hundreds)
21	10	−727	7981
28	9¾	−587	7394
Apr. 4	9⅜	−448	6946
11	9½	+790	7736
18	9⅜	−621	7115
25	9¾	+335	7450
May 2	9½	−304	7146
9	8¾	−543	6603
16	9⅜	+562	7165
23	9¼	−340	6825
30	9⅛	−735	6090
Jun. 6	8¾	−426	5664
13	9¼	+462	6126
20	9½	+458	6584
27	9⅜	−487	6097
Jul. 4	9¾	+1229	7326
11	10⅜	+1172	8498
18	11	+1652	10150
25	10½	−535	9615
Aug. 1	9¾	−273	9342
8	10	+378	9720
15	9⅜	−496	9224
22	8⅞	−709	8515
29	8⅞	754	8515
Sep. 5	9	+279	8794
12	8⅝	−331	8463
19	9⅝	+923	9386
26	11¼	+4355	13741
Oct. 3	10⅞	−1562	12179
10	10⅜	−664	11515
17	9¾	−741	10774
24	9¾	614	10774
31	9⅞	+337	11111
Nov. 7	10	+487	11598
14	9⅞	−403	11195
21	10⅞	+920	12115
28	10½	−933	11182
Dec. 5	11⅜	+1567	12749
12	11⅝	+1175	13924
19	11¾	+2576	16500
26	13	+1758	19258

1977		Price	Volume (in hundreds)	On-Balance Volume (in hundreds)
Jan.	2	13¼	+1869	20127
	9	13¾	+4632	24759
	16	13¼	−1564	23195
	23	13⅜	+1258	24453
	30	13¾	+2497	26950
Feb.	6	13¼	−1087	25863
	13	13¾	+1360	27223
	20	13⅜	−840	26383
	27	11½	−1724	24659
Mar.	6	12	+1152	25811
	13	11½	−554	25257
	20	12	+612	25869
	27	11⅜	−382	25487
Apr.	3	10⅞	−434	25053
	10	10½	−360	24693
	17	11¼	+781	25474
	24	10⅜	−470	25004
May	1	10¼	−560	24444
	8	11⅛	+632	25076
	15	10⅞	−510	24566
	22	11⅞	+909	25475
	29	11½	−759	24716
Jun.	5	12¼	+834	25550
	12	12⅝	+770	26320
	19	13¼	+1610	27930
	26	13⅞	+1638	29568
Jul.	3	15	+3964	33532
	10	13¾	−1195	32337
	17	13⅝	−611	31726
	24	14½	+1112	32838
	31	13⅛	−1831	31007
Aug.	7	12⅝	−1640	29367
	14	13	+1060	30427
	21	13¼	+975	31402
	28	13⅛	−1974	30328
Sep.	4	14¼	+888	31216
	11	13⅝	−1280	29936
	18	12⅞	−1318	28618
	25	13⅝	+1919	30537

1977	Price	Volume (in hundreds)	On-Balance Volume (in hundreds)
Oct. 2	13¾	+690	31227
9	13⅞	+764	31991
16	13⅝	−697	31294
23	13	−525	30769
30	12⅞	−472	30297
Nov. 6	12⅝	−416	29881
13	14	+925	30806
20	14⅞	+1942	32748
27	15⅝	+2041	34789
Dec. 4	15	−1391	33398
11	14⅝	−1007	32391
18	14⅜	−423	31968
25	14¼	−523	31445

Before we discuss what we can read into the on-balance volume record of Addressograph Multigraph, let's review Shaw's second assumption, mentioned in Chapter 9. It deals with the supply and demand of the stock market. He says that either the buyers or the sellers of a stock is the stronger of the two and more influential where price is concerned in the long run. If the stock keeps dropping in price, the larger number of sellers has greater influence on the price because there are fewer buyers who are willing to buy unless the price drops even more. The shares then are going through a period of distribution; the stock is moving from strong to weak hands, in Wall Street terminology, and plenty of shares are available. When the stock is rising in price, the larger number of buyers has greater influence on the price. The shares are going through a period of accumulation; the stock is moving from weak to strong hands; the stock is in great demand and the supply is falling.

Now let's look at Addressograph. Not once in the two year record shown has this stock's on-balance volume column been negative, which means the larger number of buyers has had greater influence on the price, and the shares are being accumulated. So much so, that at the end of 1977, there are over three million shares being held on to. You can see why one of the panel members of the television program "Wall Street Week" recommended it during January, 1978, as a vehicle for investment.

An important point to notice in the table for the two years is how much the volume increases when the stock goes up in price and how much volume shrinks when the price declines. This means many shares are being kept and that is a bullish sign.

Now let's go back to Shaw. He says that supply and demand are quite obvious at times, as certainly is exemplified here by Address-ograph. However, accumulation or distribution can occur with little change in price, and it is when the price is in this neutral trading range that the technician is challenged to anticipate which is occur-ring, and therefore, which way prices will go—up or down.

Better than any other method of keeping track, on-balance volume will show whether accumulation or distribution is taking place during this neutral trading range. Suppose a stock goes up five points on a zigzagging rising volume pattern that ends up with an on-balance volume gain of 50,000 shares, and then the stock goes down those same five points on a zigzagging declining volume pattern which loses 30,000 of those shares. You still have a balance of 20,000 shares that show the stock is being accumulated. Keeping track like this avoids much of the guessing.

One of the best places to use the on-balance volume technique is in the purchase of stocks that are very unpopular and whose prices have dropped very low. Nobody seems to want them. By keeping track of their volume, the earliest stages of accumulation can be detected, and the shares can then be bought for maximum profit. Technicians who believe in volume stress that low prices are not enough; they must also show evidence of accumulation of "smart money" to become eligible for investment.

To go back to Addressograph, notice that whenever there was heavy volume a reversal set in and the price dropped. Buying on heavy volume is considered unsophisticated because heavy volume means uninformed buyers have come into the market and informed sellers are leaving. After a long rise in price of a stock or of the Dow-Jones Industrial Average, heavy volume may occur with no further rise in price. This is a signal to get out. Similarly, heavy volume after a long drop when prices refuse to drop further indi-cates that the sophisticated buyers are stepping in and a reversal will soon take place. This is the time for you to get in too.

CHAPTER 16

You and Your Stockbroker

If you are going to be an investor or trader in stocks, you are going to need a stockbroker to carry out your buy and sell orders. The brokerage house which employs this person should be a member of, or have a connection with, a major stock exchange.

Your job will be to shop around to find a stockbroker with whom you feel at ease. You need to find a person with whom you do not feel embarrassed if you make a wrong decision and a stock goes down instead of up after you buy it. You need to feel free to call up and cheerfully say, "Oops, I goofed," and sell out before your loss is too great. No defensive feeling on your part and no sticking with a loser because of what your stockbroker might think of you.

One of the writers about the stock market says there are two kinds of brokers: the good and the glib. The good brokers are knowledgeable about investing and have not only made money for their clients, but they have also made money for themselves. They don't remain brokers too long, he says, because they make enough money to go into other businesses.

The glib brokers are much more common than the good. They are good salesmen and are interested mainly in making commissions. If asked for advice, they usually endorse the stock recommendations put out by the firms they work for. This writer cautions against following their advice, since these brokerage-house research departments are set up to accommodate big clients who generate big commissions, like mutual funds, pension funds, banks, trusts, and insurance companies. By the time the small investors get the recommendations, it is too late to make much profit, if any.

Another practice he cautions against is a special deal that is some-

147

times offered by brokers: that of buying listed stock at the market price without paying any commission. He says this is offered because the brokerage house has privately bought up a large block of stock from one of the big clients mentioned above in order to keep the price up. Dumping too much stock at one time would severely depress the price, so the brokerage houses try to protect their big clients.

For the knowledgeable investor, which I hope you will become, the glib broker is fine. You are not going to ask for recommendations because you have your own list of companies which you are following closely. When you have come to a decision about buying or selling, you will call up and give your order. Glib brokers can competently follow orders and are very helpful about sending you any information they can get about a specific company. And several times a year they can get you a copy of the Standard & Poor's *Stock Guide*. Knowledgeable investors do not need to pester their brokers constantly, especially during market hours when they are busy. An occasional chat after the market has closed can lead to a good relationship between the two of you.

Finding a broker to suit you means more than looking in the yellow pages of the phone book. The best way to find one is by personal recommendation from someone you know. Your doctor can be a good source, since most of them make enough money to look for investments and most of them put part of this money in the stock market. Your family lawyer or your banker should be able to make some recommendations too, or at least give you the names of a few firms that are reputable.

Most people wander into one of the recommended firms and speak to the broker whose turn it is to handle these walk-ins. From then on this person becomes their broker. But there are better ways.

First shop around, visit the various firms' board rooms, pick up the literature they have in their racks for free distribution, and get some idea of their research organization. Next talk to some of the brokers, but make no commitment until you find the one with whom you can feel at ease. The best way is to talk to the office managers first, tell them what you have in mind for an investment plan, and ask them to recommend the representative in their office they think would be the most suited. Then talk to the persons who have been recommended and choose among them.

One of the things you need to understand is that stockbrokers earn their living through commissions generated when their customers buy and sell their stock. Sometimes they have been accused of "churning" the accounts of their customers by doing excessive trading to generate commissions. This need not be a worry to you, as you are going to make your own decisions about buying and selling.

Some of the writers on investment complain about the commissions paid. It is true the small investor pays proportionately too high a percentage and should complain. Until something can be done about it, you will just have to consider this as part of the cost. If you look upon investment and trading as a business, as I do, even a part-time business, you realize that the commissions paid your broker are about the same when compared to the percentage paid on real estate, or the rent and utilities paid in a shop. You might argue that you pay the real estate commission only when you sell, not when you buy; but I have never heard of anyone whose price on a house doesn't try to cover the commission too, so you probably paid most of that when you bought.

Should you feel that commission rates are too high, you might look into the discount brokerages which are springing up and which offer a minimum of services. They cater to the smaller number of investors who are able to make it on their own. However, you might wait until you have become experienced and confident of your own abilities before trying them. Until then, consider the higher commissions as part of the cost of investing.

After you have decided on a brokerage firm and a broker, you now have to decide on what to do with your securities. You can choose to have them put in your own name, receive them from your broker, and then guard them carefully. A safe deposit box is the best place. If you lose them, it is costly to have them replaced. If you decide to sell them, you must deliver them to your broker either in person or by mail in a manner which will protect them from loss. This can be done either through registered mail or through your bank.

Your second choice is to put your securities in what is known as "street name." This means they are in the name of the brokerage house, whose duty it will be to send you all your dividends and annual reports. The advantage to you in this arrangement is that the securities are held in safekeeping by your broker and convenience in buying and selling is greatly increased. Nor will you have to worry about losing the certificates since you never get them. The firm will send you confirmations about the shares you own and the dividends you receive. Should the firm run into financial problems, you are protected from loss up to $50,000 by the Securities Investor Protection Corporation.

You will be expected to pay for your stock within five business days, according to the rules set by the Federal Reserve Board. It will take longer for you to get your money after you sell the stock. Frequent traders leave the money in their accounts with the firms to avoid the nuisance of writing checks. Unless you plan to buy another stock soon, or unless you can't trust yourself not to spend the money, you might as well put it in a bank to draw interest.

CHAPTER 17

How To Begin Your Investment Program

Anyone who is an expert in anything has been willing to put in a lot of time and effort to learn. Don't expect anything less from yourself if you wish to become an expert in the stock market. Half-way measures or a half-hearted approach will not give you the necessary expertise.

At the beginning of the book I suggested your saving the financial pages of the Sunday paper. Now you are going to make use of them. You also need a pencil, the loose-leaf noteboo for your records, and a small calculator.

You will begin by deciding whether ou will use the Dow-Jones Industrial Average or the Standard & Poor's 500 Stock Index. Many technicians use both if both are given in their papers. You will then start recording the dates and the gure for each, and when you have accumulated enough, you will begin calculating the moving averages. If you wish to use an earlier starting date than you have in your papers, you will find it simple to research the back issues of *Barron's* at the public library.

You will be doing exactly the same recording and figuring for the advance-decline moving average.

At the same time you will need to decide on the companies you will follow for your investment list. You may select from the groups I presented in an earlier chapter; or you may have your own preferences. Pick only stocks you would like to own. Price might be one of the things you will consider. Your personal prejudices on social issues, tobacco, or liquor, or pollution, could also have some bearing on the companies you choose. If you feel strongly on these issues, don't waste your time following companies whose stock you never intend to buy. There are too many other companies to choose from that can please you.

There are limits for these selections.

1. Remember these stocks must be listed on the New York Stock Exchange.

2. You are going to select stocks that are reasonably active, that trade at least 5000 shares a week.

3. You are going to select stocks that are volatile or cyclical if you plan to trade. You will select those that swing widely enough so that you will find trading profitable even if you don't hit the very bottom or top. The width of the swing should depend on the price of the stock. A 30 per cent swing on 100 shares of a higher-priced stock, say from 40 to 52, can be very profitable. The same percentage swing from 4 to 5½ could be just as profitable, and perhaps more likely to occur, providing you use as much money as in buying the higher-priced stock. For the same money you could buy 1000 shares of the lower-priced stock and end up with the same profit.

Check the stock digest for the current price range and for the previous year. Or look at some of the other references mentioned earlier. If you use a chartbook, look for the cyclical patterns with large moves that have wide swings in price. If you do not have a chart book, you can look in your newspapers at the yearly highs and lows. These too can give you an idea of how wide the annual swing has been, and you should pick out those that are potentially profitable.

With each company you select, you will start recording the dates and prices of the stock. When you have accumulated enough figures, you will start the 10-week moving average line and then the 40-week moving average line on each.

These weeks and months while you are gathering your information can be a period of training and apprenticeship. As you write down the weekly prices for the different companies you have chosen, you will notice a pattern emerging that most of your stocks are following. Then as you begin your moving averages, more clearly defined patterns will emerge. But you still aren't confident of what you are doing, so there is no reason to risk your money yet.

George Seaman, in *A Treasury of Wall Street Wisdom*, says this is the time for you to be doing your investing and trading on paper. In your notebook keep a page or two for your imaginary buying and selling. Enter the purchase order as though you had actually given it to a broker and add a half point for commission and taxes. And do be honest with yourself and your records. This is not a game but a skill you are trying to develop.

Enter your sales the same way, subtracting the half point for commissions. Then figure out how many times you were right and how many times you were wrong—not how much money you made or lost. If you were right more times than you were wrong, you can begin to think of using real money.

Do not plunge in with all your capital. Buy only a small number of shares, an odd lot, to see how well you do. If this trade is profitable, you will have gained confidence in yourself and you can increase the amount of money you invest. If you lose, don't become discouraged. Many writers feel it is better to lose at first so you don't become too optmistic and take a chance on losing all your capital. If you had purchased only a small number of shares, your loss should be small but the experience invaluable. Expect to make mistakes, expect to take small losses; just analyze what went wrong and learn from it so that you don't repeat the same mistake in any future purchase.

It is believed that perhaps the most unfortunate beginners in the field of stock investing are the persons who first become interested in the market in the middle stages of a bull market. They make profits on most transactions during the first year or so and come to think of the normal trend as upward. They think of all reversals as buying opportunities and of the general market as active and exciting. It usually requires a year or two of a bear market and some long periods of extreme dullness plus the loss of a substantial portion of their capital to give them the "feel" of bear markets and of extended periods in which the major trend is in doubt.

Losses in the first several years of investing are normal. The wise person does not allow them to deplete his capital so seriously that a comeback is impossible. Decide how much you are willing to lose and stick to it.

Gerald Loeb suggests another way of gaining experience. He suggests investing in only one stock at a time, buying one hundred shares of an average-priced stock and selling it before buying another. In this way a beginner is forced to close one commitment before opening another and does not risk too much capital to put the investment plan into effect. You are forced to make decisions about which stock to buy, when to buy it, and whether to keep it or sell it at a loss or at a profit. And you need to decide whether you are better off in another stock than the one you have chosen.

Loeb feels this is much more valuable than the paper transactions because actually being in the market tests your psychological reactions to a fear of a loss or to a desire for more gain. He says this means frequent swapping. This means selling short as well as buying long; this means paying close attention to the importance of timing; and this means staying out of the market during periods of uncertainty.

To review what you will be doing, you are going to maintain on a regular weekly basis the following moving averages:

1. Using the Dow-Jones Industrial Average or the Standard & Poor's 500 Stock Index, or both, you will have:

    a. a 10-week moving average line

    b. a 40-week moving average line

2. For the New York Stock Exchange weekly summary of advancing and declining stocks:

    a 10-week moving average line

3. For each of the individual companies you have selected:

    a. a 10-week moving average line

    b. a 40-week moving average line

The first thing you, as an investor or trader, are going to need is knowledge of what the primary trend of the market is. This you will learn from the 40-week Dow Jones moving average line and from the 10-week advance-decline line:

1. If both the above average lines are declining, you know we are in the midst of a bear market or in a reversal of a bull market and the buying of stock must be postponed.

2. Wait until the advance-decline line turns up, or until the 10-week Dow-Jones line turns up and moves above the 40-week average line before buying any stock. Most of the time the advance-decline line reverses first, but there have been several times when this has not happened, so this signal to buy must be used in conjunction with the Dow-Jones line to find the bottom.

3. As long as the advance-decline line keeps advancing, we are in a bull market. As shown in Chapter 8, these advance-decline line reversals signal the phases of the bull market. They also signal rallies in a bear market. Do not buy when the line tops out and begins to fall. Wait until it begins to advance again.

4. As long as the Dow-Jones 10-week line is above the 40-week line, we are in a bull market and it is safe to buy stocks.

5. A reversal in the advance-decline line or a declining 10-week Dow-Jones line are not signals to sell. Selling is determined by each individual stock, since they peak at different times and each gives its own signal.

6. Remember that the market does its best to confuse investors. Trading in the market is an art for which you must develop a "feel." Do not expect to make all your trades profitably. Granville feels that seven out of ten profitable trades is an acceptable average that most investors can attain. So if you get a buy signal on a stock and it doesn't work out, consider this one of the learning experiences that will help you expand your knowledge of the market. Remember we are working with probabilities. And the probabilities are in your favor; you will be right the greater percentage of the time.

7. The stock market does not go straight up or straight down, but pauses from time to time in a period of indecision. The investor needs to be particularly alert at these times to see which way the market will go. If the pause ends with the market continuing its rise, the investor will wish to remain fully invested. If the market turns down after the pause, the investor will wish to sell the stock as close to the top as possible. Each stock will top out at its own particular time and then should be sold.

8. During these phases of indecision the 10-week line may drop below the still advancing 40-week line. Do not buy additional stock at this time, nor necessarily sell what stock you have. Let the individual stock tell you what to do. This drop is just a caution signal until the market clarifies.

CHAPTER 18

Your Buying Strategy

There is a bit of folklore on Wall Street which carries some good advice for beginners. It says that at the end of a market decline, the best stocks to buy are those which have suffered the least and those which have suffered the most.

Those which have suffered the least have done so because the so-called "smart money" has been investing heavily in them and so has kept the price up. This is known as the "buy high, sell higher" philosophy. It implies the selection of the best-performing stocks, those that in the recent past have been doing the best on the exchange. This strategy of going along with the leaders is most satisfactory for the more aggressive investors. Research has shown that those stocks which have performed the best are most likely to have the momentum to keep rising through the bull market.

The following chart of NCR Corporation is a good example of this upward momentum. Notice how well the price held up during the 1977–78 bear market; in fact, at the bottom of the bear market its price never dropped below the rising trendline. Then at the first sign of the 1978 bull market, the stock took off like a rocket.

A point of warning is essential. Stocks rising this steeply may also be the ones to fall the farthest during the next bear market. They particularly need to be watched carefully in the third phase of the bull market so they can be sold before they begin a downward slide. For example, review the NCR chart again and notice the movement of the stock in the 1970 bear market and how far the price fell. Note also the large reversal in the 1974 bear market.

156

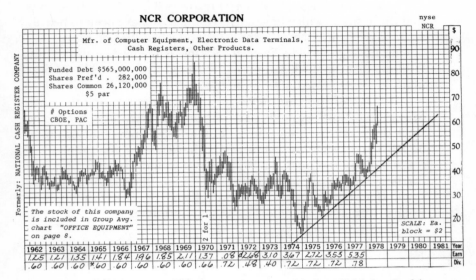

NCR CORPORATION

nyse
NCR

Mfr. of Computer Equipment, Electronic Data Terminals, Cash Registers, Other Products.

Funded Debt $565,000,000
Shares Pref'd . 282,000
Shares Common 26,120,000
     $5 par

Options
CBOE, PAC

Formerly: NATIONAL CASH REGISTER COMPANY

The stock of this company is included in Group Avg. chart "OFFICE EQUIPMENT" on page 8.

2 for 1

SCALE: Ea.
block = $2

Year	1962	1963	1964	1965	1966	1967	1968	1969	1970	1971	1972	1973	1974	1975	1976	1977	1978	1979	1980	1981
Earn	1.25	1.21	1.35	1.41	1.84	1.96	1.85	2.11	1.37	.08	d2.68	3.10	3.67	2.72	3.53	5.35				
Div.	.60	.60	.60	*.60	.60	.60	.60	.60	.66	.72	.48	.40	.72	.72	.72	.78				

Another chart which illustrates the "buy high, sell higher" philosophy is the Fairchild Industries, Inc. one. Here too the stock never dipped below its rising trendline in the 1978 bear market and seemed to explode when the bull market began.

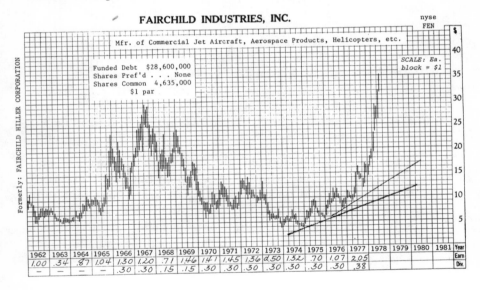

FAIRCHILD INDUSTRIES, INC.

nyse
FEN

Mfr. of Commercial Jet Aircraft, Aerospace Products, Helicopters, etc.

SCALE: Ea.
block = $1

Funded Debt $28,600,000
Shares Pref'd . . . None
Shares Common 4,635,000
     $1 par

Formerly: FAIRCHILD HILLER CORPORATION

Year	1962	1963	1964	1965	1966	1967	1968	1969	1970	1971	1972	1973	1974	1975	1976	1977	1978	1979	1980	1981
Earn	1.00	.34	.87	1.04	1.30	1.20	.71	1.46	1.41	1.45	1.36	d.50	1.32	.70	1.07	2.05				
Div.	–	–	–	–	.30	.30	.15	.15	.30	.30	.30	.30	.30	.30	.30	.38				

The second philosophy is the "buy low, sell high" one. It believes that those stocks which have suffered the most have been so heavily sold that they are now at a standstill, and when they do move, they are bound to go up. The Eastern Air Lines, Inc. chart illustrates this. It shows that the stock had never recovered from the 1973–74 bear market. Of additional interest to the trader as 1977 drew to a close was that it had had two previous support areas showing the stock dropping to just below six and rebounding each time. When the stock dropped that low again for the third time near the beginning of 1978 and began to reverse would have been a good time for a trader to buy the stock, knowing that it would probably not drop further than its previous lows and therefore the risk of a loss was small. If it were to respond to a new bull market, it had to go up. The stock price actually went to 14 within a short time.

EASTERN AIR LINES, INC.

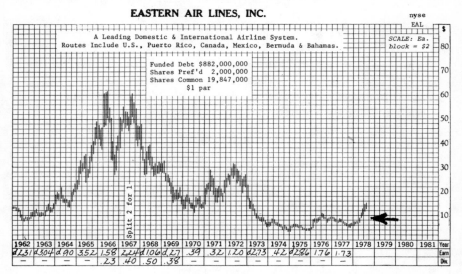

There is a third philosophy, the "just buy and don't sell" one, which is held by those who feel they should buy stocks in "good" companies and hold on to them. In past years these long-term investors have done very well. However, in today's volatile market, this third philosophy is the least profitable, and the owners of such shares should periodically check their portfolios to see if any changes are necessary. There is no reason to ride out both bull and bear markets without being aware of the profits to be made by selling out at the top and buying back at the bottom. Or even checking to see if greater dividends can be received from other investments or from switching stocks.

Buying in a Bear Market

Let's assume we had experienced the 1974 bear market. For the market as a whole the 10-week moving average line was declining as was the 40-week line, since the Dow-Jones Industrial Average had been falling consistently. When the 10-week line dropped below the 40-week line, we knew we were in a full-fledged bear market. All stocks hopefully had been sold as they topped out earlier, and we should either now be selling short or holding our money in a bank until the bear market showed promise of reversing.

I showed in Chapter 7 that the first glimmer of a break in the bear market came on November 3, 1974. This should have been the time to examine your list of stocks to see which ones would make the most profitable investments. It would be risky to invest at this time, but in Wall Street the time to make the most profitable investments is when other investors are too frightened to want to assume any risks.

The stocks in your list should have been studied to see if any were vehicles of investment at this time. You needed to look for any whose 10-week moving average line was higher than the 40-week line, no matter how small the difference. These were the stocks that had shown strength because they had gone down the least and had recovered fast. Or they might even have moved up in price in spite of the market being in a decline. These were the probable leaders in the next rally; and if the rally turned out to be the beginning of a bull market, so much the better.

A second break in the bear market decline came in December, 1974, when the 10-week line turned up for the first time. This was another opportunity to buy, as many stocks had fallen even farther than they had been in November. Besides picking out stock that showed strength, this would have been a good time to choose stock that had fallen the farthest. Addressograph Multigraph was one that had fallen from 11¾ to 3 in 1974 and was a wonderful buy on the December 15th. It also had had a previous support zone near that level in October when it had dropped to 3⅞, and so was not likely to

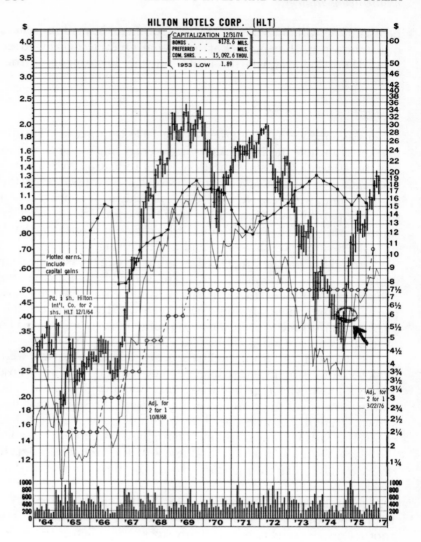

decline any farther than the 3 at which it had closed on the 15th of December. This stock lived up to expectations and had almost tripled by the following May.

Even if we had waited until the additional signals in January, 1975, there were still many opportunities for profitable investments. But had we waited until the February confirmation that the new bull market had begun, most of the cream would have been skimmed off

and much of the potential profit of the first phase of the bull market would have been lost.

If you are a chartist and rely on chart patterns for your decisions, there are four patterns to look for as a bear market comes to a close:

1. A long term decline, the longer the better, followed by a breakout, meaning it has moved above a previous declining peak. When the breakout occurs, the belief is that the stock will gain an upside impetus commensurate with the duration and extent of the previous decline. It is also believed that during the long decline the stock has been so thoroughly oversold that when the price breaks out above its previous resistance level, the stock will advance at a greater rate than it previously declined. This chart formation is held to be the most profitable of all. The Hilton Hotel chart is an example of this.

COLT INDUSTRIES, INC. (COT)

Manufacturer of steel (Crucible), machinery, industrial equipment, and other capital products.

Earns. 12 mos.
9/29/74 9.04
12/31/74 10.95

Earns. 12 mos.
3/30/75 11.70
6/30/75 10.36
9/28/75 8.51
12/31/75 7.07

Garlock
Merged
1/28/76

2. A flat base breakout is another pattern to look for. This is where the price of a stock has remained in a very restricted range of fluctuation for a long period of time, the longer the better. Once the price breaks out above this restricted range, it has great potential for profit. The chart of Guardian Industries illustrates this.

3. Coming off a double bottom is another pattern to look for. When a stock has met support at a given level following a decline, it must prove itself by holding at that level should it rise and fall back again. The farther apart the bottoms are and the lower the bottoms are the more bullish the pattern is. See the Colt Industries chart.

4. The W pattern is another profitable one. The pattern looks like the letter of the alphabet with the middle leg of the W representing a level of upside resistance. When the right leg of the W exceeds the middle leg, it signals a very important place to make a purchase.

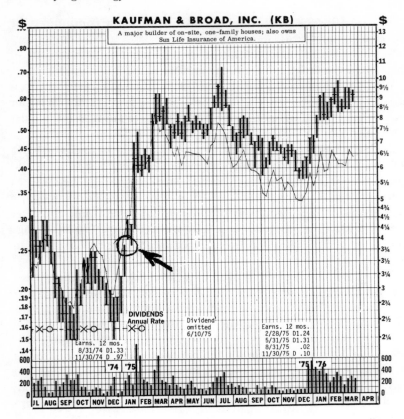

Note how well Kaufman and Broad illustrated this at the end of the 1974 bear market.

Buying in a Bull Market

Since a bull market usually lasts two or three years and has three phases, there may be times when you will have sold stock and will have money to invest again, especially if you have been doing any trading. You will be safe buying additional stock as long as the following conditions exist in the market as a whole:

1. The 10-week advance-decline moving average line is still in an uptrend.

2. The 40-week Dow-Jones Industrial Average moving average line is still in an uptrend.

3. The 10-week Dow-Jones moving average line continues to be traveling above the 40-week line.

Should these conditions exist, then you need to look for one of these patterns among the companies you follow:

1. A stock which has completed the bottom of a reversal and is beginning to move up. The 10-week moving average now is either higher than the 40-week average or is moving up rapidly toward the 40-week line.

2. A stock which had previously given a buy signal and is now in a reversal with its price at a level somewhere between the 10-week and the 40-week average prices. Choose a stock as close to the 40-week price as possible in order to limit the risk of a loss. Addressograph Multigraph in April and May of 1977 would have fit into this category. On May 15th the price was 10⅞, with a rising 40-week average line price of $11.14. There would have been little risk in this purchase.

3. Do not rush in and buy after a stock has had several sharp rises. Buy on a reaction, when the price approaches the moving averages figures. Near the 40-week line is the least risky; not quite as safe but still within a good range is a price near the 10-week line.

4. You may buy when the 10-week moving average figure rises above the 40-week average for the first time. After that wait until a reaction brings the price of the stock down to the range between the two averages if possible. This may mean there will be no stocks to buy for a period of time until the reversal sets in. You need to acquire the patience to wait.

If you are a chartist, the following patterns will provide you with the maximum profits when the second phase of the bull market begins:

1. The long-term decline followed by a breakout. This pattern is the same as the one used at the end of a bear market. It is always good for a profitable purchase.

2. The flat base breakout is also profitable. It is the same as described previously.

3. Coming off a double bottom is another pattern that is always good.

4. Cyclical stock patterns which show that the stock has retreated and lost a good portion of the gains it had made during the first phase can be profitable. These should not be bought until they again begin their upward swing.

The third phase of the bull market calls for a different kind of investment strategy. You should be interested only in those stocks whose price and 40-week moving average line are both rising fairly rapidly in parallel fashion. The stocks selected must be priced higher than the moving average line because if they are lower than the average line this late in the bull market then they are signalling that something is wrong.

This is the time to rely on high quality, blue chip issues which are not cyclical in nature. Their charts should show a steady rise with very little downside moves during reversals. The giants of American industry would qualify at this time.

The Use of Timing

Timing the primary trend of the market as a whole tells you when to buy stocks and when to avoid buying stocks. It tells you whether you are in a bull market or in a bear market and warns of possible reverses of either. It does not tell you what to buy, just when to buy.

The following guide will help you keep the primary trend in mind and should assist you in making your decisions. The first column is the Dow-Jones Industrial Average index figure as you record it each week. The next two columns are the 10-week and the 40-week moving averages of the index figure. The fourth column is the advance-decline moving average line, and the last column suggests how you should use the knowledge gained. The terms + or −40 mean that the index figure or the 10-week moving average price is either above (+) or below (−) that of the 40-week average price. *UP* means that the moving average in question is registering a higher value each successive week. *Down* indicates that it is registering successive lower numbers.

DJIA Index	DJI Moving—Averages 10-week	40-week	A-D Line 10-week	Investment Program
+40	+40	UP	UP	Bull mkt. Stay invested
−40	+40	UP	UP	Bull mkt. Stay invested
+/−40	−40	UP	UP	Uncertain, no new purchases
+/−40	+40	UP	DOWN	Uncertain, no new purchases
+/−40	−40	UP	DOWN	Bear Mkt. Short sales only
−40	−40	DOWN	DOWN	Bear Mkt. Short sales only
+40	−40	DOWN	DOWN	Buy—this may be just a rally
−40	−40	DOWN	UP	in a bear mkt. or the first phase of a new bull mkt.
+40	−40	DOWN	UP	Buy. Second sign of bull mkt.
+40	+40	DOWN	UP	Buy. New bull mkt. ahead

Timing the primary trend of each individual stock in your list tells you what your position toward that particular stock should be. The following guide will help you:

Price	Individual Moving Average 10-week	40-week	Investment Program
+40	+40	UP	Hold stock regardless of market as a whole
−10	+40	UP	Hold if bull mkt. Sell if bear mkt.
−40	+40	UP	Hold if bull mkt. Sell if bear mkt.
+40	−40	DOWN	Buy if bull mkt. Sell short if bear market
+/−40	+40	UP/DOWN	Buy if bull mkt.
−40	−40	DOWN	Avoid regardless of market as a whole

Low-Priced Stocks

Low-priced stocks have great appeal to investors, especially to new ones. They require a relatively small capital investment. They can be bought in round lots (meaning in 100 share lots) without paying the one-eighth point penalty on odd lots (less than 100 shares.) Also they are more volatile than the higher priced stocks and will show a greater price range within a given year. Their appeal to unsophisticated investors brings about a great demand which can result in a spectacular advance.

Like a lot of excessive Wall Street phraseology, these inexpensive stocks are sometimes called "cats and dogs" as if they are of no value. Yet they have their place in every trader's portfolio and can be more profitable than the IBM's if they are bought and sold at the right time.

The best right time is at the beginning of a bull market. In the 1970 and 1974 bear markets, prices were so depressed that there were hundreds of stocks that would have been profitable. With so many choices, the field needed to be narrowed to those that would provide the maximum percentage gain. This could be provided best by the low-priced stocks, those under ten or twelve dollars. As I pointed out, Addressograph Multigraph went from 3 on the 15th of December to 8⅞ at the end of May, an increase of 195 per cent in less than six months. During that time IBM went from 167 to 218, an increase of 30 per cent.

Another good time to look for low-priced stocks is in the month of December. This is the time many stocks hit new lows because of the taking of losses for tax purposes. With the middle of the month being the best time, many bargain hunters look at the list of new lows listed daily in *The Wall Street Journal* and other publications around December 15th and choose from the companies listed. Research has shown these depressed stocks frequently rebound twice as much as the general market by February 15th, with lower quality stocks gaining more than the blue chips.

The New York Stock Exchange has an excellent pamphlet "Low Prices on the Big Board" which lists 244 stocks priced at $20 or less a share. They have been chosen because of their established earnings, their dividend yield, and their rate of growth. This could be an excellent source for you to use in choosing your companies to follow. The address is 11 Wall Street, New York, New York 10005.

One important point to remember about low-priced stocks is that they usually top out some time late in the second phase of the bull market. Therefore, they make the best buys at the end of a bear market and at the beginning of a new bull market. They can also be bought when the second phase of the bull market begins. They should be avoided for the third phase. If the price of any stock has still remained low after the majority of other low-priced stocks already moved up during the first two phases of the bull market, then you can assume there is obviously a problem in the company which has kept the price of its stock low, and it should not be considered for investment.

Higher-priced Stocks

After concentrating on low-priced stocks in the first phase of the bull market, traders now need to turn their attention to higher-priced ones. In the second phase of the bull market the best opportunities for profit are in those stocks in the $15 to $30 price range, especially the better grade cyclicals in this price range.

In the third phase of a bull market you need to rely more on high quality blue chips. Your buying should be centered on advancing stocks above $30 per share. These stocks are usually the last to top out in a bull market. The 30 stocks which make up the Dow-Jones Industrial Average are good examples of the type of companies to invest in at this time.

However, in the 1975–1977 bull market there was no real third phase, as sometimes happens, and the blue chips failed to make their customary last advance. In fact, they led the market decline and did poorly compared to less expensively priced shares.

Institutional Stocks

Institutional fund managers in recent years have been disturbed by their poor records. Many of the funds have not been able to perform as well as the average of the market as a whole. To try to correct this, many funds have become index funds. This means that the managers buy stocks which enable their portfolios to have a similar composition and weight as the Standard & Poor's composite of 500 stocks. By doing this they hope the value of their portfolios will go along with the swings of the market averages and they will therefore perform as well.

To achieve this end, these fund managers will have to buy the stocks of many smaller companies instead of just the "favorite fifty" of the 1960's and 70's. This means that many of the new stocks these funds will buy will show the impact of institutional trading by having greater price swings. The greater volume should drive prices higher than they would normally have risen. The small trader should be aware of this change and try to take advantage of it.

The stocks which are heavily owned by institutions are good candidates for short sales during reversals and in bear markets. These funds find it difficult to get out of losing situations and force prices farther down when they sell.

Remember what I said earlier about the funds necessarily having to move slowly in buying or selling stock to avoid upsetting the market. Your strategy for buying stocks of interest to institutions is to buy them only on their reverses since the institutional buying will cause spurts in price. When selling or selling short, use rebounds because if institutions sell also, the stock could plunge sharply. You need not rush into making decisions as the funds take quite a while to move in or out.

Averaging Up or Down

One of the poorest strategies to follow is that of averaging down. To explain this: It would mean you buy a stock at 20 and hold on to it even when it drops. You buy again at 15, which enables you to average out at 17½. The thinking behind this is that when the stock goes back up to 20, you have made a profit. The only problem is that the stock may never go back up to 20; it may drop down to 10. Then you have thrown good money after bad and compounded your loss.

What strategy should you have followed? You should have sold the stock at about 17½ the first time it dropped and taken your loss. Then you should have waited until the decline had ended and it started going back up. You could have then bought it back at 11 or 12, after it had started moving back up again, and followed it up.

If you want to do any averaging, average up. Say the above stock is now at 15 and you are sure it will go all the way up to the original 20. Buy again at 15; this averages your two purchases at 13 or 13½ and makes a very profitable transaction.

Diversification

One of the important questions facing investors is, "How many different stocks should I buy?" The advice from the writers of books on investment seems to range all the way from one or two up to 12 or 15. The following points will help you make your decisions in this area.

1. Diversification is a necessity for the beginner. If you have enough money, you should invest in a number of stocks, say four or five or even more if you feel you can handle it. This will help you develop a feel for the market.

2. Winners cannot be picked out unerringly in advance. Therefore, the only sound plan is to have a number of lines out into companies that look like they are going places, and whose stocks' advances in price reflect this confidence.

3. Too many small holdings encourages carelessness. They can lead to a variety of small losses without your realizing they can total a large sum.

4. Selection of too many issues has been used as a hedge against ignorance. Some investors think this is a safety measure. This is a false belief. It is too difficult to keep a close watch on a broad list and to have to make important decisions about very many issues.

5. No one stock selection can be perfect, so some diversification is needed. Concentration on a limited number of issues allows the investor to have better control of his portfolio by taking profits as issues work out, by cutting losses quickly, by deciding to switch to more attractive alternative opportunities that may arise.

6. Concentration on just one stock at the beginning of a bull market is not desirable. If you are unlucky enough to have made a bad choice, you stand to lose too much of your capital. Diversification spreads the risk and helps you find winners on which you

can concentrate. You may then sell the poor stocks and invest more in the ones that are doing well. In this way you may end up with only one or two stocks, but you don't start out that way.

The Options Market

Trading in put and call options has increased tremendously the past few years. Although you might want to wait until you become more knowledgeable about the market before you consider either of these, you should at least know what they are.

Perhaps the words "puts and calls" may be unfamiliar to you, yet most of you are aware of the use of options in the business world. They are used frequently in the real estate business. An option is simply a set amount of money you pay the owner of a piece of property for the right to buy his property for a given price within a prescribed period of time. If you decide not to make the purchase, you lose your option money. The owner keeps it for his part of the bargain.

In the securities business a call option is a contract you make through your stockbroker with the owner of a particular stock to buy a given number of his shares at a fixed price within a fixed period of time. The Chicago Board of Trade and the other principal markets dealing with options have the option costs quoted daily on the stocks they handle in many local newspapers and in *The Wall Street Journal*. Any unlisted stocks you might wish are handled through the over-the-counter market, and the costs are usually about 10 to 15 percent of the value of the stock.

A put option is the reverse of a call option. Buying puts gives you the right to sell a given number of shares at a fixed price within a fixed period of time. This will be discussed at greater length in the chapter on selling short.

The principal reason for buying a call option is that it gives an investor who thinks a stock is ready to make a big upward move a chance to make a sizable profit on the swing while limiting the possible loss. Suppose the company in which you are interested is selling for $50 a share, and you expect it to rise rapidly. You do not have the $5000 to buy 100 shares, but you do have $500 plus commission to buy an option for six months and ten days. (This time was set for tax reasons, but the law has since been changed. The time limit has not.) This $500 minus commission goes to the owner of the stock who is willing to sell the shares to you.

If the stock rises as you expect within the fixed time, say to 75, you sell back the call option. You need not go through the process of buying the stock at 50, selling it at 75, and paying commission on both transactions; just selling the call option takes care of the matter. You now have $2500 from which you subtract the $500 the call cost and the two commissions on buying and selling the option, which means you wind up with about $1900 as profit. Not bad for a $500 investment.

Suppose instead of rising as you had anticipated, the price of the stock dropped to 42. You do nothing, and simply let your option expire. You have lost your $500, but you could have lost more had you actually bought the stock instead of the option.

Sometimes it is possible to salvage part of your money. You know the stock must rise above 55 before you can begin to show a profit. Suppose the stock rises to only 53. You can sell the call at that price and lose only $200 plus commissions instead of the whole $500. This is a lot better than letting your option expire and losing all your money.

Trading in the options market calls for a highly developed sense of timing; so for the time being you should leave this for the more sophisticated traders. If you as a beginner buy stock instead of options, you at least own the shares. Even if they drop in price, they are not likely to lose all their value, and you can hope the next bull phase will restore them to their original price or better.

New Issues

Although phenomenal profits have been made in new issues when the market for them was hot, you would be wise to ignore them entirely. The problem with new issues is that many of them fall apart during their first bear market and never recover because the companies go into bankruptcy.

If a new issue represents a new business that is being formed, you should know that about 80 per cent of all new businesses fail, some sooner, some after a struggle. The causes are many: inexperienced management, product problems or defects, inadequate financing, poor market analysis, lack of effective marketing effort, etc. There are more people with the ambition and opportunity to start new businesses today than there are people with the ability to nurse them along to the point where they become profitably running enterprises. As a result, there are many new companies selling stock to the public which are unable to compete with already established companies, so they fail and their stockholders lose their investment.

Some new issues represent private companies, perhaps family held businesses, which are going public for the first time. These usually come out when the demand for the stock of other companies in the same industry is strong, and this creates a great demand for their new issue. These new shares are likely to be overpriced, and even though the demand may push their price higher, they do not represent a safe investment. The time to buy these shares is after the market has declined considerably, because frequently the price will fall below its initial offering. This would also give you an opportunity to check the fundamentals to make sure the company is viable enough to survive.

Buying on Margin

Sometime in your investment career you might have to make a decision about whether or not to buy on margin. This means borrowing from your broker part of the money you need to buy stocks. Margin refers to the amount of cash you put up, not to the amount you borrow.

To prevent a catastrophe such as occurred in 1929, the Federal Reserve Board regulates the percentage your broker can lend you. This may range from as much as 50 percent to as little as zero depending on how high the Board thinks the speculative fever in the market is. In addition, the Federal Reserve Board has set down some rules that must be followed:

1. Your initial margin payment must be at least $2000.

2. Your equity in the current market value of the stock you have bought must never drop below the $2000. Should the price of the stock drop and your share be worth less than the above amount, you will receive a margin call and have to put up enough cash or securities to make up the difference.

3. Your equity must never be lower than 25 per cent of the current market value of the stock.

Most investors buy their stocks outright, but there is a sizable minority of active traders who use this credit from their brokers to help finance their transactions. This gives them more leverage and enables them to make more investments, which can mean a greater potential for profits—and for losses. Not only do they pay the going rate of interest, but they are required to answer the margin call and put up additional cash or securities if their equity drops below 25 per cent or take a chance of being sold out by their broker.

Buying on margin is not for the beginner. It is for sophisticated investors who are active in the market and understand the risks involved. For the small trader the interest is likely to eat up much of the profits, and buying on margin should not be used to any extent. But it is a technique all investors in the market should be aware of, providing they also know its possibilities and its limitations.

CHAPTER 19

Your Selling Strategy

Knowing what to buy is important. To help you decide you keep following the whole market with moving averages and an advance-decline line, and you are also following your individual stocks with moving averages. When both the timing of the market as a whole and the timing of your individual stocks indicate to you that now is the time to buy, you buy.

But knowing when to sell is even more important than knowing what to buy. According to Gerald Loeb, in *The Battle for Investment Survival*, a great many more errors are made in the selling of stock than in the buying. If you do not buy a stock, you have lost an opportunity; however you still have all your capital intact. But selling a stock you already own calls for much more decision-making and can be a much more traumatic experience.

Here are three selling decisions which might confront you: The first might come if your stock is rising in price. You may feel the price it has already achieved is about as high as it will go, and you lose confidence in the uptrend. So you sell, only to find the price is continuing to rise. If you have made a reasonable profit, have no regrets about selling too soon; no one can possibly guess at the tops. However, there is no reason not to consider the same stock for investment again. Simply wait for a reversal and buy it back when the price drops to the moving average range.

The second time for a decision might come if your stock has not gone up as you had expected. If after a reasonable amount of time had passed, say about three months, and your stock is standing still while others are rising, you might consider selling it and looking for another stock in which to invest.

The third time to make a decision comes when the price has declined and you face a large loss. Sell. When the price is rising or is standing still, the decision to sell need not be made immediately, but when you face a considerable loss, your decision must be immediate and unequivocal. Losses must always be "cut" before they become too deep. Loeb says this is the one and only rule of the market which can be taught with the assurance it is always the correct thing to do. He sees the acceptance of losses as the most important single investment device to insure safety of capital. It is the first key to success.

So *before* you buy, you plan your selling strategy. You plan how much you can afford to lose and still have enough money left to continue your trading. You *never, never* permit yourself to be "locked in" to a stock, meaning you have lost so much money, you can't afford to sell because your losses would be a large percentage of your investment. Now you have lost twice. You have lost heavily on the stock you still own, and you have lost the profit you could have made had you bought another stock.

How Much Loss To Take

Before you buy you decide *first* how much loss you are willing to take. It depends on the price of the stock. If you have paid say 30 for a stock, a 10 per cent loss is sufficient. Ruthlessly sell at 27 if the price begins falling. If you still like the company, wait till it stops falling and then buy the shares back. Say it continues to drop to 20, then reverses; at that price you are $700 ahead and you can use your $2700 to buy back that much more of the stock. In fact, if you waited to make sure the reverse had really started and then bought when it rose to 22, you can buy 122 shares. Should the stock continue to rise, you not only make a profit on the price of the shares, but also on the increase in number.

You keep that 10 per cent loss in mind and make use of it at all times. Suppose you bought another stock at 25 and it went up to 35. The 10 per cent loss you permit yourself means that if the stock drops to 31½, you sell. In this way you don't ride a stock all the way back down, and you have protected a profit.

If the stock sells for about 15, you might feel that the 10 per cent loss is not enough leeway for swings to take place. Then you might want to allow yourself a 15 per cent loss. This means when the 15 price declines to 12¾, you sell. No riding the stock down; no saying to yourself it is bound to turn. *You sell.* If you want to buy it back later, fine. Each transaction stands on its own feet and no regrets. Each one is a new hand to play.

For a very low-priced stock, say 6 a share, you might want to allow a 20 per cent loss. You bought because you were sure it would double, but it dropped to 4¾. *Sell it.* You took a chance of doubling your money, you had studied the situation, but you were also prepared to take a 20 per cent loss. So you take it and have 80 per cent left to continue your trading. Maybe your timing was wrong, and the bear market wasn't over. The stock may drop to 3½. Buy it back at the low price when the bull market begins, and double your money then.

Stop-loss Orders

Many people feel they are not able to make quick decisions about selling their stocks at the right time, so they give their brokers what is known as a "stop-loss" order. This can be illustrated by going back to the variously priced stocks just discussed for purchase and sale. Suppose the first stock you bought was the one listed at 25 which rose to 35. When you bought the stock at 25, you could have told your broker that you did not want to lose more than 10 per cent, and you would have put in a stop-loss order at 22½. When the stock moved up to 30, you could have changed the stop-loss order to 27. When it continued its rise to 35, you could have changed the order again to 31½. In this way the decision is taken out of your hands and you know your profit is protected.

Had you bought the stock priced at 30 first and put in a stop-loss order at 27 immediately upon purchase—26⅞ would have been better, as explained later in this chapter—you would have been sold out automatically when the price began its downward slide to 20.

Other people do not use a stop-loss order unless they are going away on a vacation. For one thing, they enjoy watching their stocks daily and making their own decisions. For another, they feel it is too easy to get sold out too soon. If at any time during the day your stock had dropped to 31½, the shares would have been sold, even if it had opened at 32 in the morning, dropped to 31½ around noon, and risen later in the day to 32½. They don't want a slight interday dip to force their stocks to be sold.

You, as a beginner, should seriously consider using stop-loss orders until you become more confident in your ability to make decisions. Many writers maintain that emotions prevent too many traders from selling out at the right time unless they use stop-loss orders. All kinds of excuses are used for not selling, like "Maybe I'll wait another day to see what happens," or "It's sure to bounce back," to "I can still get the dividends while I'm waiting for the price to come back." A stop-loss order can help you with this indecision.

In placing your stop-loss orders, an important point to consider is that people are inclined to think in whole numbers, 20, 21, 22, 23, etc. The next most commonly used point is the ½ fraction. Least used are the ⅜ and ⅞ fractions. Many times potential buyers wait for a stock to drop to a whole number, and when it does, they buy, forcing the price back up. You can take advantage of this by placing your stop-loss order just below a whole number or a half-point, at 21⅞ instead of 22, or at 21⅜ instead of 21½. You are protected against being sold out if the stock drops to a whole or half number and then rebounds.

Round numbers, 20, 30, 40, etc., are even more likely stopping points. Therefore a rising stock will frequently encounter resistance at round numbers. Don't wait to sell at 20 or 50, but place your sell orders at 19⅝ or 49⅝. The stock might find a strong resistance to any more rise just before the round number and drop sharply. Conversely, a falling stock is likely to find much support at a round number, so place your stop-loss order at 29⅞ instead of 30⅜ or 30⅛, even if this would mean taking a slightly larger loss than the 10 per cent if the support area were penetrated.

If you decide against giving your broker a stop-loss order and wish to use a mental order instead, you can do what the great technician John Magee advocated. You can use the daily closing price only. Having decided at what point you will sell, if the closing price hits that point or falls below, you can call your broker the following morning before the market opens and tell him to sell your shares. You are then not whipsawed by the interday price ranges. You have reached your decision objectively, and you can take advantage of the preferable morning hours.

If you find, for some reason, that you are unable to follow the stocks you have bought in a daily paper, just make the best of it. Simply check your Sunday paper and use that price to determine whether you need to sell. Then call up your broker Monday morning and give the order. You will be joined by thousands of investors who use the week-end to study their stocks and decide on a course to follow.

Another, more sophisticated method of protecting yourself from losing more than you wish is through the use of put and call options. This is explained in the next chapter on selling short.

The Factor of Time

A stock which doesn't work out as originally anticipated is almost as undesirable as one showing a loss. Having your capital tied up for a long period of time keeps you from using it for another, possibly more profitable, investment.

Time plays an important part in an investment strategy. Suppose you buy a stock and double your money in a year. You have then made a 100 per cent gain on your investment, figured on a yearly basis. But if that same stock doubles in six months, your gain is then 200 per cent, figured on a yearly basis too. The less the time, the greater the percentage of gain, and gains or losses should always be figured in per cent rather than dollar amounts. Here are some examples to help you measure your own rate of gains or losses, again figured on a yearly basis:

Purchase Price	Selling Price	% of Advance Over Cost	Divided by No. of Days Held	% Rate of Gain
20	40	100	365	100
20	40	100	180	202
20	30	50	75	243
20	23	15	12	456

When you study the above figures, you can see that long-term capital gains are not as profitable as many investors think they are. In fact, even with the payment of income taxes, short-term gains can frequently be more profitable than long-term ones. This should alert the investor into taking a profit rather than refusing to make a decision and so drift with a long-term. There is no virtue in holding onto a stock for many years because it is higher than when you bought it. Unless you are holding it because it is paying very high dividends, you can probably do as well by putting your money in a savings account. Nor is there any virtue in holding on to a stock that is going nowhere. This means a stock that is just not moving in a bull market when many others are. After a reasonable amount of time, say a few months, sell it and invest in one that seems to be more active.

How Much Profit to Take

Many traders try for a 100 per cent gain in price in each major movement of an individual stock, but this is an impossible goal. A much more realistic one would be 50 per cent.

Of course, this depends on when you buy your stock. If you restrict your purchases to those stocks which have declined from 30 per cent to 50 per cent of their previous gains in a reversal in the first two phases of a bull market, then you feel it reasonable to expect the stock to at least attain its previous high again in the next phase, and hopefully to go up even more. After selling it, you can look for another good stock which is in a decline for your next investment.

Should your stock greatly increase in price, you should be alert to the fact that the doubling in price from a previous major base is often a target for traders. Should a stock have dropped to 8 and then reversed, and you bought it at 10 or 11, keep the figure 16 in mind as a target where many traders will sell. You can then keep that as a possible goal at which you too should sell. If you still like the stock, you can buy it back at the reversal.

This is a good place to remind you again of the "technical rebound rule" which tends to work with considerable success. It says that after a stock has experienced a rapid advance or decline, it tends to retrace a third to two-thirds of its original move. For example, if a stock rises rapidly from 30 to 60 many traders will immediately redeem their stock in order to secure profits. If the price then declines, as expected, bargain hunting investors who missed the first move wait for a good place at which to make their purchase and traders who did make a profit try to judge where to reinvest to try for additional gains.

Professional traders compromise the one-third, two-thirds reversal figure into a 50 per cent guideline. They will therefore expect the above stock to find support and begin to advance again when it drops to approximately 45, half of the advance from 30 to 60. This rule enables them to select in advance a target area from which a rally is most likely to develop. The rule is also very important to the short seller, since it provides a reference point regarding the potential repurchase of the stock.

Stock Splits

Stock splits play an important role in a selling strategy. A split is simply dividing a high-priced stock into two or three so that the price of the shares will be cheaper and therefore easier to sell. One writer compares it to changing a $10 bill into two fives. The company now has twice as many shares, but each one is worth half as much as the original. The buying public considers splits as good news, because they now feel they are getting a bargain, so they are eager to buy. Also the odd-lotters can buy in round lots and not have to pay a premium.

News of a stock split is another automatic sell signal to the sophisticated trader. These splits are usually announced at the end of a long rise in price, and unsophisticated investors buy heavily because they feel the price will continue to go up. In actuality this split usually occurs at the top of the rise, and frequently the price drops thereafter. If the stock has had only a moderate advance, the drop may not occur. But should you own a stock that shoots up in price on news of a split, you would be wise to consider selling.

Stock splits are considered to be an extremely reliable indicator for timing in a bull market. They do not occur in the first phase because stocks are already low then. Stock splits begin in the second phase of the bull market and are heaviest during the third phase. Dividing a stock selling at 50 into two shares selling at 25 enables those who have made a handsome profit to more easily unload their shares. Unsophisticated investors are unaware of the timing, and so do not realize the market is about to reverse.

Large Dividends

Smart traders consider the announcement of an unusually large dividend as a sell signal. Often companies raise their dividend payments at or near market tops, causing many investors to buy at the wrong time. The sophisticated investors realize the price of the stock will probably fall after the dividend is paid, so they sell.

Tax Selling

Many investors delay selling at a loss until the end of the year, perhaps because of a wishful hope that the decline will reverse itself before that time arrives. Instead the decline usually continues into the new year, so as the year draws to a close they sell in desperation. This plays into the hands of the sophisticated investors who wait until November or December to buy these depressed stocks, knowing that January or February will probably bring a rally, even if only a temporary one. Even a 20 per cent gain in such a short time can bring a nice profit to the trader.

There are a number of tax selling strategies which occur at the end of the year, and you might someday wish to take advantage of some of them. Keep in mind the Internal Revenue Service permits losses of $2,000 on stocks to be charged against a married couple's or individual's annual income, with unlimited loss carryover. This will be increased to $3,000 in 1979.

1. If you have realized a substantial profit during the year, you might want to sell any stocks on which you have sustained a loss. This would lower your taxable income.

2. Those investors who are in the higher tax brackets and who have suffered heavy losses during the year might sell stocks in which they have a profit in order to balance the loss. Since they are allowed only $2,000 in stock losses and must carry over the balance, the sale of profitable stocks would offset some of the carry-over loss and would mean no tax payment this year on their profit.

3. Some increase in volume of sales in December may be due to tax switching rather than tax selling. If it is to your advantage to take a loss and if you have a large unrealized loss in U.S. Steel, for example, you may sell that stock and immediately reinvest in Bethlehem Steel with the thought that the future market action would be similar with both companies. You could then claim your loss.

4. Another strategy is to sell a stock on which you have lost money and replace it with a fresh number of shares in the same company. This is called a "wash sale" and the Internal Revenue Service says that, for you to be able to claim the loss, the purchase of new shares must come either 31 days before the sale or 31 days after.

Let's assume, for example, that you had bought 100 shares of a stock at 25 and it has dropped to 15. You would like to claim your loss, yet you still want to own the shares because you feel they will eventually show a profit. You could sell your shares in November and buy them back in December, 31 days later, and claim your loss. You might gain also on the deal if the price has dropped even further in December when you are ready to buy.

Another way to do it is to buy another 100 shares in November, wait 31 days, and sell the first 100 shares in December. You are then left with the second 100 shares and can claim a loss on the first 100 shares.

The net result of this tax activity near the end of the year often is to depress further those stocks which have been especially weak during a large part of the year because those are the stocks in which more investors are likely to have unrealized losses. This period of heavy tax selling may provide an excellent buying opportunity. Conversely, stocks which have pushed into record high ground late in the year create situations in which no one has an unrealized loss; therefore, selling pressure is likely to be greater in these stocks after the beginning of a new year. This gives the trader a whole year in which to use these profits for investment purposes.

It is good business practice for you to know at all times an approximate amount of realized and unrealized gains and losses for the current year. Maintaining a running record will enable you to keep tax considerations in mind in planning your purchases and sales, and you may sometimes profit from last minute tax activity on the part of those who have been less prudent than you.

CHAPTER 20

Short-Selling

Short-selling stocks is one area which seems to arouse a lot of emotion. For one thing, you are selling stocks you do not own by borrowing the shares from your stockbroker's firm with the hope of buying them back later at a lower price. This means you are expecting trouble in the market, and your short-selling might be interpreted as a lack of faith in our economic system. Nothing is further from the truth.

From your study in the earlier chapters about the Dow Theory and timing, you learned the stock market must go through bear cycles as well as bull cycles. You also learned there are reversals in all bull markets. The best way to profit from these price slides is through short-selling. You are not expressing a lack of faith in the market; you are instead showing a knowledge of how the market works.

Another emotion which affects short-selling is fear for the amount of loss you might sustain. When you buy stock outright, the most you can lose is the money you have put in. In other words, if you buy 100 shares of a $20 stock, the most you can lose is the $2000 if the company goes out of business. Theoretically you can lose much more in short-selling. Suppose you sold the $20 stock short and the price ran up to $60 before you bought back, you would then have lost $4000. But anyone who did not know enough to buy back before the price reached $60 has no business investing in the market at all.

Some detractors feel that short-selling is unpatriotic because it goes against the American way of doing business. You are doing things backwards—selling first and buying later. They also feel that it is unfair because you are taking advantage of other persons' losses.

183

Even the Internal Revenue Service discriminates against it by taxing these profits as short-term capital gains, no matter how long you may have waited to buy back the stock.

Those who favor short sales say that American businesses do this all the time. Many companies, especially in the mail-order business, sell in advance before they manufacture their product and use your money to help pay for the raw materials for the articles. Or if they are jobbers, they may not order the merchandise until after they have made their sales. Magazine subscriptions are given as another example of this short-selling; the publisher may have your money for years before completely filling the order. As for taking advantage of someone else's loss, bargain-loving Americans haunt all kinds of sales for this purpose.

Actually, short-selling is a necessary element in the market and is being done all the time by the specialists. This is part of their obligation to help maintain an orderly market. They must sell short to provide shares for all buyers if there are no other sellers available. They must buy back all shares which have been sold short if there are no other buyers available. This is their function. The only exceptions are the institutional funds; the specialists do not need to handle their huge blocks when they come on the market.

Short-selling should be considered a sound approach to managing money during declines. Since the stock market is going down anyway, there is no reason for you not to take advantage of this phase. Otherwise, during these bear markets and during the sometimes severe reversals which occur between the three phases of the bull market, you would have to look for the few stocks that buck the falling tide, or you would plan to stay out of the market entirely.

How to Sell Short

A falling Dow-Jones Industrial Average moving line and a falling advance-decline line have convinced you that a bear market has begun. You have been watching some stocks that have begun to reverse, and you are convinced they are going lower. You don't own the stocks, but you want to remain in the market and make money as their prices fall. So you look through your list of stocks for those where the stock price has dropped below the 40-week average line.

If you have a book of charts or are a chartist yourself, there are a

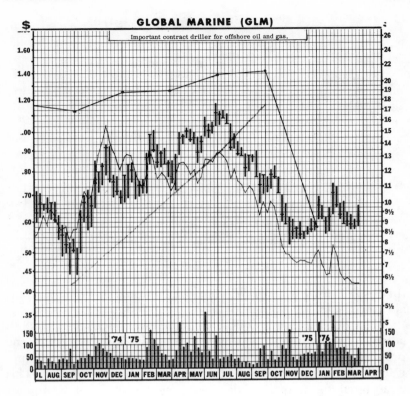

GLOBAL MARINE (GLM)

Important contract driller for offshore oil and gas.

number of chart patterns to follow for successful short-selling. Actually, they are the exact opposite patterns from those adhered to in the bull upswing.

1. The long-term advance followed by a major reversal is the exact opposite of the long-term decline followed by a breakout pattern. When this long-term rising trendline is penetrated on the downside, this is a major signal for a continuing decline ahead. Selling short this pattern should be profitable. Global Marine shows this pattern in its chart.

2. The flat top failure occurs when the stock has moved in a very narrow price range at a high level for a long period of time; and when the price does break out, it does so on the downside. This pattern is the exact opposite of the flat base breakout which occurs at the beginning of the bull market. When the flat top failure occurs,

the result is usually a rapid decline, which would make for a profitable short sale. An example of this is Dymo Industries.

3. The decline from a double top is the exact opposite of a bullish
advance from a double bottom. This double top indicates that the
price has twice failed to penetrate a resistance point at the top.
Usually the second top fails to rise quite as high as the first top. This
is a signal for a further decline. Note the chart of Computer
Sciences.

4. The M pattern is the exact opposite of the bullish W pattern.
The key to go short comes when the decline of the right leg falls
below the temporary support level in the middle of the M formation.
Deltona Corp. shows this pattern.

5. Another short-sale candidate is a stock pattern which shows the
price falling below one support level after another. The company
seems to be in great trouble. Once this type of slide begins, it
continues for some time. This occurred to General Instrument until
it finally met support at 7.

6. Cyclical stocks at historic highs make for good short sales when a
bear market begins. These can be such groups as automobiles,
chemicals, electronics, machine tools, steel, and many others. If they
have risen higher than they have ever been before, they usually
reverse quite far and make good candidates for short sales.

COMPUTER SCIENCES CORP. (CSC)

Leading component in computer services industry - programming, management, leasing, time-sharing.

Electronic Data Systems is an example of these cyclical stocks. So too is MGIC Investment.

Suppose a bear market has begun and you pick out a stock that seems to be a prime candidate for a short sale because it has dropped from 28 to 20 and is now below its own 40-week moving average. You then call your stockbroker and tell him or her you want to sell 100 shares short. The broker borrows the stock, usually from the shares held by the brokerage in its margin accounts, and lends it to you to sell. You must send him a check to cover the price plus commission.

As with a regular transaction, you have already decided how much loss you are willing to take, say 10 per cent through 15 per cent. You place your stop-loss order at 23⅛—remember the round number

often acts as a resistance point—and if the stock rises that high, you buy it back and take your loss. If it drops as you had anticipated, you can buy it back later at the lower price, take your profit, and pay your commission.

However, selling short is not as easy as selling long. (This is the Wall Street term for having bought first, then selling stock you already own.) The Securities and Exchange Commission has a regulation which says that the order cannot be executed while the stock is falling, but must wait until there is an up-tick—even one eighth of a point higher than the previous sale is sufficient. This might mean a delay in execution, and you would get the stock at a lower price than you had anticipated because it dropped a number of points before its first up-tick.

A way to avoid this is to wait for the first rally in the bear market and place your order before the rise is completed. Another way to

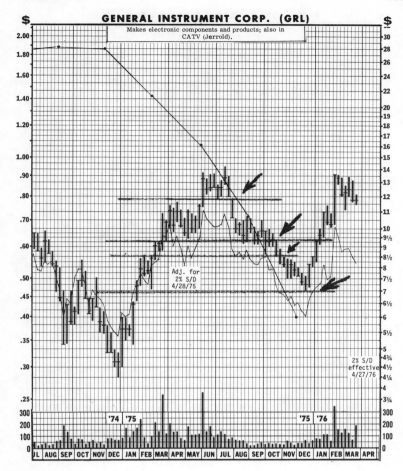

GENERAL INSTRUMENT CORP. (GRL)

Makes electronic components and products; also in CATV (Jerrold).

Adj. for 2% S/D 4/28/75

2% S/D effective 4/27/76

avoid this is to place a limit order in which you state the price at which you are willing to sell. If it isn't executed, you have a choice of changing your price or switching to another stock. But you have at least avoided a potential loss if you were forced to sell at the beginning of a rally.

I spoke earlier of the fear of a limitless loss. To avoid this dire happening, there are some iron-clad rules you must follow:

1. Never short a company that has only a limited number of shares available. Theoretically someone with a large amount of money could buy them all up and refuse to let you have any unless you pay

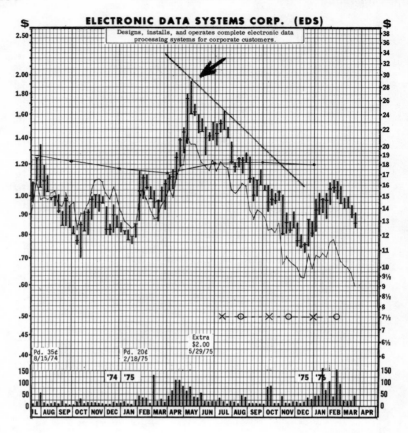

ELECTRONIC DATA SYSTEMS CORP. (EDS)

Designs, installs, and operates complete electronic data processing systems for corporate customers.

through the nose. Stick to those listed on the New York Stock Exchange, which must have a minimum of 1,000,000 shares and at least 2000 different holders of stock. The larger the capitalization of the company, the better. Then you can be sure there are shares available when you want to buy back. If no one else sells them to you, you know the specialist must.

2. The money you pay the brokerage firm is put into their margin account. If the stock rises above the amount permitted you to borrow on margin (at the present time 50 per cent), the margin clerk must call you to put up more money. The most important rule is for you never to put up more money when you do get a margin call. To begin with, *had you planned your strategy BEFOREHAND*, had you

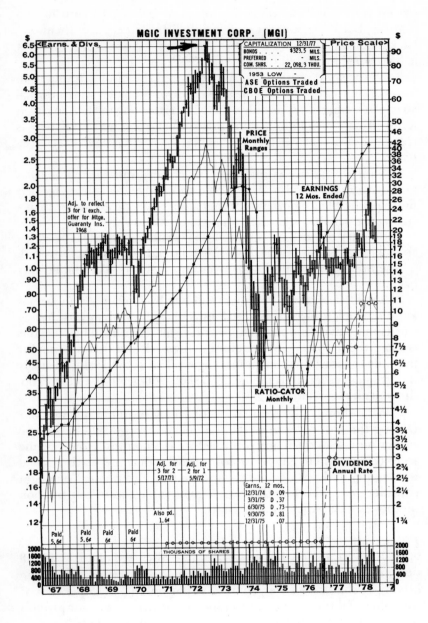

MGIC INVESTMENT CORP. (MGI)

placed your stop-loss order, you would never have let your loss go that far, but if for some reason it did, *THAT'S IT*. Have them buy back the stock, take your loss, and chalk it up to your carelessness. At least you are protected from the limitless loss.

3. Never short a stock that has advanced the most. Although we know that what goes up must come down, a stock with unusual strength frequently dips only slightly and is among the first to rise in a rally. Don't rush into shorting this kind of stock; wait until there is clear evidence that the stock has topped out and has now reversed its trend.

4. Short those stocks that look bad from fundamental analysis and/or from technical analysis. Some knowledgeable traders feel it is more profitable to short a stock that has already fallen rather than a stronger stock that is just beginning to break down.

5. Be wary of stocks which show heavy volume on rallies or which show heavy volume on the downside followed by an abrupt reversal. These are signs the decline is over and a short-seller should buy back.

6. Some traders who sell short will buy back when a rally begins and then look for bargains to go long. Others feel this means chasing stocks that have dropped in hopes they will rebound. They feel this is too difficult to do. They prefer buying back and then waiting for the rally to fade and then go short again. The second rally is usually the greatest reversal in the bear market. Following the next drop, the bull market should begin.

7. What should your strategy be for selling short in a bull market? During the first reversal of the bull market, you would have to be rather nimble to catch any profit before it rebounds. However, the second reversal might show some stocks that are having great weaknesses and that do not rebound for the third phase. You might consider going short on these while maintaining your long position on those stocks which show strength.

Put Options

In the chapter on buying strategy, I discussed the use of call options and how much additional leverage they give you in the buying of shares because you need to pay only 10 to 15 per cent of the value of the stock. Of course, should the price rise, your profit is that much less too than if you had bought the shares outright.

The same strategy is available for selling short: the put option. This gives you the privilege of selling 100 shares of stock at a fixed price within the option period. The cost of a put may be just a little less than a call, and it serves the same purpose: it gives you the opportunity to sell 100 shares short for only about 10 per cent of the selling price plus commission, and it limits your loss to just the amount you have invested.

The put and call options can also be used as stop-loss devices. Say you buy 100 shares at 30 and want to limit your loss to 10 per cent. You can buy a put option at 30 for $300. This gives you the privilege of selling 100 shares at 30 for the life of the option and limits your loss to the $300 plus commissions no matter how low the stock might fall. It would also work in reverse for a stop-loss if you are selling the stock short. You would buy a call option at 30 for $300. This would give you the privilege of buying 100 shares of stock at 30 for the life of the option and would limit your loss in the same way.

You can also use the put option to protect a profit. Say your 30 stock has gone up to 45 and you want to protect your 15 point profit. You can buy a put option at 45, which gives you the privilege of selling 100 shares at 45 no matter which way the price might go. This could be a way of carrying profits over to the next year for tax purposes if you are in a high tax bracket. It is also a way to ensure your keeping most of the profit should the price reverse and fall.

The use of put and call options have soared in popularity in recent years, especially since the Chicago Boards Options Exchange opened in 1973. Subsequently, other option markets have been opened. These markets establish a central point for trading options and for disseminating the prices daily. These are listed every day in *The Wall Street Journal* and weekly in many Sunday newspapers.

Timing Your Short Sales

As I have stated before, a complete bull-bear market cycle lasts from 3½ to 4½ years. With the exception of the cycle from the 1966 low to the 1970 high, which lasted 3 years and 7 months, the others have usually lasted from 4 to 4½ years. The length of the bear market within this cycle, which is the most advantageous time to do short-selling, depends on how long the previous bull market has lasted. Following are some examples of how you can time the bear market which follows the bull market in the cycle:

1. The 1962 bull market began in July of that year and lasted until February of 1966, a period of 3 years and 7 months. This meant the bear market following it had to be short in order to fit into the proper time span, and it was. It lasted exactly 8 months.

2. The 1966 bull market began in October of that year and lasted until December of 1968, a period of 2 years and 2 months. This meant the bear market following would be longer, and it was. Normally it should have lasted close to two years, but as I mentioned in the first paragraph, this was the exception. It lasted only 1 year and 5 months,

3. The 1970 bull market began in May of that year and lasted until October of 1973, a period of 3 years and 5 months. This left at the most a year for the following bear market, which lasted exactly that length of time—until October 1974.

4. The 1974 bull market began in October and lasted until January, 1977, a period of 2 years and 3 months. This means the bear market following should last from a year and a half to two years. It lasted 1 year and 4 months, another short one.

Learning to sell short makes for a much more knowledgeable trader. It sharpens your perspective about the phases of the bull and bear markets and enhances your ability to pick out profitable long positions as well as short ones. It will sharpen your timing. And it can be profitable for you with only reasonable care.

CHAPTER 21

The Human Element

Successful people are envied because they are considered lucky. Most are lucky because they are prepared. Behind that seeming nonchalance are years of so thoroughly steeping themselves in what it is they want to learn, that when they do act because of a hunch about it, their actions are based on facts and feelings they have developed through much study.

The same holds true for successful investment and trading in the stock market. People who make money here are lucky primarily because they have thoroughly studied the subject. This does not necessarily mean spending many hours reading financial news, interesting though some of it can be. Nor does it mean poring over company reports and trying to base intelligent investment decisions on them. There is an easier way.

The techniques given in this book are all investors really need to know in order to achieve successful results in the stock market. Any investors who consistently perform the mathematical computations recommended here for the entire market and for the individual stocks will be doing all the studying necessary as they review weekly what their figures are telling them. As they see the patterns emerging, they will develop through the years this feel for the market that will enable them to achieve large and consistent profits.

Any losses they may have—and about a third of any investor's transactions will be unprofitable—will be strictly limited, but the profit potential in the other two thirds can be extremely high in some cases. How much profit can be consistently made? A reasonable expectancy would be from 20 per cent to 30 per cent of their capital, with a possibility of doing even better in some years. All that is necessary to achieve these results is to develop this feel for the market by being willing to devote a few hours each week in making the recommended calculations and paying no attention to the news about all the things that are supposed to affect the market.

Do most investors succeed in making such large profits consistently? Unfortunately not, according to statistics. The Internal Revenue reports far more losses shown on individual returns than profits. The fault does not lie in the stock market itself, nor in a systematic approach to investing as shown in this book, but in the individual investors themselves.

Perhaps not all people should be in the stock market. If your spouse is strongly opposed to your using family savings for this purpose, you need to come to an understanding about whether or not you can use any of the money and how much. A frank discussion of how you plan to go about it is important, and this is one area in which this book can help by showing how much more can be gained than lost through using its system.

Those who have no money left over after ordinary living expenses should also not be in the market. Buying stocks for only a short period of time with the expectation of making a quick profit before the money is needed can often lead to disappointment. You must use only such money as you can afford to lose, not any money needed for necessities. Nor should you play with someone else's money. Pooling your money with that of relatives or friends to invest for them can lead to excessive worries over losses and fearfulness in making investment decisions. At least wait until you've gained enough experience to become extremely confident in what you are doing.

Another group which should not be in the stock market are people whose emotional qualifications are not suited to the risk-taking involved in this type of investment. If you are not going to be able to sleep because of anxiety over your investments, then you should not be in the market. Or at least, not too heavily involved in it. And in times of uncertainty, a vacation from the market entirely would be good for your emotional health.

To be successful investors in the stock market calls for effort. Not only must they study the market as outlined, but they must also study themselves. They must study their own reactions in times of stress and learn to control their emotions so that they can coolly and logically respond to situations. Instead of selling in a panic at the bottom of the market, as most investors do, they had long since taken their losses and were waiting for that bottom so they could begin their buying at rock bottom prices. Nor did they let greed overtake them when a bull market was roaring; they were willing to take their profits and run before a reversal set in.

Above all, they must not be impulsive. They must check carefully before making a decision, and not rely on vague hunches before getting in or out of a situation. They must be pessimistic and prepare for the worst by deciding beforehand how much of a loss they are willing to take. By preparing for the worst, they will know how to deal with it should the worst happen.

Many unsuccessful investors act like compulsive gamblers, whom many people believe have a self-punishing wish to lose. This may account for the losses of some investors, but the majority simply lose because they just don't want to put forth the effort to study a situation. They would rather rely on hearsay or tips, but mostly on vague hunches. In order to change their luck the first thing they must do is to come to grips with themselves.

Now let's talk about you, the beginning investor. Do you really want to make stock-market profits? Do you really want to be one of the minority of successful investors? You and you alone are the only one who can make that decision. If it is not important to you, no advice in the world will enable you to become proficient in the ways of the market. But on the other hand, no one can prevent you from making money if you are determined to succeed.

Great fortunes have been made and are still being made in the market. It can be mathematically demonstrated that investing a thousand dollars in stocks and having the after-tax capital gains grow at the rate of 50 per cent a year, can lead to a million dollar fortune in less than 20 years. This may sound incredible, but it is not impossible in the hands of an astute investor.

Many fortunes have also been lost in the stock market. Some are lost because their owners treated the stock market like a gambling casino. Others because their timing is so poor and their expectations so unrealistic, they seemed preordained to be losers.

In the stock market you as an investor will set your own odds. You must follow a system much like the one illustrated in this book; you must believe this system will be successful despite occasional losses; and above all, you must be willing to let the market tell you what to do and when to do it rather than the other way around.

Let's assume you have made up your mind that you do want to be a successful investor. Your next decision must be that you are willing to take full responsibility for your own investments. This means you do not ask your broker for advice or allow him to make investment decisions for you. With the system outlined in this book you should gain confidence in yourself about when to buy and sell, about what stocks to buy and sell, and about what profit or loss you are willing to take. You must be willing to accept responsibility for your own decisions.

The third decision you are going to make is that you will approach investing in a rational, unemotional manner. You will study the panic selling at the bottom of a bear market and the frantic buying at the top of a bull market, but you will not allow yourself to become involved in these emotional binges. You will teach yourself to become detached from your emotions and from the actions of others so that you will make your decisions automatically and logically, without hesitation and indecision. This is why following this book's system is so important. It gives you a weekly statement about the condition of the market and of your individual stocks upon which to base an investment decision. It may be wrong at times, but it is never uncertain; you should never be confused about what action to take.

This does not mean you will always be able to control your emotions. Remember you are human, and you will do stupid things just like all other humans. But study yourself. If you find you are inclined to be too pessimistic and tend to despair and panic when a crisis occurs, then you need to bolster your confidence by studying the investment system advocated in this book and learning that it will give sufficient signals to avoid a devastating loss. You may continue to worry, but at least it will keep you from going into a state of panic.

This system will also help you if you tend to be too optimistic. You will learn that stocks do not rise indefinitely, and the time to buy is not when they top out but when they bottom out. You will learn not to be triggered into impulsive action but to weigh carefully the alternatives before making a decision.

If you are like most people, you work pretty hard at your job to earn your daily bread. For many their work can be dull, frustrating, deadening. So they dream of easy wealth through investing in stocks and make purchases whenever they have enough money put aside. But they seem unwilling to make any effort to sensibly base their investment decisions. Instead they rely on broker's recommendations, tips, conversations overheard, or stories in the paper. Even if they were willing to invest in an organized, systematic manner, many do not know how to go about it. This is one advantage you have over others if you follow the advice given in this book.

Even if these investors do take the time to investigate before making a purchase, they usually base their decisions on unimportant matters. They investigate factors within a company that ought to make its stock go up or down, not the timing or other market factors that actually are making the stock go up or down at the moment. What these investors should do is study the price movements of the chosen stock and of the market as a whole and wait until the time is right before making their purchases.

Remember that because people you know are buying stock is no reason that you should too. Someone is selling the stock to them, and the seller may be the one who is right about the market, not the buyer. Not all people can be right at the same time or we would not have a market. The stock market is just an auction place, and for every decision to buy there must be a seller—and also the reverse. If everyone decided to buy at the same time, we would not have a functioning market place; nor can everyone sell at the same time. Buyers must have someone willing to sell to them, and sellers must have someone willing to buy. When too many people buy, prices rise sharply in price till they reach a bull market top; when everyone want to sell, a bear market panic sets in and prices drop till they hit rock-bottom. This, of course, creates a wonderful buying opportunity for the knowledgeable investor.

When you leaf through a paper like *The Wall Street Journal*, you realize the financial world is vast and that you have a very limited understanding of what is happening in that world. Yet your success as an investor depends on your making decisions within your very limited knowledge. Don't let this worry you. The principal point to remember is that most of what is going on out there is unimportant to you. You need not know the "why" of stock price movements because they are beyond your control. But you do need to see the "where" and the "when" of these movements in order to take advantage of them for successful investment. This book's method of investment enables you to concentrate on the elements necessary for success and allows you to ignore those factors beyond your control.

What you can control to some degree is yourself, your emotions and your determination to succeed. You need to practice self-discipline in your struggle for stock market profits because it could become so easy to put off the weekly computations. But if you stick to your plan, you will find the effort worthwhile. All you need do is look at your figures and charts to see how great the spread between the yearly highs and lows of many stocks is and to realize the potential for wealth that exists if you could capture part of this annual spread. This can be achieved only by knowledge that comes with self-discipline and self-control.

If you want to join that select group of "lucky" people, if you are willing to put in the necessary time, if you are looking forward to the challenge and the excitement of learning a new skill, then the stock market is for you. I wish you the very best.

GLOSSARY

Accumulation: A stock which evidences higher volume on days in which the price rises than on days in which the price falls is said to be under accumulation. More investors are buying than are selling. Accumulation generally precedes important price advances.

Advance-Decline Line: The net differential between the number of stocks advancing each day and the number of stocks declining each day, or each week, kept on a cumulative basis. This is one of the major technical indicators concerning the trend of stock prices.

At The Market: This phrase distinguishes an order that is to be executed at the best possible price from an order that can be executed only at a designated price. This is also called a "market order."

Auction Market: The stock market is an auction market, bringing buyers and sellers together. Buyers attempt to buy at the lowest price and sellers attempt to sell at the highest price.

Averages: Yardsticks for measuring broad trends in stock prices. The three most widely used are the Dow-Jones average of the prices of 30 industrial stocks, the New York Stock Exchange of all common stocks listed on the Exchange, and the Standard & Poor's index of 500 stocks listed on the New York Stock Exchange.

Bar Chart: A method of recording the price and volume of a stock through the use of vertical lines, with a horizontal bar indicating the closing price.

Bear: An investor who thinks that an individual stock or the market as a whole will fall. A bear market is a sharply declining market.

Bid and Asked: The bid is the price at which a person will buy a security. The asked is the lowest price at which a person is willing to sell a security. The actual price when you buy or sell usually falls between the two.

Big Board: Wall Street term for the New York Stock Exchange.

Blue Chips: Nationally known companies with a long record of dividends and with expected continued future growth. They are most popular with the investment trusts and institutions.

201

Book Value: A company's total assets minus its liabilities and minus the liquidation value of its preferred stock, if any. The sum arrived at is then divided by the number of shares of common stock. Book value may or may not be significant in the market value of the stock.

Breakthrough or Breakout: The terms are interchangeable. They mean that either a stock price or average has moved above a previous high resistance level or has moved below a previous low support level. It implies that the trend should continue in the direction of the breakthrough.

Broker: An agent who for a commission executes your orders to buy or sell shares of stock or other securities. Other terms used are securities salesman, registered representative, account representative, or customer's man.

Bull: A person who thinks the price of an individual stock or the market as a whole will go up. A bull market is a sharply advancing market.

Call Option: An option to buy 100 shares of a specific stock at a specified price for a specified number of days. A call is bought by an investor who thinks the price will rise.

Capital Gain or Capital Loss: Profit or loss on the sale of any capital asset, including securities. Under current federal income tax laws, a capital asset, if held for a year or less, is a short-term capital gain or loss, and if held longer than a year is a long-term capital gain or loss. Short-term and long-term are treated differently in income tax reporting.

Capitalization: The number of shares of common stock which constitutes the total issue held by stockholders of a particular company.

Churning: A suspiciously excessive amount of trading in a customer's account, done probably to generate additional commissions for an unscrupulous broker.

Collateral: Property pledged to assure the repayment of a loan. It may be any property, but is usually thought of as stocks and bonds.

Commission: The charge made by a broker for buying or selling securities as an agent.

Confirmation: The form you receive from the brokerage house informing you that your buy or sell order has been executed, and giving the price and the settlement date.

Conglomerate: A corporation that owns or controls many other corporations in widely varied industries.

Convertible: A bond or debenture or preferred stock that may be exchanged by the owner for common stock in the same company in accordance with the terms of the issue.

Covering a Short Position: Buying back a security previously sold short.

Current Assets: Those assets of a corporation which may be expected to be realized in cash, or sold, or used during the normal operation of the business for the current year. They include cash, accounts receivable, and inventories.

Current Liabilities: Money owed by the corporation that are due and payable in the current year.

Current Yield: The percentage of the current price which the dividends paid by the company yields. A $50 stock which has paid a $2 dividend in the preceding twelve months has a 4 per cent yield.

Cyclical Stocks: Stocks which tend to follow business cycles or industrial cycles. They climb fast in periods of rapidly improving conditions and slide fast when business conditions deteriorate.

Debenture: A promissory note backed by the general credit of a corporation and not secured by a mortgage or lien on any specific property.

Declining Tops: A chart pattern in which each peak is less than the previous one, showing increasing weakness. It implies an ultimate decline in the price of the stock.

Defensive Stocks: Stocks which tend to be relatively stable, in terms of dividends, earnings, and market performance, in periods of a declining market. They are quality stocks which are capable of going counter to the trend.

Depletion Allowance: To compensate for the exhaustion of natural resources, such as oil, gas, timber, and metals, the government allows a corporation to deduct certain charges against earnings in order to provide an incentive to find additional sources of these.

Discounting the News: Sometimes the price of a stock rises or falls in anticipation of a specific development. When the development actually takes place, the price may scarcely move or move in the opposite direction. At the time of the announcement of the development, the price has already "discounted the news."

Distribution: The opposite of accumulation. The selling of stock when the price is high and volume is high usually precedes a falling trendline.

Dividends: A payment, determined by the board of directors, to be distributed on a proportional basis among the shares outstanding. It may be in cash or in additional shares. Preferred stock usually receives the same fixed dividend each payment period. Common stock dividends vary with the company's earnings and the decision of the directors. They may be increased, reduced, or eliminated entirely depending upon the fortunes of the company.

Double bottom: This occurs when a price drops twice to similar low points, points of technical support. If the second bottom does not go below the first, support is implied.

Dow Theory: A theory of market analysis based on analyzing the market performance of the Dow-Jones industrial and transportation stock price averages. The theory states that the market is in a basic upward trend if one of these averages advances above a previous important high, along with a similar advance in the other. When both decline in a similar fashion, a bear market is predicted. It does not predict how long either trend will continue. The theory is important because so many people believe in it.

Earned Surplus: Accumulated earnings, which may be drawn upon to pay dividends when they have not been earned in the most recent quarter.

Equity: The ownership interest of the owner of common or preferred stocks.

Equity Financing: The obtaining of funds by a company through the sale of stocks.

Ex-Dividend: The term means "without dividend." The new buyer of such a stock does not get the recently declared dividend. It goes to the previous owner who was the stockholder on record.

Fiscal Year: The accounting year of a company. This may coincide with the calendar year or be any date on which the corporation chooses to end its business year.

Fixed Assets: Assets of a relatively permanent nature, not intended for resale, and used in the operation of a business.

Flat Base: A chart formation in which the price of a stock remains in a very narrow range for a long period of time. A breakout from this formation can be highly profitable.

Fundamental Data: The economic data of a company upon which fundamental analysis is based. This covers such items as the economy, stock earnings and dividends, price/earning ratios, new products, good management, book value of the stock, and others.

Gaps: A chart pattern in which there are visible separations or skips in price. They should be carefully watched because they set up targets for retracement.

Growth Stock: The stock of a company whose earnings are growing at a relatively faster rate than the gross national product.

Head and Shoulders: A chart formation showing three distinct rises, with the middle rise being the highest. The base level of the three advances comprises the neckline. This chart formation depicts a probable market top, and the move under the neckline completes the formation with an ensuing sharp decline. These should be looked for in particular in the third phase of a bull market. The reverse formation should be watched for late in a bear market.

Hedge: To hedge means to try to minimize or eliminate a risk by taking certain steps to offset this risk. It involves a purchase or sale of stock to counterbalance the first purchase or sale.

Insider: The directors and officers of a company, and companies or individuals who hold 10 per cent or more of the shares of stock of a publicly traded company. They must report their initial position and details of any changes of this position to the Securities and Exchange Commission.

Institutional Investor: An organization or company with substantial funds invested in securities. These may be banks, insurance companies, mutual funds, pension plans, etc.

Investor: An individual whose main purpose is to obtain a safe return on his capital. He is concerned with safety of principal, liquidity, dividend income, and capital appreciation.

Leverage: A financial arrangement that increases the possible profit or possible loss from an investment. Borrowing and buying on margin is one method of increasing leverage.

Limit order: An order to buy or sell stock at a certain price or better.

Liquidation: This has several applications. It can mean winding up a company. It can also mean turning securities into cash.

Liquidity: The ability of investors to easily buy or sell stock and the ability of the market to absorb these transactions with reasonably limited price changes.

Listed Stock: The stock of a corporation that is traded on a national securities exchange. Information on the stock and on the company must be filed with the Securities and Exchange Commission.

Long: You are long on a stock when you have bought a certain number of shares and are holding them in anticipation of a price rise.

Margin: The minimum proportion of the purchase price a customer must pay to buy securities. You use your broker's credit and pay current interest rates. The percentage you must pay is regulated by the Federal Reserve Board and in recent years has varied from 50 per cent to 100 per cent.

Margin Call: If the price drops below the amount necessary to keep your margin maintenance requirements, your broker will call you to put up additional cash or collateral. If you do not meet the call, the stock will be sold.

Market Order: An order to buy or sell a stated number of shares of a security at the best price obtainable in the market at the time.

New Issue: New stocks and bonds sold for the first time to raise money for the corporation.

Odd Lot: An amount of stock less than a round lot (100 shares.) Some inactive stocks sell in round lots of ten shares, with one to nine shares making up an odd lot. The buyer of an odd lot pays a differential of ⅛ point per share.

Option: A right to buy or sell specific securities at specified prices within a specified time.

Paper Profit: An unrealized profit on a security still held. Until a stock is sold, an investor has only a paper profit.

Par Value: Par is a dollar amount assigned to each share of common stock by the company's corporate charter. Par value has little meaning to the buyers of common stock, and many are now issued without par value.

Point and Figure Charts: A chart in which price changes are plotted only when the movement up or down is big enough to accommodate the point scale a technician is using. The scale depends on the price of the stock.

Portfolio: The collection of securities held by an individual or institutional investor. These are usually carefully researched and balanced as to risk.

Preferred Stock: A class of stock which has a claim ahead of the company's common stock to the payment of dividends or the assets of the company in the event the company is liquidated.

Price/Earnings Ratio: The relationship between the selling price of a stock and the company's earnings per share.

Primary Trend: The predominant trend of the market throughout bull and bear markets.

Prime Rate: The interest rate charged by banks to their largest and best customers.

Profit Taking: Selling stock which has increased in value since its purchase in order to realize the profit. This term is often used to explain a downturn in the market following a period of rising prices.

Prospectus: An abbreviated form of the document filed with the Securities and Exchange Commission in order to sell securities to the public. This selling circular is used by brokers to help investors evaluate the securities.

Proxy: Written authorization you give a representative to vote your shares for you at a shareholders' meeting.

Put Option: An option to sell 100 shares of a specific stock at a specified price within a certain time. It is bought by an investor who thinks the price will fall.

Pyramiding: Buying more stock as it rises in price.

Quotation: A quote is the highest bid to buy and the lowest offer to sell a security in a given market at a given time.

Rally: A sharp rapid rise in the price of a stock or in the market as a whole following a decline.

Resistance: A point on a chart which acts as a barrier to an upward or downward trend. Once a price support level is broken, that support level becomes the resistance point on the recovery level.

Rights: A short-term privilege to buy additional shares given to its stockholders by a company which wishes to raise additional capital. A stockholder should take advantage of the lower price offered by exercising the rights or by selling them.

Round Lot: A unit of trading in a security. This is usually 100 shares for active stocks and 10 shares for inactive stocks.

Seat: Membership in a stock exchange which entitles the owner to buy and sell securities on that exchange. Prices and requirements vary with each exchange.

Securities and Exchange Commission: The federal agency established by Congress to help protect investors.

Secondary Offerings: The redistribution of a large block of stock, perhaps in the settling of an estate. This distribution does not go through the exchange but is handled by one or more brokerage houses.

Settlement Day: In regular trading, the fifth business day after execution of an order. It is the deadline for paying for securities you have purchased, or for delivering securities you have sold.

Short Covering: Buying back stock previously sold short.

Short Interest: The total number of shares sold short and reported by the Stock Exchange once a month.

Short Position: Stocks sold short and not covered as of a particular date. Also the total amount of stock an individual has sold short and has not covered as of a particular date.

Short Selling: Selling stock not owned by borrowing it from the broker with the hope of buying it back later and making a profit.

Smart Money: The sophisticated investor or trader who seems to have exceptional knowledge, timing, and forecasting ability, and who has the knack of making money in the market.

Specialist: A member of the New York Stock Exchange who has two functions. The first is to maintain an orderly market, if possible, in those stocks in which he is registered as a specialist. The second is to act as a broker's broker and execute all limit orders when the stock hits the limit price.

Speculator: A person who is willing to assume a relatively large risk in the hope of gain and whose main concern is appreciation of capital and not safety of principal.

Split: The division of the outstanding shares of a corporation into a larger number of shares, sometimes two for one, three for two, etc. These lower-priced stocks have greater appeal to traders.

Spread: The difference between the bid price and the asked price, or between the purchase price and the sale price.

Stock Dividend: A dividend paid by a company to its stockholders in form of additional shares of the company's stock.

Stop-Loss Order: Standing instructions to your broker to sell your shares automatically if the price drops to a specified level. The purpose is to assure yourself that profits will be kept or that losses will not exceed a given amount. A stop order may be used for buy orders too.

Street Name: Securities held in the name of a brokerage firm instead of the customer's name are said to be carried in "street name."

Support: A point on a chart which acts as a barrier to the decline in the price of a stock. Once a resistance level has been successfully penetrated by a stock advance, the retreat from that level is expected to meet support at the old resistance level.

Symbol: The single capital letter or combination of letters given to a company when it is listed on an exchange and by which it is thereafter identified in the tape.

Tax Selling: Selling a stock for the purpose of recording a loss for tax purposes.

Technician: A person who uses charts to help make decisions on what stocks to buy and when to sell. He or she may also use moving averages, the Dow Theory, and other technical tools.

Topping Out: Denotes downturn in trend after a long price run-up.

Turnover: The volume of trading in the market as a whole or in any individual stock on any given day.

Warrant: A privilege to purchase securities at a stipulated price within a specified period of time or sometimes perpetually.

Yield: The percentage of return per year on an investment.

Index

A

Accelerated depreciation:
  how to figure, 125–6
  use in balance sheets, 128
Accounts payable, 126
Accounts receivable, 124–5
Accumulation:
  definition, 201
  of stock, 66–67
  as shown by volume, 142
Addressograph Multigraph, 19
  Stock Guide yellow sheet, 24–25
  weekly prices and how to interpret them, 67–70
  moving averages and how to interpret them, 77–84
  bar chart, 89
  P/E Ratio, 136
  on-balance volume and how to interpret it, 142–146
  buy in 1974 bear market, 159, 164
Advance-decline line:
  definition, 201

method to follow market, 41
theory of, 54–55
how to construct one 55–56
the 1974–77 A-D line and how to interpret it, 56–61
to use in investment program, 151, 154–155
to use in buying in a bull market, 163
Advantages to investing in market, 9
American Telephone and Telegraph
  as an example of buying right, 9
Annual Report, 123
Assets and liabilities, 19
Assumptions about technical analysis, 65–67
At the Market:
  definition, 201
Attitude:
  toward market, 3–7

toward investing, 195–200
Auction market
  definition, 201
Averages
  definition, 201
Averaging up or down, 168

B

Balance sheet:
  personal balance sheet 124
  company balance sheet 126–
    127
Bar chart:
  definition, 201
  examples of 89–98
Barron's Financial Weekly, 18, 19,
    151
The Battle for Investment Survival,
    2, 174
Bear:
  definition, 201
Bear market:
  definition, 4
  for buying at "wholesale", 26–
    27
  Dow Theory movements, 29–
    31
  cycles, 34–36
  in charting, 100
  volume in bear market, 140–
    142
  buying in a bear market, 73,
    159
Bid and asked:
  definition, 201
Big board:
  definition, 201

Blue chips:
  definition, 201
Book value:
  definition, 202
  in fundamental analysis, 131
Breakout:
  definition, 202
  in support and resistance, 94,
    99
  in chart patterns, 161
Brokers:
  definition, 202
  in buying and selling, 13–14
  choosing one, 147–149
Bull:
  definition, 202
Bull market:
  definition, 4
  buying right, 26–27
  Dow Theory movements, 29–
    31
  cycles, 34–36
  sell signals, 73–74
  in charting, 100
  volume in a bull market, 140–
    141
  buying in a bull market, 163–
    165
Business cycles, 34
Buying strategy:
  philosophies, 156–159
  in a bear market, 159–163
  in a bull market, 163–165
  using timing, 165–166
  low-priced stocks, 166–167
  higher-priced stocks, 167
  institutional stocks, 168
  averaging up or down, 168

diversification, 169–170
in the options market, 170–171
new issues, 171–172
on margin, 172–173

C

Call option:
    definition, 202
    in a buying strategy, 170–171
    as stop-loss devices, 193
Capital gain:
    definition, 202
    reason for investing, 13
Capital gains taxes, 35, 69
Capital surplus, 130
Capitalization:
    definition, 202
    as shown in the *Stock Guide*, 19
Cash flow, 137
Cash items, 129
Charts:
    keeping track of stocks, 86–102
    line charts, 87–89
    bar charts, 89–98
    point and figure charts 98–100
    patterns to use in buying, 159–165
    patterns for short selling, 184–195
Chicago Board of Trade, 170
Chicago Boards Option Exchange, 193
Churning:
    definition, 202
    complaint of, 147

Collateral:
    definition, 202
Commission:
    definition, 202
    in buying and selling, 13
    complaints about, 149
Common stock:
    definition, 12–13
    in balance sheet, 129–30
    net income of, 134
    lists of, 110–121
Congestion, 94
Confirmation:
    definition, 202
    of averages, 28
Conglomerate:
    definition, 202
Consolidation:
    during reversals, 32
    between movements of market, 66–67
    in chart pattersn, 91–94, 97, 99
Convertible:
    definition, 202–203
Covering a short position:
    definition, 203
Current assets:
    definition, 203
Current liabilities:
    definition, 203
Current ratio, 129
Current yield:
    definition, 203
Cycli-Graphs, 110
Cyclical stocks:
    definition, 203
    in charts, 87
    for trading, 109, 152

D

Debenture:
  definition, 203
December decline, 35, 69, 166
Decimals, 77
Declining tops:
  definition, 203
Defensive stocks:
  definition, 203
Deferred charges, 128
Depletion allowance:
  definition, 203
  in balance sheet, 127
Depreciation
  in balance sheet, 124–126
  accelerated, 125–126
  straight line, 124–125
Discount brokers, 149
Discounting the news:
  definition, 203
Disparity, 61
Distribution:
  definition, 203
  of stock, 65–66
  as shown by volume, 145
Divergence:
  in averages, 41
  in volume, 141
  in price with Dow, 54–55
  with advance-decline line, 61
Diversification, 108, 169–170
Dividends:
  definition, 203
  for income, 13, 27, 103
  information about, 16, 19, 130
  announcement of large divi-
    dend, 180
Double top and bottom:
  definition, 204

in chart patterns, 94
Charles Dow, 27, 41, 64
Dow-Jones averages, 28, 41, 90,
  139–140
Dow-Jones Industrial Average,
  42–53, 146, 151, 154–155,
  163–164
Dow-Jones Industrial Average
  stocks, 121–122
Dow Theory:
  definition, 204
  how devised by Dow, 27–29
  how used, 29–33
  timing of, 34–36
  as technical tool, 41, 63, 69,
    84–85, 184
Downtick, 65

E

Earned surplus:
  definition, 204
Earnings, 133–138
Emotions:
  in market, 4
  involved in investing, 195–200
Equity:
  definition, 204
Equity financing
  definition, 204
Ex-dividend:
  definition, 204

F

The Financial Analyst's Handbook,
  65
Fiscal year:
  definition, 204

Fixed assets:
    definition, 204
    in balance sheet, 127
Fluctuation of stock, 17, 64
Fundamental analysis, 63–64,
        87, 101, 123–133
Fundamental approach to mar-
        ket, 40–41
Fundamental data:
    definition, 204

G

Gaps:
    definition, 205
    in price chart, 83
Glamour stocks, 137
Good management, 138
Benjamin Graham, 121, 131
Joseph E. Granville, 31, 141–
        142, 155
Growth companies, 104
Growth stock:
    definition, 205

H

Head and shoulders:
    definition, 205
    reversal pattern, 94
Hedge:
    definition, 205
High-low column, 16
High priced stocks, 110, 166–
        167

I

Index funds, 168
Industry groups, 111–121

Insiders:
    definition, 205
    trading of, 87
Institutional investors:
    definition, 205
    investment funds, 8–9, 110,
        147
Institutional stocks, 168
Inventories, 127, 129
Investing:
    reasons for, 6–11
    as a business, 7
    how much money to start, 10
    insurance for, 10
Investment lists, 111–122
Investor:
    definition, 205

L

Leverage:
    definition, 205
    for greater returns, 130–131
    in margin, 172
Limit order:
    definition, 205
    use of, 189
Line chart, 87–89
Liquidation:
    definition, 205
Liquidity:
    definition, 205
Listed stock:
    definition, 205
Gerald Loeb, 2, 8, 153–154,
        174–175
Long:
    definition, 206
Long term debt, 129

Losses from investing:
    for income tax, 35
    in selling strategy, 174–175
    how much to take, 174–176
Low priced stocks, 110, 146,
    166–167

                    M

John Magee, 177
Margin:
    definition, 206
    for buying stock, 172–173
    for short selling, 190
Margin call:
    definition, 206
Market calendar, 27, 32–33
Market cycles, 34
Market order:
    definition, 206
Market bottoms and tops, 55
Market trends, 91–92
Marketable securities, 124
Moody's *Stock Survey*, 19, 123,
    128
Moving average computation,
    43–49
Moving average lines:
    for keeping track, 41–42
    10-week line, 43, 73–74, 83–
        84
    40-week line, 43, 73–74, 83–
        84
    for individual stocks, 72–84,
        152, 154

                    N

Net worth, 129

New Issues:
    definition, 206
    in buying strategy, 171
New York Stock Exchange, 2,
    11, 14–15, 16–18, 41, 54,
    103, 111, 152, 166, 190
New York Stock Exchange
    Index, 29
News affecting the market, 34
Notes payable, 128–129

                    O

Obsolescence, 127
Odd lot:
    definition, 206
    in stock splits, 180
Options:
    definitions, 206
    use in trading, 170–171

                    P

Paper profit:
    definition, 206
Par value:
    definition, 206
    importance of, 18, 131
Patents and goodwill, 128
Point and figure charts:
    definition, 206
    examples of, 98–99
Portfolio:
    definition, 206
Preferred stock:
    definition, 206
    in balance sheet, 127
    in profit and loss statement,
        134

Prepaid expenses, 127–128
Price/Earnings Ratio:
  definition, 206
  P/E ratio information, 16, 19
  in profit and loss statement, 135–137
Price range, 18
Primary trend:
  definition, 207
  keeping track of, 42
Prime rate:
  definition, 207
Profit and loss statement, 133–138
Profit taking:
  definition, 207
  how much to expect, 7–8
  how much to take, 178–179
Prospectus:
  definition, 207
Proxy:
  definition, 207
  use of, 13, 130
Put options:
  definition, 207
  use of trading, 170–171
  as stop-loss devices, 192–193
Pyramiding:
  definition, 207

Q

Quotation:
  definition, 207

R

Rally:
  definition, 207

Resistance:
  definition, 207
  areas of, 75, 83
  on charts, 87, 94–95, 99, 100
Reversals:
  in Dow Theory, 29
  characteristics of, 31–32
  in moving averages, 50–51, 83–85
Retained earnings, 130
Rights:
  definition, 207
Risk in investing, 6–9
Round lot:
  definition, 207

S

George Seaman, 152
Seat:
  definition, 207
Securities and Exchange Commission:
  definition, 207
  short sale regulation, 188
Securities Investor Protection Corporation, 10, 150
Secondary offerings:
  definition, 208
Selling strategy, 174–182
  planning in advance, 174–175
  how much loss to take, 175–176
  stop-loss orders, 176–178
  importance of time, 178–179
  how much profit to take, 179–180
  stock splits, 180
  large dividends, 180–181

tax selling, 181–182
Settlement day:
    definition, 208
Alan R. Shaw, 65–66, 99–100, 145–146
Short covering:
    definition, 208
Short interest:
    definition, 208
Short position:
    definition, 208
Short selling:
    definition, 208
    how to use, 152, 183–194
Smart money:
    definition, 208
    making profits, 33
Specialist:
    definition, 208
    activities of, 14, 184
Speculation, 3–4
Speculator:
    definition, 208
Split:
    definition, 208
    in selling strategy, 180
Spread:
    definition, 208
Standard and Poor's 500 Index, 29, 37, 41, 51, 53, 151, 168
Standard and Poor's *Stock Guide*, 18, 110, 148
Standard and Poor's *Stock Reports*, 19, 123, 128, 136
Stockbroker, 147–150
Stock exchanges, 13–15
The Stock Picture, 111
Stop-loss order:
    definition, 208

use of, 87, 100, 192
    in selling strategy, 176–177
Street name:
    definition, 209
    convenience of, 149–150
Support:
    definition, 209
    areas of, 75, 158
    in chart patterns, 87, 94–95, 99, 100
Symbol:
    definition, 209

T

Tax selling:
    definition, 209
    use of, 35, 193
    in selling strategy, 181–182
Technical analysis:
    approach to investing, 40–41, 123
    for individual stocks, 63–67
    use of charts, 86–102
Technical rebound rule, 179
Technician:
    definition, 209
    approach to trading, 146
Timing:
    in bull-bear cycles, 31–33
    the primary tool in investing, 34–39
    timing techniques, 36–39
    in technical analysis, 63–64
    for buy and sell orders, 67
    for individual stocks, 73–74
    of volume, 140
    in buying strategy, 165–166
    of short sales, 193–194

Topping out:
definition, 209
A Treasury of Wall Street Wisdom,
152
Triple top and bottom, 94
Turnover:
definition, 209
Two-tier market, 61, 69, 90

V

Value Line's *Ratings and Reports,*
19
Volume:
in charts, 86
as a technical tool, 139–146

W

Wall Street beginnings, 1
The Wall Street Journal, 19, 27,
167, 170, 193
"Wall Street Week," 2, 145
Warrant:
definition, 209
Wash sale, 181–182
Women investors, 2–3

Y

Yield:
definition, 209
in profit and loss statement,
134–137
You and the Investment World, 16